MORE PRAISE FOR *OPEN LEADERSHIP*

"The struggle in balancing openness and control is a universal human problem. While most leaders agree that greater transparency and authenticity can lead to significant benefits, many remain paralyzed by the risks involved in opening up the lines of communication with their stakeholders. Charlene shows that tapping into the power of social technologies isn't about mastering the latest shiny technologies, but instead having a clear idea of the relationships you want to form with your stakeholders. A must-read for those eager to embrace 'the new openness.'"

— Roger Martin, dean, Rotman School of Management, University of Toronto; author, *The Design of Business*

"Charlene Li is absolutely at the top of her game. She's an expert in social technology—an absolute essential in driving your company forward today. But what's more, she clearly lays out what's required to lead. Throw out the old rulebook and put *Open Leadership* into play."

— Keith Ferrazzi, author, *Who's Got Your Back* and *Never Eat Alone*

"If there's one truism that you can bank on it's this: the most important currency of the 21st century is trust. However, trust requires openness. The more you share and the more you listen, the more you will be trusted. However, becoming an open business is truly challenging. For most businesses, it's a cultural shift much more than a technological one. In this great work, Charlene Li details through rich stories just how some institutions are opening up and, in the process, earning the trust of millions."

— Steve Rubel, SVP/director of Insights for Edelman Digital

"If you are in a quandary about how to use social media and social technologies, *Open Leadership* is a book for you. It provides a road map for corporate leaders grappling with how to use social media in a thoughtful, disciplined way."

— Renée Mauborgne, coauthor, *Blue Ocean Strategy*

"Yet again Charlene Li is pioneering how companies must transform themselves to be successful in a global economy in a digital world. Her insights will inspire executives to rethink old approaches and adopt new ways of thinking and operating: *Open Leadership* is about how companies can leverage multiple networks of customers, researchers, developers, manufacturers, and other partners, etc., to drive innovation, achieve efficiencies, and grow."

— Larry Weber, chairman, W2 Group, Inc; author,
Sticks & Stones

OPEN LEADERSHIP

OPEN
LEADERSHIP
HOW SOCIAL TECHNOLOGY CAN TRANSFORM THE WAY YOU LEAD

CHARLENE LI

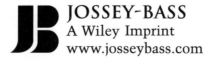

JOSSEY-BASS
A Wiley Imprint
www.josseybass.com

Published by Jossey-Bass
A Wiley Imprint
989 Market Street, San Francisco, CA 94103-1741—www.josseybass.com

Readers should be aware that Internet Web sites offered as citations and/or sources for further
information may have changed or disappeared between the time this was written and when it is read.

Limit of Liability/Disclaimer of Warranty: While the publisher and author have used their best
efforts in preparing this book, they make no representations or warranties with respect to the
accuracy or completeness of the contents of this book and specifically disclaim any implied
warranties of merchantability or fitness for a particular purpose. No warranty may be created or
extended by sales representatives or written sales materials. The advice and strategies contained herein
may not be suitable for your situation. You should consult with a professional where appropriate.
Neither the publisher nor author shall be liable for any loss of profit or any other commercial
damages, including but not limited to special, incidental, consequential, or other damages.

Jossey-Bass books and products are available through most bookstores. To contact Jossey-Bass
directly call our Customer Care Department within the U.S. at 800-956-7739, outside the U.S.
at 317-572-3986, or fax 317-572-4002.

Author is represented by literary agent Kevin Small of ResultSource.com.

Jossey-Bass also publishes its books in a variety of electronic formats. Some content that appears in
print may not be available in electronic books.

Library of Congress Cataloging-in-Publication Data

Li, Charlene.
   Open leadership : how social technology can transform the way you lead / Charlene Li. — 1st ed.
      p. cm.
   Includes bibliographical references and index.
   ISBN 978-0-470-59726-2 (cloth)
   1. Leadership. 2. Online social networks. I. Title.
HD57.7.L5 2010
658.4'092—dc22   2010007009

Printed in the United States of America
FIRST EDITION
HB Printing   10 9 8 7 6 5 4 3 2 1

CONTENTS

To my parents, Daniel and Janet Li,
for the values and love that have carried me through life.

INTRODUCTION

In the aftermath of Hurricane Katrina, people demanded answers to burning questions. Why wasn't the country more prepared? Why were citizens of the richest country in the world left abandoned for days when it was clear that a disaster had occurred? In the middle of this maelstrom was the American Red Cross, facing criticism for its emergency response. The executive team wanted to be more transparent about the work it was doing and was also worried that detractors on blogs, discussion boards, and social networking sites were hurting the reputation of one of the country's most respected organizations. So in November 2006 they hired Wendy Harman as the organization's first social media manager. "I was hired in part because the leaders knew that people were saying really bad things about the Red Cross's response to Katrina," Harman recalls, "and they wanted someone to make it stop." There was a lot to do—when she arrived, Harman had to lobby IT to get access to the social media sites she was supposed to manage; in their efforts to maintain security, the Red Cross had blocked employee access to sites like MySpace and Facebook.

But although Harman did indeed find some very issue-specific and narrow complaints against the Red Cross in the social networks, for the most part people were passionately positive about the organization and wanted to be involved in the Red Cross's efforts to provide effective disaster relief. So Harman quickly shifted her focus. "I went to my bosses and said, 'We have a huge opportunity here. There are people who want to help the Red Cross and who are online every day.'" To help make her case, she culled the most relevant mentions from an average of four hundred comments every day and distributed them via email to the top leadership. She also gathered articles and insights citing the benefits of social media and stuffed them into a four-inch binder that she circulated around the organization.

But most important, Harman addressed with persistence and patience each concern and fear her executives had about engaging in social media, from malware downloads to confidentiality of clients shown in pictures uploaded to Flickr. She made sure that the proper processes and procedures were in place before entering each new media channel. And over the course of two years, Harman gradually added a blog, Flickr, Facebook pages, and Twitter accounts, getting the organization to open up to the new world of social media.[1]

Then the calls started coming in from local Red Cross chapters hoping to jumpstart their own social media efforts. The American Red Cross is made up of over seven hundred local chapters and regions, and Harman was concerned that people would have inconsistent experiences when interacting with the Red Cross online. "We had a lot of people naming themselves 'Clara Barton,' the founder of the Red Cross, or some other sort of random clever names." So she wrote a handbook that laid out guidelines, procedures, and best practices on how Red Cross chapters could and should use social media, and she put it online for anyone to see.[2]

With the equivalent of an operating manual in hand, Red Cross chapters quickly started creating blogs and their own Facebook pages, and even setting up Twitter accounts.[3] More important, the large base of Red Crossers—people who are employees, emergency responders, or just blood donors or contributors—became part of the Red Cross's outreach. When the Red Cross puts up a disaster warning on its Facebook page, a typical volunteer return comment is "My bags are packed and I'm ready to go." Facebook echoes that comment back to the volunteer's friends, further amplifying the Red Cross's message of readiness and response.

A big payoff for the Red Cross's increased openness to social media came when retailer Target ran a Facebook-based fundraising contest for select organizations, among them the American Red Cross. The result: the Red Cross raised $793 thousand from that campaign alone. Says Harman, "If we hadn't been in this space, we wouldn't have been invited to be a part of it. We were able to leverage our community and tell them to vote for us."

What's fascinating about this story is that the American Red Cross started engaging in social media because it sought to control it, but realized over time that it was better to be open and engage with those who were already engaging *them*. But here's a critical point: the Red Cross didn't simply throw open the doors overnight. It was only when Harman was able to put in place the proper procedures, policies, and guidelines that defined how everyone should and shouldn't behave, that the Red Cross felt comfortable letting go of the impulse to control.

Today, Harman receives the full support of the organization, starting at the top with president and CEO Gail McGovern. And the impact of that support was seen during the Haiti earthquake response in January 2010, when the Red Cross activated mobile giving and raised over $10 million in three days, driven in great part by people sharing this easy donation channel on Facebook and Twitter.[4] Moreover, the Red Cross used these new channels to keep people informed about the relief efforts taking place, answering questions ranging from how donations were being used to the situation on the ground. By letting go and embracing social technologies, the Red Cross was better able to complete its mission.

THE PURPOSE OF THIS BOOK

Open Leadership is about how leaders must let go to succeed. It's for leaders like those at the Red Cross who are seeing the ordered world they understand crumbling in the face of customers, employees, and partners empowered by new tools that were almost unimaginable fifteen years ago. They know that greater transparency and authenticity can bring significant benefits to their organizations, yet they have a gut-wrenching fear that such an opening up involves tremendous risk as well.

This book lays out how organizations and their leaders can approach being open in the face of social technology adoption. It picks up where my previous book, *Groundswell,* left off, by showing readers just *how* they can use these new technologies—Facebook, Twitter, YouTube, Yammer, Jive, new mobile services, and many, many more—to improve efficiency, communication, and decision making for both themselves and their organizations.

I have been talking almost nonstop about the ideas in *Groundswell* since Josh Bernoff and I wrote the book in 2008, and I've spoken to hundreds of groups, ranging in size from five to five thousand interested listeners. I found that people originally picked up *Groundswell* because they wanted to learn more about Web 2.0 and social technologies. But they soon came to realize that tapping into the power of social technologies isn't about mastering the latest shiny technology; it is actually about having a clear idea of the relationship they want to form.

Energized and empowered, these people underlined and dog-eared *Groundswell* studiously and set about to implement social technologies in their organizations. There they ran into the curmudgeons—people who, no matter how much they appreciated and understood the benefits of social technologies, simply couldn't force their heads into a new mind-set and new way of thinking. Or they ran into an executive who simply feared what engaging the groundswell would mean in terms of exposing the company to risk. Essentially, they realized that their companies didn't have the right culture and mind-set—and more important, the right leadership— to engage the groundswell.

These dedicated, loyal souls came back to me, asking me to write the next book to support their efforts. But they didn't want another treatise on social technologies. They wanted something that would explain to their executives how to change and open up their organizations. No matter how compelling a technology or potential relationship might be, in the face of an immovable mass called company culture, and without the right organization and leadership in place, any digital strategy will fail.

Being open should be not a mantra or philosophy, but a considered, rigorous approach to strategy and leadership that yields real results. This is *not* about total transparency and complete openness, whereby everyone from customers to competitors has access to all information and everyone is involved in all decisions. Such an unrealistic extreme of complete openness is untenable if a business is to sustain its competitive advantage and ability to execute.

At the other, equally unrealistic end of the spectrum is the completely closed organization, in which information and decision making is centrally controlled and everyone follows every instruction not only perfectly, but happily. Every organization from Greenpeace to the CIA falls somewhere along this continuum from closed to open.

So put aside the calls to be more transparent, to be authentic, and—my favorite—to be "real." The question isn't whether you will be transparent, authentic, and real, but rather, *how much* you will let go and be open in the face of new technologies. Transparency, authenticity, and the sense that you are being real are the by-products of your decision to be open.

GREATER OPENNESS IS INEVITABLE

As your customers and employees become more adept at using social and other emerging technologies, they will push you to be more open, urging you to let go in ways in which you may not be comfortable. Your natural inclination may be to fight this trend, to see it as a fad that you hope will fade and simply go away. It won't. Not only is this trend inevitable, but it also is going to force you and your organization to be more open than you are today.

In the past, organizational leaders had the luxury of remaining ensconced in their executive suites, opening up only when they felt the need to. Today there is information leakage everywhere, with company miscues and missteps spreading all over the Internet in seconds. And all involved—from employees and customers to business partners—feel entitled to give their opinions and get upset when their ideas are not implemented. What's really going on here? The fundamental rules that have governed how *relationships* work are being rewritten, because of easy, no-cost information sharing.

The challenge therefore is to redefine how those relationships will operate. Just as the Red Cross had to lay out the new rules for social engagement, organizations and their leaders need to lay out the commitments they expect from these new relationships.

It is critical that your organization not enter into these new open relationships without guidelines. Simply opening up and devolving into chaos, or worse, "letting this take its natural course" are certain recipes for disaster. Being open requires more—not less—rigor and effort than being in control. This book will show step by step, with case studies and examples from many different industries and countries, how to bring the rigor of this new openness to your relationships, both inside and outside of the organization.

WHAT'S IN THE PAGES AHEAD

Part One of the book examines what it means to be open. Chapter One shows why greater openness is inevitable in the face of growing adoption of social technologies. I explain the impact that empowered consumers have had on companies like United Airlines, and go into more detail on how Barack Obama was able to manage millions of volunteers in his presidential campaign. In Chapter Two, I define what it means to be open, with case studies from companies as diverse as Mullen Communications and Facebook, Yum! Brands and Cisco. At the end of Chapter Two, I invite you to conduct an openness audit to understand where you are and aren't open today—this is the starting point to understanding how open you will need to become.

The hard work comes in Part Two, in which we determine your open strategy, weighing the benefits against the risk, and also understanding the implications of being open. One company I spoke with got the "social media" bug in 2009 and devoted a quarter of its marketing budget to developing Facebook pages, creating blogs and private social networks, and managing Twitter accounts. At the end of the year, they had a lot of activity and "buzz"—but little idea of what it was getting them as a company beyond greater engagement with their customers. To make matters worse, they felt obligated to maintain these new conversations and relationships at significant expense. The problem was, this company's approach to openness lacked a coherent strategy. Don't make the same mistake!

In Chapter Three, I explain how to create your open strategy—determining when it makes sense for you to be more open and engaged and when it doesn't. Organizations like Kohl's, Ritz-Carlton, and Toronto General Hospital are all using social technologies to become more open to their customers as well as their employees. In Chapter Four, I tackle the issue of how to measure the benefits of being open, and I show how organizations like SunTrust and Dell are becoming more open and are also seeing a significant positive impact on their business. Included in this chapter are details on how to measure and calculate the benefits of social technologies and being open, and also on how to use metrics to manage engagement and increase overall customer lifetime value.

One big concern that comes up around the topic of being open is the tremendous risk involved, especially when employees are free to say what they like in an open forum. In Chapter Five, I'll detail the guidelines, policies, and procedures that companies like Microsoft and Kaiser Permanente have used to be able to engage with greater confidence. In particular, I'll explain how pharmaceutical company Johnson & Johnson was able to navigate its legal department and government regulations to start using social technologies such as blogs.

Part Two concludes with Chapter Six, which explains the nuts of bolts of managing your open strategy, ranging from creating robust profiles of how your customers and employees engage to organizing for openness. Organizations like Ford, Humana, HP, and Wells Fargo shared their secret recipes for how they've orchestrated openness within their organizations.

But it's not enough to have a coherent strategy—you also need open leaders to execute it. Empowered people and organizations are stressing out today's leaders, challenging traditional command-and-control styles. However, they are called upon to do more than simply let go—in essence, leaders are saying, "I am responsible, so I have to have control. But if you are telling me to be open and give up control, then *what is my role?*" This is the crux of the problem: these new relationships are forcing leaders to rethink how they lead and how to get people to follow.

Leadership requires a new approach, new mind-set, and new skills. It isn't enough to be a good communicator. You must be comfortable sharing personal perspectives and feelings to develop closer relationships. Negative online comments can't be avoided or ignored. Instead, you must come to embrace each openness-enabled encounter as an opportunity to learn. And it is not sufficient to just be humble. You need to seek out opportunities to *be humbled* each and every day—to be touched as much by the people who complain as by those who say "Thank you."

In Part Three, I explore what it means to be a leader in the context of these new empowered relationships. Chapter Seven lays out what it means to be an open leader and details the characteristics, skills, and behaviors of effective open leaders like Cisco's John Chambers and Kodak's Jeffrey Hazlett. Chapter Eight explains how to identify and nurture open leaders within your organization, and I tackle what it means to be authentic and transparent. I'll look at how companies like United Business Media and Best Buy develop "zealots" among their employees.

One essential idea I explore is how to successfully fail. In fact, I think it's just as essential to consider and plan out how to *fail well* as it is to plan how to succeed—because the reality of business is that you *will* fail, at times, and how you lead and recover through that failure will say more about your ability as a leader than how you lead in times of plenty. This is all the more important for an open organization, as its failures will be more likely to be played out on a public stage. In Chapter Nine, the same organizations and leaders that saw success in earlier chapters—Cisco, Facebook, Kodak, and Microsoft—demonstrate why their ability to embrace failure leads to their success. One telling example is how an organization like Google—one of the most successful, innovative companies today— encourages its organization to take risks and fail.

The last chapter of the book examines how leaders are transforming their organizations to be more open—driven not because of a belief in an ideal, but out of economic and marketplace necessity. Organizations like Procter & Gamble and the State Bank of India have entrenched cultures that in some cases have developed over centuries of careful adherence to an organizational credo. If you are a leader facing daunting organizational and managerial challenges, I hope you'll draw inspiration from how these case studies for how you can turn around your organization.

BEGINNING THE JOURNEY

Being open is hard. But if you can understand not only the benefits, but also the process, it can get easier. You may be in a leadership position—a manager or CEO—of a business that is trying to use social technologies to introduce a new product or to counter a customer backlash. You may be an HR manager or company strategist eager to tap into the ideas of your workforce. Or you may be a church committee leader who is trying to energize listless volunteers, or a school administrator working with vocal parents agitating for change.

The struggle in balancing openness and control is a universal, human problem. As a parent of growing children, I sometimes long for the days when I could simply strap a discontented toddler into a car seat and drive off to my destination. Just as children grow and develop their own voices that need to be heard, our customers, employees, and partners want to be brought into the inner sanctum of the organization as well. My hope is that this book will provide guidance and support as you begin your journey into a new world of openness. Bon voyage!

Charlene Li
May 2010

OPEN LEADERSHIP

PART I

THE UPSIDE OF GIVING UP CONTROL

WHY GIVING
UP CONTROL IS
INEVITABLE

You may not know who Dave Carroll is, but United Airlines wishes it had never heard of him.

One March day not long ago, Carroll was a United passenger waiting for takeoff. He looked out of the airplane window and couldn't believe what he was seeing. Out on the tarmac of Chicago's O'Hare airport, he saw baggage handlers tossing suitcases, sometimes dropping them on the ground. Among the items were guitar cases—and the alarmed Carroll, an independent Canadian musician and songwriter, realized that these were *his* guitars being thrown back and forth.

Carroll called over a United flight attendant and asked her to check into what was happening outside. As Carroll related in an interview, "She physically held up her hand and said, 'Don't talk to me, talk to the gate agent outside.' Everybody I talked to after that said either they were not empowered to do anything, or they didn't care."[1]

Sure enough, when Carroll landed in Omaha, his final destination, he opened his guitar case and found his beloved Taylor guitar badly damaged. Carroll was in a hurry to get to his gig, and he was booked with back-to-back with shows, so it wasn't until three days later that he contacted United to report the damage. But United refused to compensate Carroll for the $1,200 repair—the company had a standing policy to not accept claims more than twenty-four hours after a flight, because as time passes it becomes increasingly difficult to pinpoint responsibility for damage.[2] Because Carroll submitted his claim more than three days after the damage occurred, United said that it would not pay for damages that could have been caused elsewhere.

Carroll pressed his case for months but made no progress. By November 2008, nine months after the incident, he finally got to talk to someone with some decision making power. But alas, it went nowhere. The United representative explained that her hands were tied because of the policy—and politely, but firmly, said there was nothing else that United could do.

Now, if you were a frustrated, deeply wronged *musician* like Carroll, what would you do? You'd write a song about the experience! Carroll actually did more than that—he also made a music video called "United Breaks Guitars" and posted it on YouTube.[3] He felt better, and he really didn't think that more than a dozen people or so would see it.

That was on July 7, 2009. Within three days, the video had over one million views, and Carroll's anthem became a viral sensation. By the end of 2009, there had been over seven million views and hundreds of news stories about Carroll's experience.[4]

Understandably, United was aghast. The company immediately reached out to Carroll, who explained that his biggest desire was to have United's baggage damage policy changed. Tony Cervone, United's SVP of corporate communications, told me, "We engaged directly with Dave as soon as this came out, and said, 'What happened and let us understand this better.' We listened, and then we changed a couple of the policies almost immediately." Indeed, United's willingness to engage Dave Carroll helped to quell the rising groundswell of anger. Carroll posted a heartfelt video statement that explained the incident, applauded United Airlines for its efforts in reaching out to remedy the situation, and even praised the professionalism of United's employees.[5]

United was in a tough situation. The airline industry gets luggage and people to their destinations without a hitch most of the time, and when things do go wrong, the airlines do their best to remedy the situation. But today, all it takes is one (talented) person to replace "Fly the friendly skies" with "United breaks guitars."

THE NEW CULTURE OF SHARING

What's really going on here? The answer, both simple and far-reaching, is that there has been a fundamental shift in power, one in which individuals have the ability to broadcast their views to the world. This shift has come about because of three trends:

1. MORE PEOPLE ONLINE. Not only is the number of people going online growing, but the time they spend and the kinds of things they do online are both also multiplying. According to internetworld-stats.com, 1.7 billion people globally are active on the Internet.[6] Penetration ranges from 6.8 percent in Africa and 19.4 percent in Asia to 74.2 percent in North America.

2. THE WIDESPREAD USE OF SOCIAL SITES. These days, it's hard to find any Internet user who hasn't watched at least one video on YouTube. Adoption has been quick: in September 2006 only 32 percent of all active Internet users around the world had watched a video clip online; by March 2009 it had grown to 83 percent.[7] Similarly, social networking site usage has jumped, growing from

27 percent of global online users to 63 percent of all users ages eighteen to fifty-four globally. So when people go online, they are now spending a disproportionate amount of time on content that they have created themselves.

3.   THE RISE OF SHARING. More than anything else, the past few years have been dominated by the rise of *a culture of sharing.* The activity of sharing is a deeply ingrained human behavior, and with each new wave of technology—printed paper, telegraph, telephones, and email—sharing gets faster, cheaper, and easier.

Now there's a new dimension to sharing. Until about five years ago, unless you knew how to program a Web page, sharing was limited to the number of emails you could send out. And if you sent out too many, you would start to lose your credibility.

Now widespread distribution of information online is as easy as updating your status to your friends on Facebook and Twitter, which you can access from just about any device (Web browser, mobile phone, even your TV).[8] And new services make it easy to upload not only text, but many different types of content: upload a photo to Flickr or a video to YouTube directly from your mobile device, or create a podcast by simply calling a phone service.[9] All of these new features have made sharing not only simple, but also scalable. This technological leap has given anyone armed with a mobile phone the ability to share with the world.

GOING PUBLIC

Social media has not only empowered your customers but also given your employees new ways to collaborate with each other—a good thing—and new opportunities to publicly grumble about their jobs—a not-so-good thing. Problems that once were resolved through private channels like phone calls and emails are now played out in public. You never could control what people said over their backyard fences about your brand, your company, or your management style, but until recently the public impact tended to be minimal.

Take, for example, what people think about their jobs. You've probably complained about your job to friends and family members, sharing with them your frustrations at work. In the past, the effect of disgruntled employees was mostly limited to their immediate circle of acquaintances.

But today, one need only go to a site like Glassdoor.com to get the inside scoop on an organization. Employees anonymously review companies and their leadership and also share their titles and salaries, in an effort to help others who may be negotiating a job or raise. Here's an example:

NOT A FUN PLACE TO WORK

PROS
- Interesting technology.
- The people at our location are fantastic.

CONS
- Senior management (officer level) does not communicate in a constructive way.
- It is obvious that senior management does not value the employees of the company.
- Since our company was acquired by Company X, morale and productivity have plummeted.

ADVICE TO SENIOR MANAGEMENT
- Allow business units more autonomy in day-to-day operations. Set goals for business units, then provide the freedom and the resources to get the job done.
- Recognize and reward productive employees.

SAYING GOODBYE TO CONTROL

Business leaders are terrified about the power of social technologies, but they are also intrigued and excited about the opportunities. I've spoken with hundreds of leaders about their desire to tap into the power of social technologies to transform their businesses. They like the idea of being able to hear instantly what their customers are saying about them. They're curious about the ability to obtain new ideas from customers or to lower their support costs by having customers solve each others' problems.

A few have actually taken the steps to embrace social technologies and are doing well; many others began the journey enthusiastically, only to fail. There is neither typical rhyme nor reason in these successes or failures—the size of the company, industry, or even prior experience with social technologies did not dictate the outcome. Instead, my research shows, the biggest indicator of success has been an *open mind-set*—the ability of leaders to let go of control *at the right time, in the right place, and in the right amount.*

The first step is recognizing that you are not in control—your customers, employees, and partners are. If you are among the many executives who long for the "good ol' days" when rules and roles were clear, indulge yourself in that kind of thinking for just a few more minutes—then it's time to get to work. This is a fad that will not fade, but will only grow stronger, with or without you.

LETTING GO TO BUILD RELATIONSHIPS

At this point, you may be thinking that engaging with these newly empowered people is too risky, that your organization isn't ready to deal with unruly mobs. Or as one executive commented, "It is one thing for customers to be aiming a gun at me. It is another thing to invite them onto my site and hand them the gun myself."

The reason to get proactive about giving up control is that by doing so you can actually regain some semblance of control. It seems counterintuitive, but the act of engaging with people, of accepting that they have power, can actually put you in a position to counter negative behavior. In fact, it's really the only chance you have of being able to influence the outcome.

The key is to think about the challenge of letting go as a relationship issue. Management gurus James Kouzes and Barry Posner, the authors of *The Leadership Challenge,* write, "Leadership is a relationship between those who aspire to lead and those who choose to follow."[10] At a time when customers and employees are redefining how they make and maintain relationships with social technologies, it's high time that organizations rethink the foundations of business relationships as well.

To understand how these new relationships will work, think about the most fulfilling relationship you have in your personal life. Do you control it? Do you dictate the terms and expect the other person to follow you blindly? Or do you continually invest time and hard work and endure many trials to grow and develop that relationship?

Business is no different—it too is built on relationships. There are relationships between individual customers and the organization as well as relationships with employees and partners. And leadership is defined by the relationship crafted between a leader and the people who decide to follow that person—happily or unhappily. In the context of relationships, how much control do you truly have? You can't make customers buy your products (contrary to what your marketing department may think). You can't make your employees support a strategy; they can simply act in a passive-aggressive manner and choose not to follow.

Face it—you're not in control and probably never really were, even though a recent marketing conference promised to teach attendees how to "take back control."[11] So what are you really letting go of? In order to be open, you need to let go of the *need* to be in control. But to fill that void, you need to develop the confidence—to develop the trust—that when you let go of control, the people to whom you pass the power will act responsibly.

MOVING THE NEW RELATIONSHIPS FORWARD

It's clear that we need to think about relationships and leadership in a new way. Companies are used to broadcasting messages to customers, focused on driving a specific action or transaction. Or they tell employees what work they should be doing, or they dictate the terms of how partners will work with them. Although there have always been ways for customers, employees, and partners to communicate back and forth with the company, those channels were minor compared to the volume and weight of the messages being issued by the company. The result: many traditional business relationships lack depth and real engagement. When asked to describe the nature of relationships with customers, many businesspeople will use words like "short-term," "transactional," and "impersonal."

Now imagine a new type of relationship, one built on multiple shared experiences—a relationship in which trust is developed and flourishes. Wouldn't it be great if you could describe your business relationships with words like "loyal," "engaged," and even "passionate" and "intimate"?

Not only is this possible, but it's happening today. More and more companies are realizing that in this new open world customers, employees, and partners are taking on roles different from that old one—the passive recipient of company missives. They now feel empowered because of a culture of sharing that allows them to spread their thoughts far and wide. Thanks to technology, they are becoming engaged with each other and with those organizations that embrace relationships in a deeper, more meaningful way.

YOU'VE SEEN IT ON AN INTERNATIONAL SCALE

The most telling example of this new type of relationship and engagement was seen in Barack Obama's presidential election campaign in 2008.[12] From the beginning, it was designed to embrace a grassroots movement, which was an outgrowth of Obama's community organizing experience. It also prioritized being open about the strategy, with campaign manager David Plouffe laying out the game plan in multiple venues—including YouTube.[13] The logic: the McCain campaign already knew what the strategy was, so the Obama people reasoned they might as well make known the "master plan" so that people could support it in their own way. From the importance of winning Iowa to sharing the detailed budget of how millions of dollars would be spent in Florida, again and again the Obama campaign was open about what it was doing on the campaign.

Obama and his team were comfortable with letting go of control because they spent an inordinate amount of time making sure people were aligned not only with the goal (to get Obama elected) but also, and more important, with the underlying *values* of the campaign. Michael Slaby, the CTO of the Obama campaign, shared with me, "If you do a good job of teaching your values and mission to the people at the bottom of your organization, then once you give them control, they will do the right things with it." With a relatively unknown candidate, the team realized that they needed to help people get to know Obama as a person, so they created a private social network and tapped sites like Facebook and MySpace to extend the campaign into a personal space.

Core values of the campaign were respect and humility, which meant that when someone engaged with campaign staff or volunteers, they needed to reply. "These are basic things that you do when you are in a relationship with another person," Slaby said. "Companies and campaigns typically don't dialogue well, but I think we did a good job of participating with people across all the environments in which we were working."

We all witnessed the results of that new personal relationship as Obama's campaign activated people who had been silent watchers of presidential politics for decades. Some people shared their enthusiasm by putting a virtual sticker on their social networking profiles. Others set up profiles on MyBarackObama.com and asked friends and family to donate. And a few created videos as their own testament to the campaign, ranging from the frivolous (like Obama Girl) and fun ("Wassup 2008") to the moving, as exemplified by rapper will.i.am's video, "Yes We Can," which drew millions to the campaign.[14] The Obama campaign did more than just deploy technology in a savvy new way; it used technology to reach out and create a relationship where there wasn't one before by welcoming people closest to the front lines who were previously disenfranchised in the political process.

THE LEADER'S DILEMMA

During the campaign, Obama was able to manage the balance between letting go and maintaining control, but as evidenced in the first year since taking office, running a country openly is vastly different from running a campaign. Balancing letting go with being in command has been a problem that harkens back to the very start of the information age, when the printing press allowed people to transfer and share information at scale for the first time. Education was restricted because church leaders and aristocrats worried that if the lower classes learned to read they could become dissatisfied with their lot and organize themselves.

But once books became more widespread, the people in power found it more and more difficult to maintain absolute control. Professor Samuel Huntington, in *Political Order in Changing Societies* (1968), wrote about the "king's dilemma" to illustrate the challenge of ruling an enlightened, connected populace.[15] A forward-thinking king, who gives rights and freedom to serfs and makes them citizens, may end up abdicating his throne as these citizens agitate for more and more freedom over time. But a worse fate awaited those who clamped down on reform and repressed the populace; the pent-up demand for power, coupled with new ways for people to self-organize and communicate, led to an explosive reaction, usually with the result of the leader losing not only his throne but his head as well.

Many companies today face the same dilemma in that they are structured in classic command-and-control organizations that were set up in the post-war industrial age. These centralized hierarchies worked well to organize complex supply, manufacturing, and distribution processes that relied on consistent methods and precise controls to maintain quality. Although teams could have some discretion on how to get things done, good management meant strict adherence to predetermined measures of success. In addition, the high cost of communications and information meant that only the most precious, important information moved up and down corporate hierarchies—leaders relied on a clear "chain of command," and any information that flowed outside of that chain was slapped down.

Two things have happened to put pressure on this traditional mode. First, the parameters of success have changed from process control to innovation. You simply can't "Six Sigma" your way into new markets. Instead, organizations need to develop the organizational flexibility to adapt to fast-changing situations. Second, businesses are now more likely to be delivering services than manufacturing objects. A skilled and motivated workforce on the front lines quickly chafes under strict limitations and hierarchies, unable to do what they think is needed because of headquarters' disconnected notions of what really works in the market.

A long line of management gurus have studied and recognized the limitations of this organizational structure. In 1946, Peter Drucker described, in *Concept of the Corporation,* the strong management approaches of General Motors, but also recommended that the company decentralize authority because the people with the most information and expertise weren't being heard.[16] Robert Greenleaf's "The Servant As Leader" essay in 1970 turned leadership on its head, positioning executives as the humble stewards of the corporation, not the almighty heads of them.[17] And in his 1982 book *In Search of Excellence*, Tom Peters encouraged organizations to replace top-heavy management with employee- and customer-led teams.[18]

But despite the admonitions of these respected management experts, the call for change has so far gone largely unanswered, because it hasn't been practical. Executives often ask, in so many words, "I'm responsible so I have to have control . . . if you're telling me to give up control, how can I manage the discrepancy between control and results?" The problem is, these leaders are asking the wrong question. They should instead be asking, "How do I develop the kind of new, open, engaged relationships I need to get things done?"

THE NEW RULES OF OPEN LEADERSHIP

What's changed today is that new technologies allow us to let go of control and still be in command, because better, cheaper communication tools give us the ability to be intimately familiar with what is happening with both customers and employees. The result of these new relationships is *open leadership*, which I define as:

> *having the confidence and humility to give up the need to be in control while inspiring commitment from people to accomplish goals*

Open leadership fosters new relationships—and to understand and govern how these new relationships works, we need new rules like the following:

1. RESPECT THAT YOUR CUSTOMERS AND EMPLOYEES HAVE POWER. Once you accept this as true, you can begin to a have a real, more equal relationship with them. Without this mind-set, you will continue to think of them as replaceable resources and treat them as such. And if you ever need a reminder of what that customer and employee power looks like, just go read a social media monitoring report on your company from a vendor like Radian6, BuzzMetrics, or Cymfony—you'll quickly be humbled by the power of these people.

2. SHARE CONSTANTLY TO BUILD TRUST. At the core of any successful relationship is trust. Trust is typically formed when people do what they say they will do. But in today's increasingly virtual, engaged environments, trust also comes from the daily patter of conversations. The repeated successful interchange of people sharing their thoughts, activities, and concerns results in relationship. New technologies like blogs, social networks, and Twitter remove the cost of sharing, making it easy to form these new relationships.

3.   NURTURE CURIOSITY AND HUMILITY. Often, sharing can quickly turn into messaging if all of the outbound information isn't accompanied by give and take. Expressing curiosity about what someone is doing and why something is important to that person keeps sharing grounded and focused on what other people want to hear, balanced with what you want to say. The natural outgrowth of curiosity is humility, which gives you the intellectual integrity to acknowledge that you still have a lot to learn, and also to admit when you are wrong.

4.   HOLD OPENNESS ACCOUNTABLE. In relationships, accountability is a two-way street—it makes clear the expectations in the relationship, as well as the consequences if they are not met. So if your product causes someone problems, what's the first thing you should do? Apologize and figure out how to resolve the problem. Likewise, if you give someone the ability to comment on your site and they misuse it, they should understand that you will deny them future access.

5.   FORGIVE FAILURE. The corollary to accountability is forgiveness. Things go wrong all the time in relationships, and the healthiest ones move on from them, leaving behind grudges and blame. This is not to say that failure is accepted; rather, that it is acknowledged and understood.

You'll find that you are not alone in your concerns, nor unique in your belief that there is an upside to letting go. Find out how other people responded to these questions by going online to open-leadership .com. You'll have the opportunity there to share your own concerns and hopes as well.

We've seen some of the opportunities and dangers of this new, open world. To better understand the threats and opportunities, in the next chapter I'll define in greater detail exactly what I mean by being open.

ACTION PLAN: UNDERSTANDING THE CHALLENGES OF OPEN LEADERSHIP

With these rules in mind, you can ask yourself the following questions. They will give you a starting point, as well as a preliminary roadmap to help you reach where you want to go.

- What are your biggest challenges and fears when it comes to your customers or employees using social technologies?
- How would you describe the nature of the relationship today with your customers? With your employees? With your partners?
- How would you like those relationships to look and feel two years from now? What are your biggest fears about giving up control?
- What is the one thing about which you are most nervous about giving up control?
- Where do you see the greatest opportunities in letting go and being open?

THE TEN
ELEMENTS OF
OPENNESS

While I was writing this book, I had the opportunity to address a group of Harvard Business School alumni in Silicon Valley about the concept of openness. I asked, "How many of you work for what you consider to be an open organization?" Only three of the hundred or so people in the room thought they did—and they worked for Mozilla, Twitter, and IDEO.

This highlights a fundamental problem with the topic of openness: we lack a basic framework and vocabulary on which we can base discussions and decisions around openness because there are so many different ways to be open. For instance, Mozilla, Twitter, and IDEO look at openness in three very distinct ways, two of them based in technology. Mozilla's product is built via open source, so improvements to the Firefox browser can come from anywhere. Twitter has very open application programming interfaces, allowing anyone to build on top of Twitter's basic structure and use its data, even off of its site. And IDEO, a design and innovation consulting firm, has a famously open work culture that encourages innovative "design thinking."

To begin to define openness, let's start with the fundamental problem we examined in Chapter One—that you and your organization already exercise less and less control over your business situation in light of empowered customers and employees. Your focus must shift from trying to retain what little control you have to choosing where and when you will be open so that you can embrace these newly empowered players.

At the center of this problem is confidence. When you open up and let go, you have to have faith that the people to whom you pass the power will act responsibly. This also requires a heavy dose of humility, which is the understanding that there are equally capable—or actually more capable—people who can do the things that you do.

All too often, people believe that being open is just the first part of the definition I gave in the last chapter—*Having the confidence and humility to give up the need to be in control*—which is why they often fail. Without the second part—*while inspiring commitment from people to accomplish goals*—which enables openness to lead to results, your efforts will be fruitless and unfocused. So as I further define openness in the pages ahead, I also explain what openness is trying to accomplish.

THE CONTRADICTORY NATURE OF OPENNESS

As we begin, I want to take a moment and emphasize that organizations can be open and closed at the same time, and this is to be expected. For an organization to be open and still accomplish things requires that some controls be in place, and this is one of the biggest mysteries of business: How can you be open while still running a tight ship?

I had a chance to begin to answer this question firsthand when I spent twenty-four hours at sea on the nuclear aircraft carrier USS *Nimitz*. I was on the bridge speaking with Captain Michael Manazir about the intricacies and challenges of running a carrier when he stopped, looked down at the flight deck, and frowned. He excused himself, picked up a nearby phone, and spoke softly into it. After hanging up, he returned to the conversation, explaining, "One person down there didn't check everywhere to make sure that everyone was out of the way before the plane took off. I told them to tell him that his head needs to be on a swivel, turning all the way around, all the time."

There's no doubt that Manazir runs a tight ship. He has to, as he is responsible for the safety and well-being of five thousand people on board. Moreover, the USS *Nimitz* is the crown jewel of the navy, and when fully armed represents one of the most powerful military arsenals in the world. Like most jewels, it is protected vigilantly: the navy keeps the carrier safe, positioning a battle group of destroyers, battleships, and submarines around the *Nimitz* to protect it from threats.

You might think a person or organization with that much at stake would be secretive and paranoid. And when I received the invitation to visit the *Nimitz,* along with fifteen other bloggers, I assumed that there had to be a catch—that the navy probably wanted us to spread some prescribed recruitment and mission messages. But we found just the opposite: a crew that was surprisingly, disarmingly, and refreshingly *open.* Captain Manazir welcomed us with a brisk overview of how the ship worked. Manazir was very approachable and easy to talk to, and I was impressed by his directness, energy, and confidence in his crew as, over and over again, he encouraged us to talk to as many people as possible, to ask any question we wanted.[1] "This is your navy," he said, "and it's your right to know how it works for you."

19

And we saw everything! From Vultures Row, high above the flight deck, we watched pilots take off and land. Outfitted with helmets, hearing protection, and white vests (to make it easier to find us in case we fell overboard), we went on to the flight deck, where we stood feet away from the roaring engines of a jet catapulting off the runway. You don't just *hear* a jet accelerate from 0 to 140 miles per hour in less than two seconds—you feel it vibrate in your very bones.[2]

There were no preconditions and no restrictions other than to safeguard our well-being (such as staying out of the way of aircraft taking off and landing). In fact, the only thing the navy would not let us see were the nuclear reactors—but then, only a select group of engineers gets to see them.

The navy's openness was most amazing to me when we visited the pilot squadron room of the Strike Fighter Squadron 97 (aptly named the "Warhawks"). They were confident and jocular, as you would expect "Top Gun" pilots to be. The pilots shared their love of flying, but they also shared their fears, especially of landing a fighter jet in the dead of the night on a heaving ship. In an interview with another blogger, Navy pilot Lieutenant Luis Delgardo, who flies an F-18 fighter jet, was especially candid about his flying experiences:

"Landing at night—it just fills you with terror. Sometimes I'll be screaming into my mask in the last few seconds before I touch down. And you remember that fear, so it's very difficult to sleep. But the next day you wake up, and you remember that you gotta do it. In this job, there is no choice. There is a mission that has to get done. As much as I enjoy it [my job], I look forward to not having to do it one day because it takes away from you. Every flight is almost as if you die a little death."[3]

Such candor is welcomed in the navy, because it's that sharing that helps the crew connect with and support each other throughout the long tour of duty. Captain Manazir had confidence in his crew to do and say the right thing in front of strangers because their training and commitment to the navy's mission ensured that they would know what they could and couldn't discuss.

Although there is this very open type of communication, each person on board the ship has a highly specified, prescribed job (such as loading a missile onto the left wing of a fighter jet) that they rehearse under many different scenarios. And as Delgardo shared in the preceding quote, he doesn't have another choice but to fly and to do so when he's commanded, even though every fiber of his soul is telling him not to do it.

So, is the navy open? The crew of the USS *Nimitz* have very little decision making discretion about their jobs, yet they understand that this is essential to their accomplishing their shared mission and goals. At the same time, the navy service members are very, very open to sharing and communicating their experiences, hiding little, and they are very forthcoming about themselves and their feelings. So the navy is open in some ways and not at all in others.

THE TEN OPEN ELEMENTS

To help make sense of the navy's seemingly contradictory ability to be both open and closed at the same time, let's look at what I see as the ten elements of being open, which fall into two broad categories: information sharing and decision making (see Figure 2.1). In the case of the navy, the service is open when it comes to sharing nonclassified information. But there is a strict hierarchy when it comes to making decisions, and service members exercise very little discretion in their day-to-day responsibilities.

Within each element or component of openness, we'll take a look at what it means to be open and also examine what you are really letting go of as you become more open. In many cases, you aren't *giving up* control—you are *shifting* it to someone else in whom you have confidence. As you read, note which types of openness excite you the most and also those that create the greatest anxiety. At the end of this chapter, you'll have the opportunity to conduct a self-assessment to audit the openness of your organization. There is not one exact

FIGURE 2.1. Defining Openness: The Ten Open Elements

Information Sharing	Decision Making
• Explaining	• Centralized
• Updating	• Democratic
• Conversing	• Self-managing
• Open Mic	• Distributed
• Crowdsourcing	
• Platforms	

"metric" for openness, but you'll be able to start gauging where you fall on the closed-open continuum. Keep your completed openness audit close by, as it will be a starting point for your openness strategy.

OPEN INFORMATION SHARING

Information is the lubricant of any organization. Without it, the company comes to a screeching halt. In the past decade, the flow of information around the company and into and out of the organization has vastly accelerated with the advent of new technologies, starting with the widespread adoption of email and accelerating with social technologies.

I define the six different elements of information sharing primarily by the goal and the nature of the sharing. We'll first take a look at information that originates from within the organization (explaining, updating), and then move to instances when information comes from outside the organization back into it (conversing, open mic, crowdsourcing). Last, we'll take a look at how technological openness can create platforms where different groups and people can work with each other using common standards.

EXPLAINING: CREATING BUY-IN

The purpose of this type of information sharing is to inform people about a decision, direction, or strategy with the goal of getting recipients—employees, associates, distributors, and others—to buy into the idea, so that everyone is working toward the same goal. This is typical of the open book management (OBM) approach, which John Case defined in his bestseller by the same title as a "philosophy of involving every employee in making a firm more successful by sharing financial and operational information."[4] Although there have been many books explaining how OBM works, up to now it was an option that few companies pursued, namely because it's hard to give enough information at a granular enough level to make the knowledge actionable.[5] In addition, it was hard to see your employees as partners vested in the success of the company if you saw them only once a quarter when you met to discuss financial results.

As I suggested in Chapter One, a key difference today is that a new generation of workers is coming of age that believes "sharingness" is next to—or more important than—godliness. Moreover, the demand to be more open about how an organization makes decisions and operates is coming from people both inside *and outside* the organization.

One leader who believes in this wholeheartedly is Jim Mullen, who founded Mullen Communications, with headquarters in Boston. He says the most important thing he's learned in his thirty years of running a company is that "the more power you give away, the more power you ultimately have." For example, he shared Mullen's quarterly financial information with all of its employees, even though the agency was privately held. He also shared the Association of American Advertising Agencies' annual salary data with all the employees and based their compensation on the inter-quartile mean figures. This meant that everyone in the company knew within a fairly narrow range what everyone else in the firm was earning—and also what other ad agencies in the region were paying their employees.

Why did he do this? Certainly, Mullen was creating focus around a goal and removing distractions such as who is making what salary, but he was doing more—he was building a relationship. "I felt that if you shared information you actually created a trust, and the more information you shared, the greater trust you created in people. Because data is factual, as opposed to opinion, it is extremely persuasive." In this way, Mullen practiced two of the new rules of open leadership that I discussed at the end of Chapter One—namely, he recognized that his employees had power and that he needed to actively practice sharing with them to grow and shape the relationship.

Managing leaks. Of course, this approach to information sharing runs counter to the traditional way of doing business. As Intel's Andy Grove memorably counseled, "Only the paranoid survive."[6] While Grove's book counseled a constant look over your shoulder and dissatisfaction with a comfortable business-as-usual attitude, many executives took the message to be something like, "If you want to survive, be suspicious of everybody . . . including your employees, customers, and partners." Which leads directly to the mindset of "The more secretive, the safer."

Paranoia has its place—especially in the context of today's highly porous communications environment, in which an errant employee email can wreak havoc on company confidential information. And although the open book philosophy strives to share as much information as possible, there are practical limits. To examine this, let's take a look at Facebook, whose mission is "to give people the power to share and make the world more open and connected."[7]

Facebook's platform has evolved from being a closed social network for college students to one that allows developers and companies to use the company's data on sites outside of Facebook and to create money-making businesses that are worth millions.[8] Internally, Facebook practices open book management, with CEO Mark Zuckerberg holding a public question-and-answer session for the entire company every Friday for an hour.

The concern, though, is that sensitive information could be leaked. "Our default is that we would like to talk about everything," explains Lori Goler, the VP of human resources. "But we have also come out and said, 'Here are some things that we are probably not able to talk about.'" For example, Zuckerberg will update employees about progress on finding new office space, but hold back on specific details, explaining that it could affect lease negotiations. And clearly, not only is any information regarding potential strategic moves— such as discussions around investors, acquisitions, or an IPO—too sensitive to share, but to do so may be illegal. So although Facebook is eager to share information widely, it remains sensitive to business realities.

As someone who has been covering Facebook for years, I've found that there is astoundingly little leakage, given the amount of information available. How do they manage to do this? Goler says that Facebook repeatedly emphasizes that information is shared only because people keep it internal to the company. "We have had a couple of situations where we wish we could have shared information without it becoming public. One or two emails Mark sent to the company appeared in the press in their entirety, and that is really bad behavior because it puts in jeopardy our ability to share everything internally. So we said, 'Guys, we want to be able to share everything with you, but if you are not going to treat it with respect, then you are putting that privilege at risk.' I think there is a lot of peer pressure to not share things and to treat the information with respect." In this way, Facebook is practicing one of the five new rules of open leadership: holding openness accountable.

As these examples show, the key benefit to this type of sharing is aligning goals by sharing the logic, thinking, and decision making process behind the decision or action. The key difference today is that the give-and-take that typifies OBM happens more regularly, not just once a quarter when the executives of the company descend to share the results. It's the constant checking-in that leaders do—made possible by blogs, podcasts, and Twitter accounts—that enables them to share their thoughts and decisions.

Technology has also made it possible to extend this type of sharing outside the organization—providing updates and customer service through new channels. Customers and partners want to hear more details more regularly, especially if they are making long-term plans based on products or services being provided by partnering organizations. Facebook recently opened its product development timeline, exposing future improvements six months in advance so that developers could make better plans for upcoming changes.[9] Although competitors can easily see what Facebook is going to do in the near future, it was more important for Facebook to inject confidence and certainty into its developer relationships. Facebook was also confident in its innovation pipeline, so that competitors would also be trying to keep up, rather than trying to leapfrog.

UPDATING: CAPTURING KNOWLEDGE AND ACTIONS

In the normal course of work, people provide each other with updates on what they are doing. This includes the everyday information debris that all too often clutters our email inboxes—sales support requests, product and project updates, the endless "cc'ing" of people to make sure everyone is included.

It's time to end the madness!

New publishing tools like blogs, collaboration platforms, and even Twitter provide updates that are easily available whenever someone needs them. These updates have the added benefit of being archived, searchable, and discoverable, meaning they capture the knowledge, expertise, and actions that happen in the ordinary course of business. Imagine, for instance, that you're a new employee coming onto a project and need to make a contribution quickly. By reaching into the team collaboration platform or reading people's internal micro-blogging updates, you can quickly get up to speed.

Let's take a detailed look at how that works, with two examples of the updating process both inside and outside an organization through two specific channels: blogging and internal networks.

Blogging provides updates. Paul Levy, the CEO of Beth Israel Deaconess Medical Center, maintains a highly active public blog called "Running A Hospital," covering topics from the hospital's efforts in lean process improvement and an award they won for their new ICU, to discussions about whether he gets paid too much.[10] He began blogging because he wanted to "share thoughts with people about my experience here and their experiences in the hospital world."[11] Although few health care executives are comfortable talking so openly about medical concerns, technology, and treatment, Levy embraces the scrutiny, arguing that rather than just be attacked, it's better to state a point of view and to create a framework.

In the book *Sticks & Stones* by Larry Weber, Levy explained how he balanced blogging with being a CEO, saying, "There are lots of parts to the job of a CEO, but one of them is, in the crassest possible terms, to position your company in the best possible light in the public environment; among your consumers, potential consumers, and potential adversaries. What better way to do that than to write when you want, about the topics you want, in your own words? You're not being edited by reporters or anyone else; you can get your message out in thirty seconds, and the whole world can see what you've said."[12]

Levy understands that a key part of his job as the CEO is simply communicating the mission of his organization and providing regular updates on how his hospital operates. This is slightly different from visibility into decisions, which involves a top-down flow of information. With updates, the information can come from anywhere. What Levy is doing is creating a unique culture of sharing, and he's doing this by setting the example from the top.

One key concern that arises over and over again is that employees will not know what to do with publishing tools that are given to them and thus may end up writing or saying something inappropriate that will harm the company. We'll look at the need for policies and procedures in Chapter Five, but consider how infrequently this actually happens today, as well as what you realistically can expect to control. Most employees have access to any number of free publishing tools—Facebook, Twitter, blogs, discussion forums, even plain old email—through which anyone can share company secrets and say inappropriate things. Yet it rarely happens. There are inherent risks in giving employees a soapbox to shout from, but you should also consider the benefits this type of sharing can bring to your relationship with customers.

Internal updates speed up product development. In another example of sharing, Brian Robins, the chief marketing officer of the technology company SunGard, told me that the firm's development teams started using Yammer, an internal version of Twitter, to support short conversations and updates between employees. Anyone in a company can start a Yammer network and begin inviting colleagues, and Robins says SunGard's developers started using Yammer without any kind of corporate sponsorship or mandate. "They were using it to share information about projects they were working on. I looked through many of the examples, and the developers are asking technical questions of other developers: 'Does anyone know how to do this?' or 'Has anyone used this or that tool or object?'" It was so effective that SunGard rolled out Yammer access to its twenty thousand employees across more than thirty countries, where it's starting to affect all aspects of operations from sales to customer service.

CONVERSING: IMPROVING OPERATIONS

Senior executives like to say that they want to be closer to customers and employees. They want to know what customers think about the firm's products, services, and experience and how the company can improve. Today, anyone with a computer can provide feedback to the organization—comments on blogs, discussion forums, review sites—and, even better, the company can talk back. By conversing openly, an organization engages in these conversations with the intent of improving operations and efficiency.

As we saw in the previous chapter, customers are quick to air their grievances in public. So companies like Comcast have led the way in responding in those same channels. Frank Eliason, the senior director of national customer service at Comcast set up a Twitter account, aptly naming it "ComcastCares."[13] In addition to monitoring blogs, Frank and his team actively seek out customers who are having problems with Comcast and have written about it in social media like blogs or Twitter. They then start the conversation with a simple question: "Can I help?" These three simple words have fundamentally changed the relationship.

Although this may sound like a lot of work, Eliason explained that it's better for Comcast to proactively find and address these problems before they escalate. As such, they have ramped up the team, shifting and adding resources as demand grows. An important benefit has been to demonstrate Comcast's desire to provide excellent customer service and shifting—ever so slowly, one person at a time—the public perception that Comcast has poor customer service.

The hardest part for Comcast? It had to adjust to the fact that it was publicly discussing negative comments and problems for the whole world to see. But Eliason argued that since these comments were already public, it behooved Comcast to be there as well to engage these customers in a conversation.

Putting community to work. Customer service is historically a cost center for most organizations. But many companies—especially technology companies with a base of tech-savvy customers—are turning to their expert customers and partner networks to take on that support work. From its inception, SolarWinds, a network management software provider, built a twenty-five-thousand-member user community of network administrators who help each other with their problems, be they large or small. This has allowed them to support a customer base of eighty-eight thousand companies with just two customer support people, as most of the problems that arise are aired and addressed inside the user community.

SolarWinds is able to do this by constantly investing in and managing the health of the community. They frequently provide experts with content and training and use recognition to highlight the best experts. They also monitor the health of the community, tracking response time, issue resolution, and user satisfaction. But, unusual among companies, they also tout their user community as a key competitive advantage—when the company went public in May

2009, they dedicated a part of their precious investor presentation time to explaining the value of their user community. "When you strip away everything that we do, our community is in many ways the key long-term competitive advantage that we have," said Kenny Van Zant, SolarWinds's senior vice president and chief product strategist. "They not only provide user support, but they also serve as a sounding board for new products and services."

Collaboration platforms provide structure for conversations. Conversations can also be quite helpful internally; they differ from the internal updates discussed earlier in that the conversations are centered about a specific topic or problem. For example, Yum! Brands—the world's largest restaurant company in terms of system units and the parent company of A&W Restaurants, KFC, Long John Silver's, Pizza Hut, and Taco Bell—wanted to build a knowledge base and internal network that would allow its 336,000 employees in 110 countries to be able to connect with one another in a way they had never been able to before. As Barry Westrum—dean of the Yum! Know How and Innovation Center—put it, the goal was to get the company to "work differently," not only taking the best practices from one division or geography to another but coming together to solve tough problems as well.

Using a community platform from Jive Software, the network, called iCHING, went live in early 2009. The goals at first were modest. Sharing had traditionally taken place at summits where all the leaders in a function, like marketing, would gather. But these were held only once every two or three years. "We were just looking for a place where we could speak the same language on a 24/7 basis," said Westrum. On iCHING, which involves about six thousand restaurant corporate employees around the world, you can pose a question at the end of your business day and find seventeen responses from around the world waiting for you when you arrive the next morning. Groups gather together to solve problems, not because they were identified and prioritized by executives and managers, but because people on the front lines self-identify problems and ask for help.

And increasingly, traditional enterprise applications are getting conversational. For example, as this book went to print, Salesforce .com announced that its Chatter collaboration platform will integrate real-time updates and conversations from people directly into the interface, using sales opportunities or customer service incidents as the context for conversations. Is there a hot deal in the works, or is a key customer having a service problem? Rather than carry on the discussion via email, people will have those conversations around work processes that already exist, where information about the account or customer is readily at hand. Even one-off updates are put in perspective when they are tagged and shown in the context of a deal or customer service problem.

OPEN MIC: ENCOURAGING PARTICIPATION

You may have been to "open mic" night at a local comedy club, where talented artists are mixed in with many, many duds. Micah Laaker, a director at Yahoo!, has adopted the phrase "open mic" because it so aptly captures the essence of the next type of shared information, where anyone and everyone is welcome to come forward and participate with no preconditions.[14] The epitome of this is YouTube, where you can find jumbled together the following: Randy Pausch's Last Lecture, a jubilant wedding entrance dance, a how-to on inserting a central vascular line with ultrasound, and, to the delight of children (young and old), silly videos such as one of a hamster on a piano.[15]

News outlets have long encouraged people to send them tips, but increasingly they also ask them to submit complete news segments, turning over the reporting of a story directly to them. CNN's iReport.com is the news channel's online user-generated site, and although anyone can upload a video, CNN staff do go through and vet a few that they then feature on the main site. One reporter, Chris Morrow in San Diego, is a freelance journalist who produces high-quality news videos (complete with transitions and graphics) from her home.[16] CNN iReport becomes a platform for Morrow to promote her work, and for CNN it's a way to diversify their news coverage at little cost.

Other companies are following suit. Premier Farnell plc, a UK-based multinational marketer and distributor of electronic products to engineers, has approximately 4,100 employees around the world. The firm bought several thousand video cameras, gave them to employees in every office, and encouraged them to record what they considered to be their best practices and upload the video to their internal video sharing site, appropriately called "OurTube." Allowing individuals to have an unfettered voice that was shared—unedited—with the organization via the Internet brought about profound changes in the company culture, which we'll discuss in greater depth in Chapter Eight.

What's hard about open mic sharing is filtering through all of the submissions to find the best and most relevant content. Unless you have the resources of a CNN, you'll need a system where people rate and rank the material or provide reviews so that the good content rises to the top. Reputations—like the one that Chris Morrow has on CNN iReport—become essential, so there should also be ways to highlight and follow particularly good talent.

CROWDSOURCING: SOLVING A SPECIFIC PROBLEM TOGETHER

The goal with crowdsourcing is to grow the sources of new ideas and gather fresh thinking to create or improve a new product or service. This was always possible (think of the Pillsbury Bake-Off, in which customers compete for prizes with new recipes they create). But the difference now is that this is happening on an unprecedented scale and is directed at encouraging a coherent contribution from an individual toward a specific goal, such as improving a piece of open source code, submitting an idea for a thirty-second ad that will air on the Super Bowl, or uploading mobile phone pictures from a concert.

Doritos, for example, brought back its user-generated content (UGC) Super Bowl ad contest for the 2009 game broadcast. Two unemployed brothers, Joe and Dave Herbert, created a hilarious spot, "Free Doritos," spending less than $2,000 to make a commercial that beat out all of the Madison Avenue agencies to garner the top spot in *USA Today*'s Ad Meter survey of the most-liked commercial during the game; it was also voted the show's favorite ad by YouTube and Hulu audiences.[17] As a result, their commercial won the Doritos contest's $1 million prize. Of more interest to Frito-Lay's management, however, was the comScore survey of the effect: Doritos showed the biggest improvement in consumer perception among advertisers on the Super Bowl show.

Most companies can't afford to run a high-profile contest the way that Doritos does, which is the key reason why UGC contests peaked around 2007. But crowdsourcing has since taken on a different flavor, in that it's solving everyday problems. Take, for example, logo design. Many companies can't afford to spend much more than a few hundred dollars on a good logo, so they turn to "logo factories" or to a local office supply store with in-house design capabilities for a logo that costs as little as $99. At the same time, there are many designers who would like the chance to create logos but lack the relationships and visibility to reach clients.

Enter crowdsourcing sites like crowdSPRING and 99designs.[18] These sites create a marketplace for design, where clients can submit design requirements and designers submit their ideas. Rather than put all of its eggs in one basket, the client can choose from potentially hundreds of options, but only one designer gets paid in the end, and the art work is transferred to the buying client. The work is highly variable, and is sometimes derided as "spec work,"[19] but when I used crowdSPRING to obtain a logo, the winning design was done by the creative designer for a large ad agency. His reason for participating and submitting a design? He wanted to keep up his "design chops." The cost to me: $800 for two logo designs. The value of being able to review 146 different, unique designs: priceless.

Today, crowdsourcing is gaining a foothold for the design of logos, letterhead, and even site design. In the future, I anticipate that the technology platforms and interest in crowdsourcing will lead to more complex projects—such as designing entirely new products or services—and will attract the attention of teams of people as well as individuals.

PLATFORMS: SETTING STANDARDS AND SHARING DATA

eBay is a great example of an open platform—by standardizing how items are listed and how transactions are handled, the company has enabled millions of individual sellers to trade online. The goal behind open platforms is to create standards, protocols, and rules that govern how organizations and people can interact with each other.[20] There are two primary types of open platforms: (1) open architectures that structure and define the rules and interactions, and (2) open data access that makes available data so that other entities can freely use it. In the technology world, these two types of open platforms often dominate discussions around "openness," fueling long debates about how open one company is versus another. I'll give a few examples of each type of open platform, then explain how they change business relationships.

Open architecture. This type of openness comes as a set of standards that lay out how organizations can work with each other and, in many cases, build on top of the platform—without having to craft detailed agreements with each and every partner. One example is Firefox's plug-in capabilities, which allow any developer to extend the functionality of the Firefox browser. The specifications for doing this are clearly laid out by Firefox.

Similarly, commercial companies like Facebook and Apple allow developers to create applications that run on their respective sites and phones. The logic: Facebook and Apple have limited developer resources and couldn't possibly create as many features as their users would want. By opening up their platforms to outsiders, they have turned over the customer experience and relationship to nonemployees. But in the process they have gained so much more. They have created a much more compelling user experience overall, thereby locking in the loyalty of both those users and the developers. Today, iPhone's head start on its apps store and Facebook's half a million apps are significant barriers to entry by competitors.

There are some complaints that the iPhone and Facebook platforms aren't truly "open" in that they do not conform with industry specifications and standards. Others protest that these are proprietary platforms and clamor for a relaxing of the platform rules. Therein lies the contradiction. For the platform to work and be adopted, it must have clear rules that define that openness.[21]

Open data access. Inside of every company lies a rich warehouse of data that could be of interest and benefit to customers and partners. Some companies have what are called "application programming interfaces" (APIs) that define how data requests can be made of that warehouse. Software can make requests of another software program or database. For example, Google Maps has an API that allows its maps to be integrated into other sites—one of the first examples of this is a "mashup" at www.housingmaps.com that takes craigslist.org housing listings and overlays them on Google Maps so that the listings can be searched and browsed within a map's interface.

Many organizations have gone on to use APIs to open themselves to new partners and opportunities. Here are a few examples:

- *Twitter.* This social technology has very open APIs, which allow its entire service and experience to be rendered in a completely different environment. That means people can experience Twitter completely off of its site, on mobile phones or third-party desktop software like TweetDeck, Twirl, or Seesmic. With such widespread dispersion of users, Twitter benefits from more customized, personal end-user interfaces, but potentially could suffer from an inability to directly monetize users off of its site.
- *Best Buy.* The entire product catalog on BestBuy.com is available, including pricing, availability, specifications, descriptions, and

images for nearly a million current and historical products. Their challenge to developers is "build a better Best Buy" for their specific audiences. For example, CamelBuy.com provides price drop alerts and price history charts of Best Buy products, while Milo.com aggregates local product availability across multiple retailers. The API also had an inadvertent benefit, in that an employee in Florida decided to build a better home theater recommendation tool by using the API. He didn't have to wait for approval, ask for permission, or wait for IT to launch an official project. With data access and some basic programming knowledge, he was able to build a better experience than anything corporate marketing could come up with.

• *Newspapers.* Publications like the *New York Times* and the *Guardian,* a UK-based newspaper, make their content and proprietary databases available for anyone to access. The *New York Times* makes available data sets like its Congressional roll call votes database, as well as all the content from the *Times* back to 1981. The *Guardian* includes data like the responses from five thousand British citizens on how they think government should reform; all executive pay for FTSE 1,000 companies; and a database of the 23,574 nuclear weapons in the world and where they are located. The goal: allow other people to access and analyze the data for further journalistic use. But there's also a business motive: the *Guardian* will show its ads alongside any data that's being used, essentially changing the business model so that they deliver content and ads to where people are, rather than making them come to the *Guardian*'s Web site.

Okay, let's take a breather.

As we shift now from discussing open information sharing to talking about the final four elements of openness that are found within the broad category of decision making (look again at Figure 2.1), I'd like to emphasize how these two areas are related to each other.

Open information sharing is vitally connected to decision making, but they do not necessarily go hand in hand. Recall, for example, how open the navy is with information, but how very centralized it is in its decision making process. But here's a critical point—more open decision making processes also typically require open information sharing. If you are going to involve more people in the process, they have to have the right information on which to base their decisions.

OPEN DECISION MAKING

Like information sharing, open decision making varies significantly not only between companies but also within them. You can find one type of decision making among executive ranks and another type being used at the team level. There are four major types of decision making in organizations today: centralized, democratic, consensus, and distributed. As we go through each one in turn and examine how each type is enabled and also changed because of openness, keep in mind that no one type of decision making is best. Rather, understand that they differ in terms of the degree of control, extent of information shared, and choice of people involved as appropriate for each situation.

CENTRALIZED

A small number of people—typically the CEO and perhaps a small team around that person—have the knowledge and judgment to make centralized decisions. It is not necessarily micromanagement (although it can be), but the general sense is that for certain types of decisions, especially highly strategic ones, the person in charge can't afford to let other people make that call.

The advantage of centralized decision making is that it can be decisive and quick—and also effective, if the leader is trusted by the organization. However, it frequently carries the stigma of "command and control," whereby employees feel they are being dictated to and have little recourse except to abide and obey.

But in a world in which the marketplace is moving at unprecedented speed, few leaders can afford to act within a cocoon of information or risk not having full buy-in to their decisions. The key challenge to making centralized decision making more open is not to involve more people in the actual decision but to open up information sharing in both directions, so that those in power have the right information on which to base their decisions and also have the commitment to share it back out to the organization.

DEMOCRATIC

In democratic decision making, a limited set of choices is put forward to a group and voting is used to make the decision. The creation and selection of the choices could be a simple "yes" or "no" vote. Think of the way most public companies approve members of the board of directors, for example. But increasingly, voting is used to allow people to choose from a set of equally viable options—for example, the service provider for the company cafeteria—and the choices are then put to a vote. The result: employees feel a much greater sense of ownership in the process.

This is also becoming prevalent in decisions with customers. Walkers in the UK, for example, held a "Do Us a Flavour" campaign to crowdsource ideas for a new potato chip taste. The company narrowed the choices down to six, produced them as a sample pack, and asked people to go online and vote for their favorite.[22] Over a million people voted for the winner, "Builder's Breakfast," which tastes like eggs, sausage, bacon, and beans and is now a permanent Walkers flavor. And of course, there are the perennial talent contests like the *American Idol* or *Who's Got Talent?* TV shows whose viewers vote for their favorite performers.

Although compelling, democratic decision making isn't well suited for most situations. First, the cost of mounting the outreach to engage potential voters—even inside an organization—can be daunting. Second, this process isn't suitable for complex decisions that have nuance, and those who use it in such situations run the risk of being perceived as rubberstamping when the decision had already been made. Last, voting is open to politicking and based on popularity rather than merit, as is often seen on shows like *American Idol*. This decision making may be appropriate for picking the next best-selling artist, but not if you're trying to make strategic decisions.

CONSENSUS

In this decision making model, every person involved and affected has to agree about whatever is being decided, resulting in tremendous buy-in. One typical place where this type of decision making is often used is in hiring—everyone has to feel comfortable that this is a good person to add to the team. But it's also a cumbersome model, as it takes a tremendous amount of time and effort to corral everyone into agreement.

W. L. Gore, the maker of GORE-TEX fabric, is one of the few examples of enterprise-level consensus decision making in business, and for good reason—it's really, really hard. From the beginning, Gore has had no employees or managers—only associates. The organization is extremely flat and hierarchies are actively broken down. Decisions are made because people believe they need to be and agree to them.[23] So although the decision making process can be chaotic and slow, in the end everyone buys into it. With 8,600 associates and $2.5 billion in annual sales, Gore is able to do this because their culture supported it from the beginning. As Gary Hamel describes in his book *The Future of Management,* one employee sums up the essence of Gore, saying, "We vote with our feet. If you call a meeting and people show up, you're a leader."[24]

Other companies, like Whole Foods, Google, and Semco Bank in Brazil, have been cited as examples of companies that allow employees to self-manage. The common trait of these companies is that either they are owned by their leaders (Ricardo Semler, Semco Bank) or they began with these philosophies and cultures in place from the start (Whole Foods, Google, and W. L. Gore). But this can also happen when a small company or team decides to operate in a different way. Scott Heiferman, CEO of Internet start-up MeetUp.com, engineered a re-org of its forty-person organization. Actually, it would have to be called a "de-org," because he threw out the organization chart.

Starting in February 2008, all decisions on what features the company would add to MeetUp.com would be self-determined—if someone could convince an engineer to spend time on the project, it would get done. A year and a half after the change, I spoke with Heiferman and got an update. "[It's] working to the point where we really can't imagine it being another way. The team has the freedom to control their working destiny. In the first six weeks after we made the switch, we got more done than we had in the previous six months, and that kind of productivity has not ended."

Heiferman admits that things are at times chaotic, and that he's had to redefine his role as a leader. He is no longer the ultimate strategist and decider of what people should do; rather, he acts as a platform maker. His job is to make sure that the right protocols, the right environment, and the right infrastructure are all in place for people to create new features and make amazing things happen on MeetUp.com.

Most organizations don't have the luxury of junking the entire org chart or the ability to do so, but they can realize the benefits of self-managed teams with a variation, which I call *distributed decision making*.

DISTRIBUTED

This model of decision making is a hybrid of all of the preceding ones, in that it pushes decisions away from the center to where the information and knowledge to make decisions actually reside, typically closer to the customer. Once decisions are made closer to the edge, the actual *method* of making the decision may still be centralized, but the mere act of pushing it down into the organization means that the buy-in that usually comes with consensus decision making is achieved. Decision making inside of distributed models may look confusing and chaotic, but it's just the opposite—a tremendous amount of discipline and planning is needed to get everyone working in the same direction.

The payoff: the ability to break down complex tasks as well as speed and ability. We'll look at Mozilla, the provider of open source browser Firefox, as an example of how distributed decision making can work, and we'll also examine the transformation that Cisco is undertaking.

Distributing complex tasks. Mozilla is the organization behind the Firefox browser, which is itself created as an open source project. Mozilla has 170 employees, but their role isn't to build the browser—it's to coordinate the thousands of people who help build and market it.

The way open source works at Mozilla is that anyone is free to contribute suggestions. Volunteers routinely submit between 50 and 60 percent of all patches to Firefox. So that means anyone (including you and me) can propose a change, comment on a proposal, or even submit a change to the code (if we know how).

But when it comes to decision making, Mozilla follows a very prescribed process that is open and distributed out to hundreds of people. As Mozilla explains on its site, "The code is large and complex; the number of daily decisions to be made is enormous. The project would slow to a crawl if a small set of people tried to make the majority of decisions regarding particular pieces of code.[25] This means that the actual work at Mozilla is divided into about one hundred "modules" led by "module owners," the only ones who can authorize changes to the code. Many of these module owners are not Mozilla employees, and there's a rigorous, detailed process for choosing and replacing module owners.

This means that although anyone can make suggestions, in the end the chaos must be turned to order, with only one person allowed to make the changes. Mozilla incorporates tremendous visibility into the ongoing discussions and decision making process to ensure that everyone understands the way the decision is made. But in the end, only *one* person makes the decision.

In many organizations there is a similar structure, with leaders positioned all over the organization tasked with making decisions.

41

But all too often their decisions need to be approved or are second-guessed further up the chain of command. At Mozilla, it's clear that whatever the module leader decides, goes. Many organizations wish they could do this, but they lack the discipline that Mozilla has demonstrated in terms of transferring and distributing real decision making out into the organization. We'll take a look next at how Cisco—a very large, established, hierarchical company—is trying to instill that discipline.

Organizing for speed. Let's first understand what Cisco CEO John Chambers is trying to do. After weathering the 2001 tech melt-down, Chambers was determined to make the company more nimble and responsive to changing customer and market demands. But Cisco is a $40-billion company with 65,000 employees scattered all around the world and a deeply engrained hierarchical structure. Although Chambers is a charismatic leader deeply respected for his leadership and decision making, how could he pull this off?

In effect, he cloned himself. Or at least the decision making part.

Cisco saw that its core business of networking technology was becoming mature, so the company needed to find new market opportunities to enter and grow. To do this, Cisco created councils and boards and shifted decision making down several levels. Only nine councils report directly into the very top "operating commit-tee," made up of top executives, including CEO Chambers. These councils are typically responsible for $10 billion in revenue and each have about sixteen executives. Reporting into the councils are more than fifty boards, each responsible for $1 billion in business, and reporting into the boards are numerous working groups that come and go to support initiatives.

In total, there were over 750 executives involved in the councils and boards at the time this book was written—up from one hundred executives two years earlier. That means strategic decisions—acquisi-tions, entering new markets, creating new products—are handled by a huge number of people. Moreover, these councils and boards are almost always co-led by two people, typically one person from sales

42

and one person from product development or engineering. On the surface, it looks like Chambers created an entirely new matrix organization on top of Cisco's functional departments—in effect, duplicating the bureaucracy. Requiring consensus at the leadership level would also seem to defeat the purpose of greater speed and agility.

But the proof is in the numbers, and the numbers are shocking. In an interview with me, Chambers shared what the company had accomplished in just the prior forty-five days:

- Announced four acquisitions, with two of the acquisitions above $3 billion in value and three of the four acquisitions outside the United States
- Prepared and announced quarterly earnings
- Held a CIO conference and a service partner meeting
- Led a $5-billion debt offering
- Announced strategic partnerships with EMC and VMWare

On top of this, Chambers personally had 125 individual customer meetings in the same time period. And he isn't doing all of this by working insane hours—in fact, just the opposite is happening. "I am working less than I did two years ago," Chambers said, smiling. In fact, the amount of time spent by senior executives on strategic decisions is sixty days a year—exactly the same that it was in 2007. But the number of cross-company priorities increased from two in 2007 to thirty in 2009, a fifteen-fold increase. The speed and scale of Cisco's activities is breathtaking, but to Chambers, this is the way that Cisco should run. He said, "This is business as normal at Cisco. Name me any other organization in the world that could do this."

What exactly is in Cisco's secret sauce? Two things. First, it has codified distributed decision making into a disciplined, replicable process. Second, Cisco uses collaborative technology as the "grease" that makes distributed decision making and execution work. I'll go into more detail about how Cisco does this in Chapters Six and Ten.

ACTION PLAN: CONDUCTING YOUR OPENNESS AUDIT

Whew! This has been a long chapter, and we've covered a lot of ground and presented a great deal of critical information. Now that we've laid out the different ways in which you can be open, it's time to take an audit of how open your organization is. Use the following chart or take this audit online at open-leadership.com.

The Openness Audit

First, rate how open you are in each of the six different information sharing elements. Be sure to think about internal as well as external examples and instances. You may also want to rate how the openness of your competitors or companies that you admire. Note that these scores are not to be used on an absolute scale, but rather as a diagnostic tool for you to understand where your organization is open and where it is not. The goal shouldn't be to get a higher score, but to understand why you are more or less open in one area than another.

Second, examine how you make different decisions in your organization, documenting when and where you see each type of decision making taking place, who is involved, what shared information is used, and whether it is effective or not. You may find that ineffective decision making is happening not because of the type of decision making process being used, but because the right information or the right people are not involved. In those types of situations, before you undertake a significant change in decision making processes, you should try and see whether making changes in being more open in terms of the people involved or information shared can improve effectiveness.

Information Sharing

For each statement about each type of information sharing, rate yourself on a 1 to 5 scale, with 1 being "strongly disagree" and 5 being "strongly agree." Just as important, provide examples both internally and externally.

Interpreting your score: These scores are not to be used as an absolute scale, but rather as a diagnostic tool for you to understand where your organization is open and where it is not. In particular, understand how you do or don't have the right level of structure, encouragement, and exhibited behavior in each area.

Explaining _____ My organization is disciplined about keeping company information confidential, so that people feel comfortable sharing sensitive information. _____ The executive team takes the time to explain to employees how decisions are made. _____ Customers and partners outside the organization feel they understand how and why decisions are made by the company.	Total _____ Examples:
Updating _____ Technology and processes like community platforms and collaboration tools are in place to facilitate information sharing and collaboration. _____ Many executives and employees frequently use social technologies like blogs, video blogs, microblogging, or collaboration platforms to provide updates. _____ Shared updates are perceived as useful and not seen as public relations or HR rhetoric.	Total _____ Examples:

Conversing _____ Employees and executives are free to blog and participate in social media, both internally and externally, as long as they act responsibly. _____ The organization is committed to hearing from and talking with customers and employees—even when those conversations may be negative in tone. _____ There are community tools that engage customers and partners to talk with each other and to also engage with the organization.	Total _____ Examples:
Open Mic _____ Channels are in place through which employees and customers can contribute ideas and content. _____ The organization actively encourages employees and customers to contribute their ideas and best practices. _____ Customers and/or partners frequently contribute ideas and suggestions that are adopted by the organization.	Total _____ Examples:
Crowdsourcing _____ There is a platform for large groups of people to be able to contribute ideas, innovations, and solutions in an organized way. _____ There is a proactive process in place to seek out and try new sources of ideas and innovation. _____ Ideas from outside the organization are frequently incorporated into products, services, and processes.	Total _____ Examples:

Platforms	Total _____
_____ Architecture and data platforms are defined and open for widespread access.	Examples:
_____ Open platforms are seen as a strategic and competitive advantage for the organization and invested in appropriately.	
_____ Many employees, developers, and partners tap open platforms to create new products and experiences for customers.	
Total Score	Add all column totals _____

The Decision Making Process

Decisions are made every day in your organization. This part of the audit examines some of the most common decisions that are made in every organization. For each type of decision, identify the decision making process that is used, who is involved, what kind of shared information is used to make the decision, and how effective the decision-making process is.

To improve effectiveness, you may want to change the decision making process to be more open, but you may also want to consider who is involved or whether better information sharing could improve effectiveness as well.

Type of decisions	Type of decision making used (centralized, democratic, consensus, or distributed)	Who is involved?	What shared information is used to help make the decision?	Effectiveness (on a 1 to 5 scale, with 1 = "not effective at all" and 5 = "highly effective")
Acquisition				
Partnerships				
Branding or positioning				
Product development				
Budgeting				
Workflow design				
Hiring				
Other				

After you've completed your audit, keep it handy as you read Chapter Three. We'll be looking at the different objectives you can achieve with openness. As you read, check your completed openness audit against your strategy—are you as open as you need to be to achieve your goals?

Now let's move ahead. It's time to figure out just how open you want and need to be.

PART II

CRAFTING YOUR OPEN STRATEGY

OBJECTIVES DETERMINE HOW OPEN YOU WILL BE

Now that you understand the different ways you and your organization can be open, it's time to determine how open you *need* to be. If you completed the Openness Audit at the end of Chapter Two, you have a good idea of where you are and are not open today. The question now is, are you open enough? This question can't be answered in a vacuum, and all too often organizations get stuck in a conversation that goes roughly like this:

> **Chief Marketing Officer:** We need to get close to our customers—be more transparent with them. Why don't we start a blog and get on Twitter?

VP Customer Service: That's not going to work. All we'll get is complaints from irate customers. We can't win in that kind of situation.

VP Product Development: But we need to get feedback on what our customers like and don't like—otherwise we'll never create products better than our competitors'.

Director of Sales: Our competitors will be able to exploit areas where our customers are unhappy, and they'll swoop in to steal the sale.

CMO: Better we find out directly. We should have a place on our Web site where customers can review our products so we know what's broken and needs fixing.

CEO: But having those negative reviews on our own site will kill sales.

VP Product Development: Other companies like us are doing this. Dell, for example.

CEO: We're not Dell.

Sound familiar? You're not alone. Many companies are trapped in the strategic equivalent of a Gordian knot: they can't find the beginning of a problem so they can solve it. The dialogue just keeps going around and around in circles because everyone has a compelling reason to be open (or not), to keep control (or not). What is needed is a common framework and process whereby some clear decisions about openness can be made.

What is often missing when leaders try to decide how open to be is a coherent open strategy—something I like to call "open-driven objectives." With an open strategy, decision shifts from *whether* you should be open, to how open you *need to be* to accomplish your overall strategic goals. In this chapter, we'll look at the four key objectives that greater openness can achieve.

WHAT ARE YOU TRYING TO ACCOMPLISH?

In my work with a wide range of companies, I find over and over again that there are four underlying objectives integrated into almost every successful strategic plan. The objectives apply to both internal and external situations, to an audience primarily of employees as well as to one of customers and partners. These objectives are to:

LEARN. First and foremost, organizations know that they must learn from employees, customers, and partners before they can do anything else. As discussed in Chapter One, organizations and their leaders must be constantly open to learning. And you must do this first before pursuing any other goal—otherwise, you risk operating in a vacuum.

DIALOG. Communication—both internal and external—transforms a relationship from that of shouting out one-way messages to a dialog between equals. And along the way, people in the conversation become more and more engaged, to the point where they have a dialog without you having to be present.

SUPPORT. People both inside and outside the organization need help at different times—ranging from pre-sale to post-sale.

INNOVATE. Creativity needs to be fostered, both inside and outside the organization.

As you can see from Figure 3.1, the first objective, *learn*, is the one from which all others stem. Let's get started with a closer examination of the four core open objectives, beginning with *learn*.

LEARN: INVOLVING THE WHOLE ORGANIZATION

Look at this first objective through the lens of the new relationship you are trying to form with empowered employees and customers. How well do you understand them? Probably not as well as you

Figure 3.1. Four Open-Driven Objectives
Support the Open Strategy

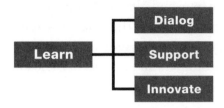

need to. Traditionally, the market research department uses tools like focus groups and surveys, and the human resources department conducts an employee survey once a year. But the new culture of sharing has created an additional, timelier way to listen and, more important, opens it up to anyone in the organization who is willing to learn.

For example, basic monitoring tools like Google Blog Search or Twitter search makes it easy to track when customers are discussing your organization.[1] For a fee, you can get real-time monitoring of social content through vendors like BuzzMetrics, Cymfony, Radian6, Umbria, or Visible Technologies.[2] Moreover, new products from Microsoft, Oracle, Salesforce.com, and a host of start-ups will integrate these monitoring tools into your sales management or customer service enterprise applications, meaning you'll be able to understand if these are your own customers that are writing about you.[3]

Imagine if you could put that real-time learning in the hands of every one of your employees. Customer service could be proactive in addressing issues, in much the same way that Comcast reaches out to people via Twitter. A salesperson could (1) identify that "Wildman369" commenting on a company blog is a prospect who was recently called on, (2) pull in that person's LinkedIn profile, and (3) use that information as a jumping-off point for the next discussion. By enabling your employees to hear and learn directly from customers, you empower them to use that information to do their jobs better.

COMMUNITIES SUPPLEMENT FOCUS GROUPS

Insights can also come from communities, both private and public. Private online communities—such as those powered by vendors like Communispace, Networked Insights, Passenger, and Umbria—pull together people, ranging in numbers from a few hundred to several thousand, for the purpose of idea generation and feedback. But these members don't simply answer online surveys or post to message boards—rather, community managers engage members through live chats, encourage storytelling with video tools and diary keeping, and ask for feedback on new product ideas.

And this isn't limited to just external customers and stakeholders. In one case Communispace manages a virtual community of four hundred employees for a major financial services company, allowing the company to engage with workers from across multiple locations. Executives from across the company received feedback on initiatives ranging from how to structure employee benefits to how well the new strategic roadmap was being received. A key part of the success of this employee community was building trust—employees were reassured directly by executives participating in the community that they wanted honest, direct feedback. The result: insights in real time that helped executives make crucial strategic decisions.

WHAT MAKES OPEN LEARNING HARD

The benefits of using social technologies for research include speed (real time, fast), scale (lots of points of input, not just twenty people in a focus group or four hundred people in a survey), lower costs (can be as cheap as simply monitoring to gain insights), and distributed (people outside of market research can access it). Fast, relatively cheap market research—what could be better?!

There are a few roadblocks that you should be aware of. First, social media monitoring results in a great deal of noise—many comments, blog posts, and especially Twitter updates—that are simply not relevant to what the company wants to know. But better analytical tools are making it easier to sift out trends and important lessons.

Second, the insights that come out of private communities are not representative, so you have to be smart about the data. The responses of eight hundred people who answer an on-line questionnaire, for example, may be much less representative of the market than the responses of four hundred people chosen to represent a market statistically. Because the eight hundred decided to answer the questionnaire, their answers are somewhat (or largely) skewed.

Last, the new distributed nature of learning threatens one important stakeholder—the market research department. In truth, these new techniques don't supplant traditional research methods like focus groups and surveys, they *supplement* them. But beyond a basic unfamiliarity with these tools, market research departments most fear losing their status as the providers and guardians of customer and employee insight. An executive can easily sway the discussion by bringing up a single customer comment, invalidating weeks of careful market research. To reassert their expertise and authority, market researchers should themselves enable *more* listening and learning opportunities across the entire organization and, in so doing, act as the aggregators and distillers of the valuable insights that come in.

DIALOG: GETTING PEOPLE TALKING

Let's talk frankly here. Nobody likes to be shouted at! Yet that's what usually happens when a message needs to get out, whether to employees or customers. At the core, marketing and communications is about building relationships, but the key is knowing how to do it in a way that feels relevant and "authentic" to someone. Basically, communications need to shift from relationships that are transactional, short-term, and impersonal in nature to ones that are more long-term focused, personal, and intimate. In essence, I'm asking that you think about humanizing marketing and communications, replacing the nonspecific "voice" of the company with a person and a meaningful relationship.

That's because with today's empowered customers and employees, organizations need to *earn* the right to have a conversation, and then only at the right time. Without a relationship in place, the best marketing campaigns will fall on deaf ears, especially as people struggle to channel the real signal in the cacophony of today's media clutter. So just as a marriage proposal on a first date is, with rare exceptions, alarmingly premature, a pitch to "Buy now!" would be spurned.

Let's take a look at what Kohl's is doing. As this book went to print, the U.S.-based retailer had almost a million fans on its Facebook page. The main landing page has typical brands and sales information, and the "Wall" has updates from Kohl's, like, "It's a sale. It's huge! In fact, it's bigger than huge!" But take a closer look at the Wall, and you'll see something interesting happening there. On one day we viewed it, there were thirty-two posts from fans. And on *half* of those fan posts, Kohl's posted some kind of response from the company.[4] Here's a sample of what that dialog looked like:

Edie: Good sale going on . . . Just left there . . .

Kohl's: What did you get!? What did you get!? What did you get!?:)

Edie: A sweater, leggings, and a top for my granddaughter's birthday!

Kohl's: You are the best grandma! Thanks for posting, Edie!

I suspect that Edie never expected to hear from the store when she posted her comment, let alone expect the corporation to talk in such a way—that's not the kind of corporate-speak we're used to! It takes one person at Kohl's just a few minutes a day to reply back to a dozen or more people, but it's this kind of dialog that is changing the nature of relationships.

And given the nature of Facebook, the impact of this dialog isn't limited to just Edie. First, anyone visiting the Kohl's Wall sees this interaction and understands that someone at Kohl's is personally interested in them and their purchases. But more important, Edie's fifty friends could see that she has posted on Kohl's fan page. In fact, the 32 posters on that one day alone included 4,109 people in their friend networks. If they are curious about what their friends were doing on Kohl's fan page, they are just a click away from finding out. (Edie had to hope her granddaughter wouldn't click through and spoil a birthday surprise!)

Even more important, people are starting to converse about Kohl's with each other. When one person posts a question, others chime in, sometimes answering before Kohl's does. Sometimes called word-of-mouth or viral marketing, this is what happens when the dialog transcends the bounds of the single conversation and takes on a life of its own with little effort or pushing by Kohl's.

UNDERSTANDING THE NEW NATURE OF ENGAGEMENT

Many organizations have a strategic objective to engage with a new market with the explicit goal of selling more products and services. But a simplistic focus on sales alone obscures the need to build a relationship that will support not just a short-term sale but a long-term, loyal relationship. Many organizations worry about what it means to truly engage with potentially millions of people in a dialog. What's involved? How do you prioritize? What do you *say?*

Engagement is a many-headed entity that shape-shifts depending on who is in the room. One way to think about how to approach engagement is to group and prioritize the types of engagement into what I call the "engagement pyramid" (see Figure 3.2). The pyramid shows how people—both customers and employees—are engaging with your company, brand, product, or even a broad topic. The pyramid is made up of five levels, with each level representing a higher degree of engagement behavior. It's similar to other audience segmentation frameworks, like the "90–9–1" participation inequality theory, which states that 90 percent of site visitors are lurkers, 9 percent participate occasionally, and only 1 percent are truly, deeply engaged.[5] The new pyramid presents engagement behavior as starting much lower in the pyramid, and it highlights ways to engage at each level.

For each of the pyramid levels there are specific activities and behaviors associated with engagement that you can easily observe.

Figure 3.2. The Engagement Pyramid

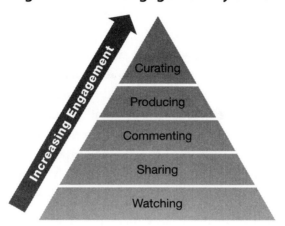

Let's take the topic of "Hawaii vacation" and see how engagement maps out at each level, showing how a fictitious hotel, "Happy Days Resort," might approach engagement and dialog at each part of the pyramid.

WATCHING. At the lowest level of engagement, people passively read blogs, listen to podcasts, or watch video content about Hawaiian vacations. They may also visit numerous sites, like the official tourist site GoHawaii.com for general island information, TripAdvisor to read reviews of the resort, or the resort's Web site to see pictures. They may even book a vacation, but there is minimal interaction with the resort outside of the transaction itself. Their goal is to get the job done, and typically the information they find is sufficient and they have no need or desire to engage any further. The thing to note about this group is that until a Watcher interacts directly with the resort, Happy Days generally doesn't realize that a particular person was even interested in a Hawaii vacation. As a result, there's little engagement with a Watcher.

SHARING. At the next level up in terms of engagement, watching becomes sharing. A recent study by ShareThis found that sharing can make up 5 to 10 percent of a site's overall traffic, and it drives up to 50 percent more page views per person than search.[6] For example, a person may be in the midst of deciding which resort to stay in, updating a Twitter account with "Researching where to stay in Hawaii." A friend who is also planning a vacation sees the update and follows the link. And it's also an opportunity for the resort to reengage with the original Sharer. It doesn't have to be complex or "sales-like" in this interaction. Imagine what you would say if you overheard two women talking while waiting in a supermarket line. A reply like, "What are you looking for in a hotel? Maybe I can help," would be a good conversation starter.

COMMENTING. After a visit to Happy Days Resort, a returning vacationer may post a review on a travel discussion site like TripAdvisor or comment about the visit on the resort's own blog. The person is just adding her comment to the many voices already chiming in about Happy Days—but her level of engagement is now higher because she's actively sharing her opinion *and* doing so in the context of an existing conversation about the resort. Depending on the nature of the comment, the resort could either thank the commenter for a glowing review or probe for more details about why the vacation stay didn't meet expectations.

PRODUCING. If you've ever written a blog, created a podcast series, or maintained a channel on YouTube, you know the amount of effort it takes to attract and engage an audience. Producing differs from Commenting in that it involves creating and producing content for a specific audience *over time,* rather than engaging intermittently. Happy Days Resort may be a producer of a blog, but the resort may also want to engage prominent travel bloggers in a dialog when they write about Hawaii vacations.

CURATING. As individuals, people who engage in curating set themselves apart, because they become highly and personally engaged in a community. They spend countless hours as community and discussion board moderators or wiki editors, not only helping make sure that the content is well organized for the site's users, but also making sure that people are participating well in the community. In some cases, this could be a paid employee managing a discussion board on the company's site. In others, it may be a highly knowledgeable and dedicated volunteer who simply enjoys helping people. For Happy Days, having a relationship with the curator of a travel community board may come in handy if there are problems that arise later.

The best part about the engagement pyramid is that it is fairly easy to identify, observe, and measure these behaviors. There's no set, arbitrary definition of what behaviors or technologies belong where, and that's appropriate, because the technology associated with these engagement levels will shift and change. Most important is identifying the mindset that accompanies engagement at each level and to engage with these individuals appropriately.

Here is a snapshot of how many people in general are active at each level of the engagement pyramid on a monthly basis, broken out for the United States, the UK, South Korea, and Brazil (see Table 3.1).[7] Data for sixteen countries and details on activities included in each category are available at open-leadership.com.

Table 3.1. Engagement Levels in the United States, UK, Korea, and Brazil

Percent of those online	USA	UK	South Korea	Brazil
Curator	<1 percent	<1 percent	<1 percent	<1 percent
Producer	24 percent	19 percent	53 percent	47 percent
Commenter	36 percent	32 percent	74 percent	53 percent
Sharer	61 percent	58 percent	63 percent	76 percent
Watcher	80 percent	77 percent	91 percent	90 percent

Source: TrendStream Global Web Index Wave 1, July 2009, trendstream.net.

USING THE ENGAGEMENT PYRAMID

There are three things to note about the engagement pyramid. First, people engage with your company and brand whether you want them to or not. And they do it all over the Internet—in fact, they are likely *not* to be doing these activities specifically on *your* Web site. To engage with them, you'll have to go to where *they* are, places where you have no direct control.

Second, you can and should consider having a dialog with people directly. I'm often asked by nervous executives, "What do I say?"—and you may be feeling that same unease, similar to the way you feel walking into a meeting where you don't know anyone in the room. You may also be concerned that you not come across as "corporate" and inauthentic. But if you've done the first objective of *learn* well, you'll have a good understanding of what topics people want to discuss. Also, by understanding where they are in the engagement pyramid, you'll also understand how to start the conversation—you'll approach the curator of a third-party discussion forum like TripAdvisor very differently than you will someone who just posted a negative review.

Last, do not become overly focused on people at the highest, most engaged levels of the pyramid. Although that group is important, your efforts should start at the base of the pyramid, making sure that you have a strong foundation of engagement on which to build your other dialog efforts. Focus on how you can get people to move from being a passive watcher to being a sharer, perhaps by simply adding "Share this" buttons to your site content so that visitors can easily post content on Facebook or Twitter. Even if all you do is enable them to forward the content in an email to someone they know, you're tapping into the culture of sharing that now permeates the Web.

OPENING UP DIALOG: EVERYONE'S A MARKETER

Now that you have some understanding of how a more open dialog can take place between you and people engaged with your company, the question becomes *who* will be tasked with that responsibility.

We'll take a closer look at organization in Chapter Six, but let's take a quick look now at how Southwest Airlines manages dialog. On their blog, there is a wide diversity of voices writing on behalf of the company, ranging from pilots and customer service representatives to mechanics and even customers. People who don't have anything to do with marketing and communications are speaking on behalf of the company.

Take, for example, Bill Owen, a lead planner in the Schedule Planning Department—which means he helps decide where Southwest's planes fly. To give you a taste of Owen's writing, here's how he started an October 13, 2009 post: "Today we started accepting bookings from March 14 through May 7, 2010. Party on, Spring Break! Hippity-hop, Easter! Hello, Passover! Time to plan a trip and book something. LET'S GO SOMEWHERE!"[8] It definitely doesn't read like a press release! Owen is one of the most popular Southwest bloggers, routinely drawing tens of comments to his blog posts. He also actively responds to comments directly, answering questions and requests. A typical dialog goes like this:

> **Alex:** Once again Bill, you amaze me at all these new additions! DEN is amazing for SWA and what not to see how fast and rapidly we are growing at DEN. Very excited to see the new destinations out of DEN and the daily flights just keep on rising!
>
> **Bill Owen:** Alex—you're welcome! I've never seen anything like our growth in Denver. Not even LAX during the "Shuttle war" days grew this fast. And I was serious about how stark the difference is inside Concourse C—it's amazing!

Why is Southwest Airlines so secure about letting Owen and others speak on behalf of the company? In 2004, Southwest allowed a film crew to tape a documentary show that had video crews following employees through an eight-hour shift, recording the good, the bad, and the ugly. Southwest had no editorial control over the programs that were eventually broadcast on the A&E network, although the airline could have the show's producers add a clarification about procedures if something was not clear. What did all this do to Southwest? Brian Lusk, the manager of online relationships and special projects, says that every Tuesday morning after an episode of the show aired, Southwest would see a spike in employment applications and in revenue bookings. So when Southwest started blogging, they saw it as a natural continuation and outgrowth of the dialog that had already started with their customers and employees.

So who are your customers and employees going to listen to? You, the monolithic brand and company? Or are they more likely to listen to people like themselves, with whom they can engage in a dialog that leads to a meaningful relationship? Marketing and communications are being transformed—it's no longer about creating and delivering messages, but about the open expression of customer and employee concerns and hope amplified through these new dialogs and relationships.

SUPPORT BECOMES PROACTIVE AND INTEGRATED

Let's move on now to the third objective, opening up the avenues to help and *support* these new relationships. Support is often thought of as "customer" support, a post-sale activity. But I think of it also as sales support, as well as support for the needs of employees. Let's start first with how customer support is becoming more open.

Ritz-Carlton is synonymous with luxury—you imagine ornate lobbies and rooms and, of course, impeccable service. That's exactly what one couple expected when they booked a room at the Ritz for their wedding night. Because of their budget, they reserved a standard room rather than a honeymoon suite, and although it was a very nice room, it overlooked the parking lot! The disappointed bride did what came naturally—she tweeted about it!

But the hotel manager was social technology savvy and was alerted about the problem almost immediately, thanks to monitoring tools. He went up to the room, apologized for the disappointment of their honeymoon expectations, and upgraded them to the Presidential

Suite! The cost to the property—minimal. Bruce Himelstein, the senior VP of sales and marketing at Ritz-Carlton, shared this with me: "With social media, we can be alerted about a problem while the guest is on the premises—when we can still do something about it." For Ritz-Carlton, proactively monitoring for property-related problems is the responsibility of the people onsite who are most likely to be able to respond quickly. This is an opening up not only of the customer service process, but also of *who* is responsible for monitoring and decision making.

INTEGRATING SUPPORT

iRobot is a $300-million manufacturer and marketer of cleaning robots, most famously for the Roomba vacuum. From the start, customers participated in a community that discussed the products, offering tips, suggestions, and advice. Maryellen Abreu, iRobot's director of global technical support, estimates that 90 percent of the questions on the community board are answered by the community, and just 10 percent by iRobot employees. "We have now more than three million units out in the field, and my customer service budget has been holding steady year over year despite the increases of number of units in the field." Supervisors will jump into the conversation when a customer discusses things like taking a unit apart for some self-service repair, which would void the warranty.

Moreover, iRobot integrates its discussion forums and community (hosted by Lithium Technologies) into its customer support system (run by RightNow Technologies). When an unanswered question is elevated from the community forum to the iRobot support center, the service representative can see information about the customer's participation in the Lithium online community, such as which questions were submitted and which ones were answered.

Support also takes place at the beginning of a relationship, such as when a prospect is still making a buying decision. For example, technology company SAP created EcoHub, a place where SAP has all its solutions available and also enables partners in its ecosystem—such as system integrators or technology or software partners—to provide additional background or solutions of their own.[9] SAP EcoHub incorporates tools like ratings and reviews by people who have actually used a particular product, as well as relevant discussion topics and blog posts from SAP's two-million-members-strong developer and business-user community. The profiles and contact information of these contributors are also available so prospects can reach out to them directly to get further candid feedback and advice.

SAP formally opened up the sales support process to reflect how complex buying decisions actually get made, which is usually in the context of the larger ecosystem of reference customers and partners. With SAP EcoHub, they integrated the larger pool of people and players who influence the buying decision, bringing everyone together. The result: prospects discover solutions faster and SAP or partner salespeople get more qualified leads. SAP didn't have to create a new support community for sales—it just needed to integrate the existing support forum into the sales process where the expertise would be easily accessible.

Take a look at your own organization and consider where open, integrated support could improve a critical process or strengthen the natural relationships you have.

INNOVATE: MOVING CROWDSOURCING INTO THE ORGANIZATION

As we saw with crowdsourcing in Chapter Two, organizations are starting to turn to their customers for ideas, leveraging crowdsourcing markets like crowdSPRING, uTest, and InnoCentive for design, testing, and ideation, respectively.[10] Although driven in part by economics, customers and employees are also clamoring to have a say in what is created.

In February 2007 Dell set up Ideastorm.com, which allows customers to submit ideas and then vote for them in a Digg.com-like model. Because of the votes, Dell gets a prioritized list of which ideas to address first. One of its first successes was the launch of a

Linux-based consumer PC in just sixty days (compared to the typical twelve to eighteen months). Because of the success of IdeaStorm, Dell followed up quickly with Employee Storm in June 2007. But more important, Employee Storm has opened up information and decisions that in the past were never discussed, substantially changing the tenor of internal communication and culture at Dell.

Starbucks has a system similar to Dell's IdeaStorm (in fact, it's based on the same platform, Salesforce Ideas) called MyStarbucksIdea .com. I'm particularly fascinated by what they did on the back end to support the site internally. First, this was Starbucks' first major foray into social media, and they didn't want to just make it a symbolic site—they wanted the top vote-getting suggestions and ideas to have resonance inside of Starbucks. So Alexandra Wheeler, Starbucks' director of digital strategy, identified and secured the participation of fifty people around Starbucks who would oversee suggestions in their areas. As a result, the innovation director for the Starbucks Card directly monitors the ideas and discussions around the product and brings relevant ones to the attention of the team. By spreading responsibility, Wheeler was able to integrate outside innovation deeply and quickly into the Starbucks organization.

But how do you encourage innovation and ideas in a working environment where people are not at keyboards all day? This was the fundamental problem facing Toronto General Hospital, where the hours are long for medical staff and there's tremendous hierarchical and stakeholder power because the stakes—people's lives—are incredibly high. If feedback got taken the wrong way, it could affect team cohesion and performance and hence patient care.

Their solution: use the services of technology start-up Rypple to gather frequent, anonymous feedback on one single question at a time, such as "What one thing can we do to reduce readmission rates?" By asking one question each week, a team is able to get much higher response rates; they can quickly share responses and brainstorm solutions together. Multiple teams request feedback each week and post the results on a physical board in the hospital where everyone can see the actions—and most important, the results of those actions. Dante Morra, the medical director of Center for Innovation in Complex Care and staff physician at Toronto General Hospital, observed, "People were quite shocked how hierarchical the organization was and how difficult it was for different team members to speak up. This process opened up the feedback channels amongst the different hierarchies, and we were able set up a model where we could create continuous team improvement."

Finally, how do you encourage innovation in an organization that believes that new ideas should come primarily from inside the company? For a century, Procter & Gamble adhered to a principle of "grow from within," whereby people began and ended their careers at the company. And for most of the company's history, this has been a fantastic strategy, ensuring a unified, global business culture. But when the then-new CEO A. G. Lafley started his tenure in 2000, the company was slowly but surely slipping in its ability to innovate— only 15 percent of new products were successful.[11] Moreover, in-house private label products from retailers like Walmart were challenging P&G's value proposition.

The solution: look outside for new ideas and discoveries. Lafley created a new program called "Connect + Develop" (*connect* externally to find new ideas, then *develop* internally in the way that only P&G could). The goal was to have half of P&G's new products developed externally. I asked Jeff Weedman, VP of global business development at P&G, how hard it was to alter the company's abhorrence of "not invented here." Very. P&G's leadership had to show by example that there was a different way of making a career within the company by asking questions like, "Did you look outside? Where did you look outside? Have you thought about partnerships?" Weedman said, "We had to let them live it themselves and make sure we chose leaders that had exhibited some of those new behaviors because that was the only way to show the rest of the organization that this was a better way to progress through the organization and be successful in the company."

One of P&G's strategies was to use a new Web site, pgconnect develop.com, to highlight some of the research needs the company wanted to address and to encourage contributions. The goal: to expand beyond the 9,000 or so internal scientists at P&G to reach an estimated two million researchers who were working on related, relevant issues. Without the Connect + Develop site, P&G's needs would never have come to these scientists' attention. The impact has been significant—65 percent of new products succeed in the market, with 35 percent of them sourced externally from P&G. And all of this was done while decreasing overall R&D costs. We'll explore more about how P&G was able to transform its company culture to be more open to the outside in Chapter Ten.

THE OBJECTIVES AND YOUR STRATEGIC GOALS

We've now gone through the four major openness objectives—*learn, dialog, support,* and *innovate.* The question that applies to all of these objectives is, again, how open do you *need* to be? If a goal is to learn, can you learn better if you can be more open? If you can, that's a good reason to be more open. But you have to weigh that against your audience and its needs and expectations. Will they participate with you? Are there risks in each of these objectives? There always are, so the real question is, how significant are the risks? Whatever you decide should be in the context of your goals.

I strongly encourage leaders to ground their open leadership strategy within the overall strategic goals of their organization. By basing your open strategy on a key strategic goal that everyone has already agreed to, you also ensure that you'll get the executive, financial, and emotional backing needed to make the tough transition toward greater openness. As we saw in Chapter One, being open is *hard,* so you'll need all the help you can get.

If it doesn't make sense, according to your strategic goals, to be more open in a given area, then don't do it. As a leader, it is incumbent on you to focus your open strategy on concrete goals. If you don't have a concrete goal for activities like having a blog or being on

Twitter, then please don't start. You'll be spinning your wheels, and worse, you may be undermining the enthusiasm to engage openly if these early efforts falter.

Let's take a minute and discuss what to do if being more open *doesn't* tie in with meeting your strategic objectives. Essentially, I'm talking about companies that are successful despite being not that open. Let's take a look at one company that is famously closed and yet wildly successful—Apple.

THE APPLE FACTOR

When I talk about the benefits of being more open, someone inevitably brings up Apple as an example of a company that is successful despite being closed and controlling. Apple is actually quite open when it comes to platform (look at the iTunes Store and iPhone Apps) and providing customer support via its Apple Forums. It also has a presence on places like Facebook and most recently Twitter.[12] But there are no official blogs, and the dialog on both Facebook and Twitter is decidedly one-way—from Apple to the world.

I would argue that, given Apple's strategic objectives, it doesn't have a driving, compelling need to be open—at least, as long as it continues to develop world-class products. Let's take the first objective of learning as an example. A recent Google search for "Apple computers" resulted in more than sixty-six million hits. A search for blog entries turned up almost twelve million. People are already saying a lot about Apple and its products. There is a tremendous amount of dialogue available. Apple's market research people can just mine it, refine it, and send the information to those places in the corporation where it will help the most. They also have excellent market research access and tools to understand the tenor of the marketplace and their users. They don't need to be more open than they already are to meet this first objective.

Similarly, in terms of a dialog about the brand and its products, there is already a tremendous amount of dialog happening about

Apple, though Apple doesn't directly participate in it. In fact, a lot of people actually like talking about the fact that Apple doesn't say anything about itself except under carefully controlled conditions.

For support, they have Apple forums. Apple users help Apple users. Apple rarely participates, because Apple enthusiasts can take care of themselves. So Apple is actually open in some ways. By allowing other people to take care of the customer support so they don't have to, they lower their costs—one of the key benefits.

Last, when it comes to innovation, Apple has the most innovative, creative minds in the business. Exposing potential ideas in an IdeaStorm .com manner in a highly competitive marketplace wouldn't justify the benefit of finding and prioritizing ideas.

When you come down to it, Apple doesn't *need* to be more open than it already is. And as long as it continues its success streak of delivering market-changing and -leading products that delight customers, it likely won't need to change its ways. But cracks show every once in a while. The poor launch of MobileMe saw Steve Jobs issue a rare apology. And as Apple faces more direct competition from formidable players like Google, I expect it will open up even more, to curry greater favor from fickle consumers.

So beware if you have a top executive who says, "I want to be like Apple. If they can be closed and be successful, then I don't have to be open." The causal relationship is reversed. Apple can pull off being less open because they *are* successful. So if your company has what I call the "Apple factor"—a combination of brilliant engineers and designers, a charismatic CEO, and a brand that everybody loves—then go for it, openness be damned! But in my experience, very few companies are successful enough in the way that Apple is that they can afford to remain closed off.

ACTION PLAN: CREATING YOUR OPEN STRATEGY

As we've discussed in this chapter, it's crucial to tie your open strategy to your overall corporate strategic goals. Here's a step-by-step action plan of not only how to do this, but also how to prioritize where and how to be open.

1. IDENTIFY WHICH STRATEGIC GOAL TO ADDRESS FIRST. Review and assess your company's corporate goals with the following questions: Which ones are behind? Which ones are having a hard time gaining traction? Wherever the pain point is greatest, that's a sweet spot for your first openness initiative because executive attention will be highly focused on achieving that goal. By focusing on and addressing a pain point, you build credibility and gain momentum to spread to other areas. Let's take two sample strategic goals to ground this discussion: entering a new market, and addressing declining employee morale in the face of tough economic times.

2. PUT IN PLACE LEARNING SYSTEMS TO SUPPORT THAT GOAL. I've found that most strategic goals get derailed early on because of lack of knowledge and information—how does the new market think about a product category, or what are employees saying about the company? No matter what you do next, put in place the appropriate learning systems so that you can get a better idea of the context that you will be operating in. This is a good time to use readily available monitoring tools to begin the learning process.

3. DETERMINE WHICH OPEN-DRIVEN OBJECTIVE CAN HELP THE MOST. Besides learning, determine which of the other objectives—dialog, support, or innovate—most closely supports the goal you want to pursue. For the new market entry initiative, it would make sense to pursue a dialog objective and identify key engagement points using the engagement pyramid. For the employee morale goal, you may want to have some elements of dialog to start, but morph quickly into a support objective so executives and employees can connect and support each other.

4. GAUGE THE NEED TO BE OPEN. This is a crucial step—to accomplish your open-driven objective, how open do you need to be? This is often driven by external factors, such as your position in the marketplace or the willingness of the audience to engage with you. For example, if you're trying to enter a market whose audience members are highly engaged in a dialog with each other, or whose existing players often engage, you will by necessity have to be more open if you hope to gain any traction. But if your audience tends to hover toward the bottom of the engagement pyramid, you will likely need to take a lighter hand when seeking to engage with them.

5. GAUGE YOUR ABILITY TO BE OPEN. This is the time to pull out the openness audit that you conducted at the end of Chapter Two. If your open-driven objective is going to be dialog, how ready are you to have the dialog that the market demands? Look at the applicable open elements; for example, sharing conversational information. If your organization scores low in this area, you may have to take the appropriate steps to improve your organization's ability to be open. Does your organization have the appropriate policies and structures in place to support openness, or is it more an issue that executives need to be more visibly supportive of an open strategy?

The next three chapters deal with exactly this issue—if you have determined that there is a gap between the need to be open and your ability to be open, how do you become more open than you already are? The first step is to understand the specific benefits of being open, which is especially important to put forward to an organization and leaders who may be beset with the inertia of precedence. In Chapter Four, we'll discuss the different ways you can—and can't—measure the benefits of openness as a foundation for putting together your openness execution plan in Chapters Five and Six.

UNDERSTANDING AND MEASURING THE BENEFITS OF BEING OPEN

Now that you have an idea of what your goals will be, it's important to understand the value of those goals and to put in place measurements to make sure that you are on track to realizing those benefits. The importance of these steps is affirmed by conversations I've had with senior executives about being an open leader or the value of an open organization. Inevitably, they want to know what the return on investment (ROI) is. But this emphasis on ROI is like asking what the value of a deeper, closer relationship is. Although

I agree that leadership should rigorously examine the benefits of openness, an undue emphasis on hard ROI does no one any good.

To illustrate this point, I'll quote John Hayes, the chief marketing officer of American Express, who eloquently explained the conundrum of measurement in general: "We tend to overvalue the things we can measure, and undervalue the things we cannot."[1] Hayes speaks a truth in business: although we strive to become more measurable and accountable, there is a limit to what is feasibly (and economically) measurable. Inevitably, we base many of our decisions on just the thinnest sliver of information and evidence or, even more likely, our gut feeling.

For example, what's the ROI of a handshake? Or think of a lunch you recently had with a colleague or direct report, where you invested time and money to develop a deeper relationship with them. How do you calculate the ROI of an internal business lunch? This illustrates the fundamental problem of being open and of business in general: some things in a relationship can be measured and managed, but many other things cannot. Companies invest an inordinate amount of money on relationships, everything from public relations to establish relationships with highly influential members of the media to the coffee pot in the lunch room to keep up employee morale. In most cases, more than half of a company's operating expenses are likely to be spent on activities that have an indirect impact on the bottom line. We may not be able to link the ROI of these expenses to direct sales, but we know there's some incremental benefit that makes them worthwhile.

The fundamental problem is that it's hard to quantify the value of a relationship, because we can tap into that value in so many different ways. Think about the closest relationships you have in your life. How do you measure their value? Even more to the point, how do you realize the value of being in a relationship? Take, for example, a Twitter follower—as an unengaged, passive watcher of my updates, that person is not that valuable. But when the follower responds to a request or retweets an update—in other words, engages with me— then I begin to realize value.

The difficulty with today's new social technologies—like Facebook, blogs, discussion forums, and Twitter—is that they appear to lack clear, direct benefits compared to more established relationship channels. In actuality, the activities taking place on those sites are inherently highly measurable, but we have not yet established a body of accepted knowledge and experience about the value of these activities versus the costs and risks of achieving those benefits. In this chapter, I'll go through and explain how the benefits of each of the four open-driven objectives that we examined in the previous chapter can be understood and potentially measured, in both direct and indirect ways.

In my research, I've found that the open-driven objectives all create some common benefits, in that they:

- *Remove friction.* By removing barriers and access to information and people, the cost of information sharing and decision making is lowered and it is also simply easier to do.
- *Scale efforts.* The culture of sharing means things spread faster and wider, with less direct investment.
- *Enable fast response.* The real-time nature of social technologies means that you can respond quickly. In fact, if you are not there to head off the growing wave, you risk being overrun.
- *Gain commitment.* Probably the hardest to quantify but the most important, as you win the hearts and minds of your employees and customers.

We'll take a look at how the benefits differ depending on whether the focus is on external audiences (customer and partners) or internal employees and stakeholders. At the end of each section there will be an example of how a hypothetical company with $500 million in revenues might benefit from each objective. These examples are also online at open-leadership.com, where you can add your own data and run scenarios. At the end of the chapter, I'll also discuss some new ways of thinking about existing metrics like customer lifetime value.

THE BENEFITS OF OPEN LEARNING

As we saw in Chapter Three, a tremendous amount of information can be gathered with free, simple tools like Internet or Twitter search, as well as with paid monitoring tools. Keep in mind that there can also be significant costs, both in terms of the time needed to filter and analyze the data as well as in the services of paid private communities, which can run into the hundreds of thousands of dollars. But before we look at the costs, let's take a closer look at the benefits.

First, there are tangible direct cost savings from money that would otherwise be spent on traditional market research methods such as focus groups, one-on-one interviews, mall intercepts, and ethnographic research, as well as polls and surveys. Take, for example, the cost of a focus group of ten people, which can run $5,000 or more for an evening, and compare it to the cost of canvassing an existing community of people who are drawn together by a common interest.

A very personal example of the direct benefit of learning is the way the title of this book was chosen. My publisher and I weren't very happy with our preliminary titles, so I first posted a request for title suggestions on my blog, followed a few weeks later with an online survey of the final four title candidates. My publisher and agent sent out emails to a selective mailing list, which drove some respondents, but the vast majority of the 575 responses came from people who read about it on my blog, on my Facebook page, or via a single Twitter update that I posted (which was then retweeted over and over again). It's a small but powerful example of the benefits of scale that social technologies bring.

The result of the survey: *Open Leadership* was the overwhelming favorite. The cost of fielding the survey was the $35 fee that I paid for SurveyMonkey.com. The cost of recruiting those 575 responses was negligible because of the existing relationship that I—and my extended network—already had in place. Moreover, half the respondents asked to be added to a mailing list to be notified when the book would be available, representing over $6,000 in potential book revenues!

But in addition to the direct hard cost savings and potential revenue benefits, there were considerable indirect benefits as well. First, there is speed. More than half of the responses came in within twelve hours of the original posts going up. Second, the posts sparked additional dialog about the book and topic, generating several case study leads as well as word-of-mouth marketing for the book in general. These are much harder to quantify; what's the value of a single case study in the book? In the end, I'm comfortable with the indirect, unquantifiable nature of these benefits because the value so far exceeds the tangible cost of $35!

I should acknowledge that there are hidden costs. I've spent considerable time investing in my network—over thirty thousand Twitter followers when the book went to print and thousands of "friends" on Facebook don't develop overnight.

CHANGING MINDS WITH CUSTOMER VOICES

Even if you have the concrete benefits at hand, you still may not be able to change the minds of executives who see the world in a specific way. The fact is that people, even those driven by numbers, are not swayed by them if they contradict the world that they believe in. In these instances, you will need to tap into the emotional power of stories to make your case, and nothing is more powerful than a compelling customer story. The beauty is that today, customers by the millions are telling their stories—and just waiting for you to join the conversation.

For example, Comcast had long come in towards the bottom of customer satisfaction ratings for its industry.[2] Comcast CEO Brian Roberts had had enough. He shifted the company mission to be, "We will deliver a superior experience to our customers every day." It's one thing to have a mission, but it's quite another to have a *person* who humanizes the customer for the company.

For Comcast, that person was Grannie Annie. Her given name is Anna May, and she's a lovely grandmother who writes a blog primarily to stay in touch with her extended family, especially her grandchildren. One day, she wrote a blog post titled "I don't like Comcast!" She shared that she was having problems with her new Comcast connection and setting up her email.[3] Frank Eliason, who runs Comcast's new Direct Care program (and the face of their Twitter account, @ComcastCares), found the post with monitoring software, reached out to Grannie Annie, and helped her resolve the problem. But he didn't stop there. He shared Grannie Annie's situation internally and recalled, "Her experience wasn't that bad. But oh, my God, it was Grannie Annie! I got hundreds of emails the day it appeared in the newsletter I send out, all of them saying, 'How could we have done this to Grannie Annie?' From then on, when we started talking about Grannie Annie, everybody was engaged."

We often talk about humanizing the company with social media, but in the case of Comcast, what they needed to do was to humanize the customer. By giving customers a name, face, and voice, they now figuratively walk the halls of the company. What's the value of being able to bring to life a company mission, to give it life? At a point like this, the benefit and ROI of such activities ceases to be a matter of debate of whether to engage or not; rather, it becomes an issue of how to participate in the most efficient way possible to accomplish the goal.

One metric frequently used in public relations is "sentiment," a measure of whether the articles, posts, updates, and reviews are positive or negative. When Comcast began its direct care campaign in 2007, they had Nielsen conduct a survey to gauge the level of negative versus positive sentiment in the online dialog. The result: 70 percent was positive and a whopping 30 percent was negative. After two years of Comcast addressing blog posts, discussion forums, and Twitter updates, Nielsen found that 90 percent of consumer comments were positive and only 10 percent negative. Comcast's Frank Eliason admitted that they use sentiment as their major measurement tool, saying, "We have never concentrated on sales and retention as a key metric for our listening programs. We know that addressing customer problems has an impact, but we haven't concentrated on measuring it that way." Instead, they concentrated on identifying opportunities to improve overall customer relations, knowing that it would eventually be reflected in improved customer sentiment.

BUILDING EMPLOYEE UNDERSTANDING

Learning is not reserved for customers only—many organizations use new technologies to be able to better understand and get closer to employees as well. SunTrust, a large bank operating primarily in the Southeastern United States, underwent a transformation process as one of its responses to the deepening financial crisis. With one of the initiatives, called "Voice of Teammate," the bank gathered feedback from the twenty-eight thousand employees at SunTrust. In the past, when SunTrust gathered employee feedback people would often wonder what happened to their suggestions. Chuck Allen, director of internal communications, told me that the bank realized this had to change: "We wanted better ways to connect with our teammates; we knew that we could do a better job of listening to and acting on feedback."

One solution was to engage Communispace to create and manage an ongoing private three-hundred-employee community. Management could ask employees for feedback and ideas—and also communicate what was done with the suggestions. One initiative they tested was a brochure that the communications team wanted to send out to every single employee's home about the current and future strategic path that SunTrust was taking. But before sending it out, Communispace took it to the Teammate community to see what they thought of it. Although they loved the content, they felt that it was inconsistent with the message that the leadership team had been espousing about both cutting costs and being efficient. Allen said, "We saved $40,000 by not printing the brochure and putting it online instead. But we also gained unspoken capital in terms of Teammate goodwill."

To recap, organizations can sometimes quantify in very direct terms the money that may be saved because of more efficient ways of learning about customers and employees. Intangible, indirect benefits—such as real-time, better, and deeper insights—are much harder to quantify, but in the long run these provide greater value to the organization.

MEASURING THE BENEFITS OF LEARNING

As I discussed earlier, it's can be difficult to directly attribute hard numbers to a specific learning initiative. But let's try, making several assumptions, namely about the value of indirect benefits. In Figure 4.1, I lay out the benefits and costs of having a paid monitoring service like Radian6, supplemented with a private insight community such as those provided by companies like Communispace or ThinkPassenger. Please note that these numbers are representative of a company with $500 million in sales and two thousand employees and are meant to give you ideas on how to estimate the value of indirect benefits. As you can see, there are a lot of assumptions that go into each line, especially for the more indirect costs. Every organization is unique, so the way that you realize and recognize value will be different from the next person's experience.

THE BENEFITS OF OPEN DIALOG

Dialog is at the core of any relationship—and because so much of it takes place outside of the organization, the engagement it creates is easily observable. There are times when an organization can directly attribute revenues or lower costs directly to specific conversations that took place, but for the most part, dialog contributes to the overall deepening of a relationship whose payoff could be months or even years away. We'll first tackle the task of correlating dialog to direct business impact and then move into more indirect benefits.

DRIVING SALES

Let's cut to the chase—you *can* make money with openness and social technologies! Take, for example, how Dell Outlet drives sales with Twitter. Using the real-time nature of Twitter, Dell started

Figure 4.1. Understanding the Benefits of Learning

Description	Benefit
Reducing the cost of focus groups	
– Assumes twelve focus groups at $5K each.	$60,000
Faster, real-time insight generation	
– Speed to market, develops one extra product per year (10 percent of new products profit of $1M).	$100,000
– Avoid a big mistake, cost savings from not doing an ad campaign.	$25,000
Developing alignment for a strategic goal	
– Reduced training classes and meeting times, employee productivity increases four hours/year/employee at $20/hour for two thousand employees.	$160,000
– Better buy-in for the goal, employee morale increases, reduces turnover, avoids recruitment costs. Assumes 1 percent decrease in turnover, recruitment costs of $10,000.	$200,000
– Strategic partners develop more solutions and can sell 1 percent more than their existing $250 million, at 10 percent profit to the company.	$250,000
Total benefit	**$795,000**
Costs	
Social media monitoring platform	
– Assumes $5,000 per month	$60,000
Private community	
– Assumes $250,000 per year	$250,000
Internal resources	
– Assumes one full-time employee at $100,000 per year)	$100,000
Total cost	**$410,000**
Net benefit	**$385,000**
Return	**94 percent**

posting Twitter-only deals to its twitter.com/delloutlet page in March 2009.[4] The number of people following Dell Outlet quickly exploded to 600,000 in June 2009 and more than doubled by January 2010 to 1.6 million. And Dell Outlet saw sales increase—after its first year on Twitter, it had sold $2 million in revenue directly at Dell Outlet from links on its Twitter page and another $1 million in revenue from people who decide to ultimately buy a different system on Dell.com, not in the outlet area.[5] Moreover, Stephanie Nelson, the Dell employee behind the Twitter page, spends only a small part of her time on Twitter, as she is responsible for all public relations activities for Dell Outlet. Clearly, Nelson was able to scale her investment in Twitter, and the return on her time was tremendous![6]

But there is more to this story than simply posting items for sale on Twitter. There are now numerous companies with Twitter deal pages, and even sites that aggregate these deals.[7] What Dell Outlet does differently is to engage visitors in a dialog and, in the process, provides sales support. Here's an example:

> **Nathan:** I'm confused why refurbished P703w printers are selling for $129–$149 when it's available here (http://bit.ly/rb1Mj) for $99.

> **@DellOutlet:** Yes, that's a limited time promo price. The Outlet prices will be adjusted at noon CT today, so check back then.

Dell is doing more than simply notifying people about items for sale—they are also providing direct sales support that could result in a sale, removing friction from the sales process. The time and effort Nelson spends on this is directly measurable in the sales that she drives from the Twitter page, but that's because of the specific nature of the page and Dell's business model—direct selling. So let's take a look next at some indirect benefits that can come from having more dialog and deeper engagement with your customers and employees.

DRIVING BUZZ

One of the most powerful aspects of dialog is that it doesn't stay still—if the topic is interesting and compelling, it naturally spreads. That was exactly what Ford was banking on when it introduced its new Fiesta model by giving one hundred online personalities a free car to drive for six months—creating a Fiesta Movement.[8] There's competition involved—each "agent," as they are called, receives points for each video, blog post, tweet, and photo uploaded or written. They also get points for comments and ratings on sites like YouTube, further helping to spread the Fiesta buzz.

The results have been astounding—on the eve of the car's launch in December 2009, there had been over six million views of YouTube videos, 740 thousand views of Flickr photos, and 3.7 million Twitter impressions. Ford had also collected eighty thousand "hand-raisers" asking for more information about the car and when it would be available—and 97 percent of them had not owned a Ford vehicle previously. Overall awareness of the Fiesta in the target Generation Y audience had reached over 40 percent, equivalent to that of a car that has been in the market for several years. And this was with zero traditional media support—the campaign is 100-percent social media–based.

But Ford doesn't just stand by these numbers; it's putting its money where it thinks it will have the greatest value. A quarter of its marketing spending has shifted to digital and social media because of this channel's ability to not only scale but also deeply engage people in a way not previously possible. Note also that Ford is the only U.S. auto manufacturer that didn't take any federal bailout money in the financial crisis. Clearly, something is going well at Ford.

MEASURING ENGAGEMENT

In Chapter Three, I introduced the engagement pyramid as a framework to understand how engaged *people* are with a particular organization, product, or topic. Organizations need a similar way to understand and measure *their* depth of engagement with customers. The key is that organizations need to do more than merely be present in many different channels—they also need to engage deeply.

In the summer of 2009, my company Altimeter Group and Wetpaint studied the online engagement of one hundred top global brands to see how deeply engaged brands were with their customers in social media.[9] The ENGAGEMENTdb Report shows that engagement is more than just setting up a blog and letting viewers post comments, or even having a Facebook fan page. Rather, deep engagement comes from activities like keeping your blog content fresh and replying to fan comments on Facebook in the way we saw Kohl's do in Chapter Three. It's not about checking off a box that your organization is on Twitter, but more about how you engage with your audience in a deeper, more meaningful way. Adding up all of the engagement scores, we ranked all one hundred companies based on their engagement, with Starbucks, Dell, eBay, and Google achieving top rankings.

But more interesting, we found there was correlation between deep, broad engagement and financial performance, specifically in revenue and profit.[10] Companies that are both deeply and widely engaged in social media surpass other companies in terms of revenue, gross margin, and gross profit performance by a significant difference.[11] Although correlation does not necessarily mean causality—after all, there's a long chain of activities between social engagement on Facebook and revenues—there is definitely a trend. We are looking at statistical significance among the world's most valuable brands, where deeper engagement resulted in statistically different financial performance.

Although these findings do not necessarily prove a causal relationship, they hold powerful implications. Social media engagement and financial success appear to work together to perpetuate a healthy business cycle: a customer-oriented mind-set stemming from deep social interaction allows a company to identify and meet customer needs in the marketplace, generating superior profits. The financial success of the company in turn allows further investment in engagement to build even better customer knowledge, thereby creating even more profits—and the cycle continues.

The difficult step is identifying the links between engagement and revenues. There are nonfinancial metrics—such as customer satisfaction and employee loyalty—that can be observed and measured; although they don't necessarily lead directly to revenues, you know there is a link. The key question to ask in your organization: How is your ability to engage openly creating new, valuable relationships? Every organization is different, so understanding where you will take dialog engagement—and being sure to measure that next step—is a crucial part of understanding the value of dialog and engagement.

Before moving on, let's consider one final benefit of increased dialog—reputation protection. As we saw in Chapter One, the potential for flare-ups like "United Breaks Guitars" is always in the background—and there's nothing you can do to prevent one from starting. But there *is* a way to mitigate the damage—by being able to engage in a dialog early, in real time.

REPUTATION PROTECTION

Jim Collins wrote in *Good to Great* that companies are like a fast-moving bus: you need to get the right people on board, because you don't necessarily know where that bus is headed.[12] Again I turn to Ford for an example. They brought on Scott Monty to run their social media strategy, and that move paid off in 2008 when Monty had to deal with a site called *The Ranger Station* (TRS), a Ford Ranger enthusiast site run by Jim Oaks.[13] In a case study, Ron Ploof tells how Oaks received a cease and desist letter from Ford, demanding that Oaks not only give up the Web site's URL but also pay Ford $5,000 in damages. On a Tuesday evening, a stunned Oaks posted his situation to his user forums: "TRS is being attacked by the Ford Motor Company."

Within two minutes, angry comments started being posted. Early on Wednesday morning, Monty learned that Ford had a growing communications crisis; Oaks's post had spread virally to other sites. With the crisis growing, Monty sent out Twitter updates to the 5,600 people who followed him. Here's a chronology of Monty's tweets:

10:54 A.M.: "I was made aware of it this morning and I'm tracking down our trademark counsel to weigh in on it. Not good."

10:55 A.M.: "I'm on it. Getting our legal team's perspective and trying to stop a PR nightmare."

11:13 A.M.: "I'm personally looking into it. Hope to have an answer soon."

11:23 A.M.: "I'm in discussions with our Chief Trademark Counsel about it right now. I'm none too pleased."

Then Monty did something that would not have been possible two years earlier. At 11:31 he tweeted, "For anyone asking about the Ford fan sites and legal action: I'm in active discussions with our legal dept. about resolving it. Pls retweet." A retweet simply forwards a message to one's followers. Some 19 of Monty's Twitter followers retweeted his message to their own communities, covering over 13,400 people.

Monty learned what provoked the original letter: the Ranger Station was selling counterfeit Ford products—decals with the Ford logo. Throughout the day, Monty worked with the lawyers and the Ford communications department to write a human-sounding public statement, called Oaks directly to discuss the situation, and came to an agreement. At the end of the day, Monty tweeted, "Here is Ford's official response to the fan site cease & desist debacle." He included the link and asked his followers to retweet; 25 did, sending the message on to more than 21,000 of *their* followers.

In all, twenty-two hours had passed since Oaks posted his first cry of frustration. Having Monty "on the bus" and able to move between internal departments and the external world was crucial. But even more important, Monty had the relationships in place to be able to get his message out in near-real time. Had Ford taken the traditional route to The Ranger Station crisis—organizing a committee to determine how to respond—it probably would have been picked up by the mainstream press, where Ford would forever be playing catch-up. Whatever The Ranger Station crisis cost Ford in Monty's time and the time of other employees—legal, communications—I will guarantee it was a pittance compared to what the crisis would have cost had it grown.

As you try to measure the benefits and ROI of a deeper dialog and relationship with customers, you must realize that you can't even begin to calculate the benefit of protecting your organization's reputation in a real-time communications world. Another way to frame the issue is to ask: What is the ROI on your fire insurance policy? You wouldn't even contemplate going without it! Reputation protection can't be a primary goal for your openness strategy, as it quickly becomes obvious that you are acting in a defensive manner rather than trying to develop a real relationship. In the end, reputation protection is a good by-product of deeper relationships, a benefit that organizations derive when key employees—and customers—come to their rescue.

MEASURING THE BENEFITS OF DIALOG

As I did with learning in Figure 4.1, I calculate the direct and indirect benefits of dialog in Figure 4.2. There are many tangible, direct benefits of increased dialog that I haven't discussed in detail but I'm also including in the chart, such as the appearance of blog posts higher in search engines. This example assumes multiple benefits stemming from the activities of one full time person dedicated to encouraging dialog, and demonstrates especially the benefit of scaling dialog among customers.

THE BENEFITS OF OPEN SUPPORT

As we saw in the previous chapter, a key benefit of providing a more open support environment is that people spontaneously join together to help each other. Lithium Technologies and FT Works produced

Figure 4.2. Understanding the Benefits of Dialog

Description	Benefit
Increased revenues	
– Assumes 10 percent profit on $3M in incremental sales	$300,000
– Encouraged additional sales from existing customers from interactions (assumes increased sales by $100 in 10 percent of interactions, 100,000 interactions a year)	$100,000
Increased awareness	
– Advertising equivalent of social media outreach (five million impressions at $10 CPM)	$500,000
Improve reputation of the organization	
– Negative sentiment reduced from 25 percent to 10 percent (assumes a thousand customers not lost, at annual value of $100)	$100,000
Avoid potential PR blowup	
– Assumes would have cost $250,000 in lost reputation and business	$250,000
Hire better people, thanks to desire to work for a good company	
– Reduces recruitment costs from $10,000/new hire to $8,000, affects 200 new hires	$400,000
Scale engagement	
– Reach more people with the same amount of resources and effort (results in 1 percent more sales)	$500,000
Improved search engine placement, thanks to greater inbound links in social media	
– Improved position in search results in 10 percent greater traffic to the site, increases sales by 1 percent from base of $500 million (assumes 10 percent profit)	$500,000
Total benefit	**$2,650,000**

Costs	
Salary + benefits of one full-time manager	$150,000
Total cost	**$150,000**
Net benefit	**$2,500,000**
Return	**1,667 percent**

an excellent white paper outlining the various benefits of support communities.[14] When one customer answers another's question in a forum (a direct deflection), it saves company staff time. When the customer finds the answer on the site without ever posting the question (indirect deflection), it saves everybody time.

How to calculate the benefits? Let's focus primarily on direct deflection benefits (see Figure 4.3, later in this section). Assuming that 10 percent of 100,000 service calls are deflected at $10 a call, that's a savings of $100,000 a year. Let's assume it costs $50,000 to set up and technically maintain a customer support forum, and that any time spent by customer service people to monitor it is easily absorbed. The net benefit is $50,000—not a bad return. There will inevitably be some customers who can't get satisfactory answers or need additional help, but the incremental cost still results in a positive benefit.

The same logic can be applied to Twitter, Facebook, or blogs—any channel where customer problems are being addressed. There are additional benefits to open support, in that it can provide information on so-called "long tail issues" that are hard to resolve, as well as identify key or emerging problem areas. Last, it can also be a source of learning and innovation, which we'll cover later in this chapter.

The future of open support is that new tools built into customer service applications, as well as sales force automation, will help prioritize workflow so that customer size, influence, and case histories are readily available within these new channels of support. Somebody answering a question in Twitter will be able to associate that Twitter handle with a customer and not only prioritize the response but also answer it appropriately given past experiences. This leads to the indirect value of providing *better* customer support that's appropriate and in line with the overall relationship you have with that customer.

ANSWERING QUESTIONS IN ADVANCE

The other major benefit of open support is in "indirect deflection"; that is, avoiding a call in the first place because the question is answered. This entails more than simply directing people with a good search engine to an answer on a discussion forum—it also involves the proactive monitoring of situations and questions that may arise. Here, speed of response is of the essence.

Comcast's Frank Eliason provides a wonderful example: an instance when one of their channels unexpectedly went off the air. Eliason recalled, "We actually found out about it via Twitter, even before our call centers got the first calls. We checked regular TV broadcast and Direct TV, as well as other cable competitors and saw that they were off the air too. We tweeted out a message that the station was down, which got retweeted to millions. We also notified our call centers, and put a message in the phone greeting so that if someone called to check what happened, they would immediately get an answer. Lastly, we also told our engineering team not to work on this, that it wasn't a problem with our system or network."

The amazing thing about this particular situation: the time it took Eliason and his team to put this entirely into place was three minutes. *Three minutes.* When they went back, charted the calls coming into the call center, and tracked how many calls they were able to deflect, the cost savings were "well into the millions," recalled Eliason, in terms of just avoiding those support calls.

THE INTERNAL BENEFITS OF SUPPORT

As we saw in Chapter Two, the updating and conversing elements of open information sharing can result in not only better communications, but also significant time and energy savings. Think of the decrease in emails, less time spent tracking down information or experts, and, best of all, fewer meetings—all from better information sharing. The cost/benefit examples are almost laughable: it is clearly evident that the benefit of using collaboration technologies is much higher than the cost.

For example, Cisco shared a detailed study of the financial impact of their Web 2.0 Collaborative Initiatives. The biggest cost savings came from remote collaboration and telecommuting, using Cisco's in-house TelePresence video conferencing tools as well as WebEx. Most of the savings came from avoiding travel between far-flung parts of Cisco's operations. But it also stemmed from greater productivity and faster results because less time was spent traveling. The cost in 2008: $75 million. The benefit: $655 million. Cisco also quantified the benefits of other internal initiatives, ranging from the executive blogs ($500,000 cost, $10 million benefit) to a Mac wiki that supports in-house Apple computer users (less than $100,000 cost, $4 million benefit). I think you get the idea! In all, Cisco estimated that its fiscal year 2008 expenditure of $82 million created $772 million in benefits—savings that flowed straight to the bottom line.[15]

The benefits of better internal collaboration and support aren't limited to savvy technology companies. TransUnion, one of the largest credit report companies in the United States, originally deployed a collaboration platform on Socialtext to keep employees, who were keen on establishing an internal social network, from sharing information on Facebook.[16] Once the system was set up, employees used it primarily to ask questions of each other, with the questions and answers recorded in a database. Additional tools allowed people to vote on their favorite answers, analyze the answers people were choosing in their attempts to solve problems, and also analyze which answers correlated with topics that were most valuable to the company as a whole.

The direct, measurable benefit that TransUnion quickly realized was problem solving. Because the company is driven by code developed for customers, employees often jockeyed and clamored to spend precious IT dollars to solve vexing problems. But with the Socialtext platform in place, they tended to turn to each other first to see if they could collaborate on the problem. The result: almost $2.5 million in deferred IT spending in less than five months. The cost: $50,000 to install Socialtext. Moreover, TransUnion identified who was best at answering specific types of questions and redefined their job descriptions so that addressing questions in the collaboration platform became part of their formal roles.

MEASURING THE BENEFITS OF SUPPORT

As just discussed, the major benefit of more open support comes from removing friction and lowering costs, which is fairly straightforward to measure. But there are also indirect benefits, such as improving customer and employee relationships and commitment, which are much more difficult to value. In Figure 4.3, I give some examples of how open-driven support can create a positive business impact with the implementation of a customer-facing support forum and an internal collaboration platform. The example also assumes two full-time people to manage these initiatives, one for each platform.

THE BENEFITS OF OPEN INNOVATION

The benefits of the last of the open-driven objectives, *innovation*, are the hardest to quantify. What's the value of an idea that hadn't been thought of before? How do you value the ability to bring a product to market faster than you did in the past? In the end, the benefits of better, faster innovation come in incremental steps that may be indirectly related to the actual openness efforts.

Let's take a closer look at Dell's IdeaStorm innovation hub. Right on the home page there's an accounting of what has been accomplished. As this book was going to press, over 13,000 ideas had been contributed, which had been voted on over 700,000 times and garnered almost 90,000 comments. In all, Dell had implemented 389 of those ideas since they started IdeaStorm in February

Figure 4.3. Understanding the Benefits of Support

Description	Benefit
Call deflection	
– Assumes 10 percent of 100,000 calls/year at $10/call.	$100,000
Identify support problems in advance	
– Notifies customers ahead of time of problem; avoids 10,000 new calls at $10 per call.	$100,000
Greater employee productivity (fewer emails, find info or experts faster, fewer meetings)	
– Assumes employees get back two hours a week at $150/employee value per hour.	$600,000
– Cost avoidance because employees find solutions.	$200,000
Better employee morale and commitment	
– Better buy-in for the goal, employee morale increases, reduces turnover, recruitment cost avoidance. Assumes 1-percent decrease in turnover, avoiding recruitment costs of $10,000.	$200,000
Total benefits	**$1,200,000**
Costs	
Discussion forum software	$50,000
Collaboration software	$50,000
Two full-time people	$200,000
Total costs	**$300,000**
Net benefit	**$900,000**
Return	**300 percent**

2007—on average about 11 per month and about 3 percent of all ideas submitted.

Dell doesn't try to measure the value of those 389 ideas—that's not what matters most to them when it comes to *running* IdeaStorm. Instead, they focus on metrics that gauge the health of their innovation community—the percent of members who actively comment and vote versus inactive members, the quality of the ideas, and—of great importance—Dell's internal rate of response to these ideas. Dell dedicates one person internally to moderate the site full time and another to make sure that Dell as a company is deeply engaged in evaluating and implementing the ideas that surface.

Herein lies the complexity of understanding the benefits of open innovation—the actual value that comes from these new ideas can be realized only within the organization, not within the open innovation process itself. You're basically fine-tuning the engine that drives innovation. I've captured some example metrics in Figure 4.4, but again, these are hypothetical examples for just a few benefits that can be easily quantified. Similar to measuring the benefits of dialog, innovation metrics will have to be focused more on activities that support open innovation efforts than those that measure the benefits themselves.

NEW METRICS FOR NEW RELATIONSHIPS

The discussion of how to understand the value of crowdsourced innovation gets to the heart of the problem—current business vernacular for ROI, value, and benefits fails to capture the essence of these new relationships. But rather than try to come up with a new way to measure engagement, I prefer to take some tried and tested measurements of value, like customer lifetime value and Net Promoter Scores, and understand how they can be modified to take into account the value that openness creates.

First, let's take a look at the new lifetime value (LTV) of customers (see Figure 4.5 and open-leadership.com for a spreadsheet you can download with sample calculations).[17] It differs substantially

Figure 4.4. Understanding the Benefits of Innovation

Description	Benefit
Diversity of designs and ideas	
– Results in products that sell better (increase profits by $1 million.	$1,000,000
Innovations developed faster	
– Gets product to market quickly in response to greater demand, $250,000 value.	$250,000
More accurate projections and predictions	
– Anticipates that a product will not be a success, so closes down development, saving $50,000.	$50,000
Customer and employee commitment and loyalty	
– Better buy-in for the goal, employee morale increases, reduces turnover, recruitment cost avoidance. Assumes 1 percent decrease in turnover, avoiding recruitment costs of $10,000.	$200,000
Total benefits	**$1,500,000**
Costs	
Innovation hub	$100,000
One full-time person	$100,000
Total costs	**$200,000**
Net benefit	**$1,300,000**
Return	**650 percent**

from looking at just the ROI of a campaign; instead, it examines the value of the entire relationship—everything from the referral that comes out of the dialog that customers have about a purchase to the insights, support, and ideas that customers may contribute during their long-term relationships with you. This "big picture" view of the customer recognizes what we discussed in Chapter One: being open requires that you look at your customers as not only a transaction, but also a relationship from which you can derive value in many different ways.

In this example, the lifetime value of one of the original 10,000 customers is $74.89. But if you add in the additional value created by those 10,000 customers in terms of referred customers, new insights, support questions answered, and new ideas, the value rises to $101.48. Understanding where value is created allows you to make decisions that a straight ROI measurement wouldn't. For example, does it make sense to invest in a deeper dialog with prospects and customers who have larger networks? Probably, but only if they will actually make referrals for your products, and at a cost that makes sense for your business economics. To help you better understand these drivers and trade-offs, there is a detailed spreadsheet of these calculations available online at open-leadership.com.

THE ULTIMATE METRIC

Finally, many companies have adopted the Net Promoter Score (NPS) as a key metric of customer loyalty and satisfaction in their organizations. The NPS asks just one question to gauge customer satisfaction: "How likely are you to recommend [company] to a friend or colleague?" on a 0 to 10 point scale.[18] People who respond "9" or "10" are considered Promoters, those who respond "7" or "8" are Passives, and those who respond "0" to "6" are Detractors. To calculate your company's NPS, take the percentage of your customers who are Promoters and subtract the Detractors. Satmetrix, which deploys and manages NPS loyalty programs, benchmarked the NPS

Figure 4.5. The New Customer Lifetime Value Calculation

+ Net present value of
future purchases

− Cost of acquisition

+ Value of new customers
from referrals

- Percent that refer
- Size of their networks
- Percent of referred
people who purchase
- Value of purchases

- Percent that provide
support
- Frequency and value
of the support

+ Value of insights

+ Value of support

+ Value of ideas
_____

= Customer lifetime value

	Year 1	Year 2	Year 3
Number of original customers	10,000	5,000	3,500
Gross profit of purchases	$400,000	$200,000	$140,000
Cost of acquisitions and retention	$150,000	$25,000	$17,500
Net profit	$250,000	$175,000	$122,500
Total lifetime value over 15 years	$748,858		
Traditional lifetime value per customer	$74.89		
Value of referrals	$30,000	$45,906	$45,287
Value of insights	$10,000	$5,438	$4,080
Value of support	$5,438	$8,156	$6,120
Value of ideas	$2,000	$1,000	$1,000
Net profit and value	$297,438	$235,500	$178,986
Total revised lifetime value over 15 years	$1,014,839		
Revised lifetime value per customer	$101.48		

Note: Total lifetime value is calculated over 15 years, but only the first three years are shown. The detailed calculations are available at open-leadership.com.

scores of several industries, with companies like Vonage (45 percent), Charles Schwab (36 percent), Apple (77 percent), and Google (71 percent) leading in their respective categories.[19]

NPS is especially interesting in that this single metric is strongly correlated with repeat customer purchases; moreover, the NPS explains differences in relative revenue growth rates. To increase your NPS score requires that you increase the number of Promoters and decrease the number of Detractors. Greater openness can directly improve NPS in these two areas—consider how updating more frequently can convert Passives to Promoters, or how conversing in a more open manner can meet the needs of Detractors.

In my consulting work, I have found that organizations that were already using NPS skipped the entire discussion of understanding the ROI of openness and social technologies and moved immediately to thinking about how openness can affect NPS. The beauty of NPS is that it is immediately and easily measurable. How does the NPS differ for your blog and Twitter users versus customers who don't participate? Are customers who use a product that has been crowd-sourced showing an increased NPS? Is the NPS of your employees improving when decision making changes are made? Having a common metric across the company provides not only a unified view but also a way to make consistent trade-offs.

ACTION PLAN: CALCULATING THE BENEFITS OF OPENNESS

As you've seen in this chapter, there are multiple ways to look at the benefits of openness. Now comes the fun part— coming up with your own measurements! As you do this, consider *why* you are developing these metrics. You may be in a justification stage right now, trying to make the case for your organization to become more open and engaged. Or you may need ways to measure your progress toward greater openness. The following five steps should get you started on the way, but note that there are no easy answers, as the metrics depend on (1) your goals, (2) how being more open impacts how you achieve those goals, and (3) how open you are today compared to how open you want to be. You'll know that you have the right metrics when they are both useful on an operational level and also provide insight into how you're making headway against your strategic goal. So let's get started!

Step 1: Define your objectives. At the end of Chapter Three, you went through the exercise of linking an open-driven objective to a strategic goal and also examined how being open can help you achieve that goal. If you haven't done that yet, take a quick look at the action plan and define your objective—you can't measure something if you don't know what it is! For the purpose of this action plan, I'm going to again use the hypothetical example of entering a new market, with the goal of increasing awareness of my brand from 2 percent to 20 percent in my target audience over the next year.

Step 2: Identify the most important key performance indicators (KPIs). This is the hardest step, as you're making a jump from the abstract objectives to the operational KPIs you'll be measured against. For example, the objective of having a dialog with a new audience needs to be more detailed than just "have deeper engagement with them." Your KPI should have very clear, quantifiable objectives; for example: "Grow the number of Facebook fans, Twitter followers, blog readers, and YouTube viewers" and "Increase the number of people sharing about our product to their friends." And it should set expectations of what those goals will be. The key: linking the indirect goal of growing social media audience size to increased awareness in your target audience. At the end of the

(Continued)

(Continued)

test period, does greater awareness stem from your greater presence in social media?

One pitfall of using these new metrics is picking too many KPIs—it's far too easy to fall victim to dashboard delirium and throw in metrics just because you can. By focusing on only the most important measurements that reflect how you are reaching your goal, you'll be able to do the next three steps—managing and optimizing the actions that matter most.

Step 3: Identify open activities that support your KPIs. If you have a page on Facebook already, does starting to actively respond to wall posts—as Kohl's does—increase the number of fans? How much time does it take? Or should you spend those same resources on a blog that has less reach but engages people on a deeper level and spurs linking, more blog posts, and high search engine placement? Or would simply writing posts that focus on specific hot topics make a difference? You can't make these decisions in a vacuum unless you can compare their contributions to your KPIs.

Step 4: Establish a baseline for your objectives and KPIs. Note that the objectives and KPIs I'm suggesting are not limited to a specific action or snapshot in time. Rather, the best metrics acknowledge it's the *change* over time that best reflects the benefit. For example, your final KPIs may look something like this: "Increase Facebook fans from 50,000 to 500,000 over the next six months by engaging at least half of wall posters in a dialog, which will eventually take up 25 percent of our community manager's time." If those efforts only get you to 250,000, you'll know that your efforts got you only halfway to the goal—and although you didn't reach your goal, you'll know more than you did before. Remember that in the absence of established value metrics and benchmarks for openness, you'll need to create them for yourself along the way.

Step 5: Optimize and adjust your KPIs and priorities. With new data and experience in hand, make adjustments as needed. Are your KPIs realistic or do you need to increase the amount of time your community manager spends in Facebook? And is there a better use of that person's time—say, driving traffic to and responding to comments on a blog or discussion board? Along the way, check to see whether the KPIs themselves correlate with advancement on your objective—is awareness of your brand growing from that initial 2 percent, and is it at 10 percent midway through the year? Which KPIs appear to be driving the most value to your overall goal?

As you can see from these five steps, measuring the benefits of openness needs to move quickly from the theoretical to the concrete and to be rooted in good business practices. The sooner you can ground your openness strategy with operational details and measurements, the sooner you can get to work realizing the value.

Now that you have an idea of how to measure the benefits of openness, we'll move on to look at how to manage the risk and uncertainty that comes from opening up your organization. In Chapter Five, we'll examine the policies, processes, and procedures that will help you manage openness.

STRUCTURING
OPENNESS
WITH SANDBOX
COVENANTS

Now that we've gone through establishing your strategy and understanding the benefits, a concern is likely overshadowing your enthusiasm—namely, that openness feels risky and dangerous. You're not alone. The most frequently asked question I get is how to deal with the sense of being out of control when you come face-to-face with openness, especially when you are asking skittish executives to jump in with you. Although outlining the benefits helps, I urge you to also put in place the policies, processes, and procedures that will help you manage openness. You have to have a plan for how you will, in effect, control openness. This is not a contradiction—in fact, I believe it is a necessity that you structure and explain openness and hold it accountable.

In this chapter, I'll lay out the reasons why structuring openness properly is needed and how to do it with your employees and with your customers. In Chapter Six, we'll look at how to operational-ize your openness strategy, but first let's get started with laying the groundwork for your new open relationships.

WHY STRUCTURE IS NEEDED

People sometimes say to me that to be open you just have to trust people. "Put your faith in people and let them do what they think is right." The problem is, what happens if what individuals think is right doesn't align with the thoughts of other individuals or with your organization's goals? Chaos will ensue. In previous chapters I've sug-gested that openness needs structure and prioritization—you have to determine what you will be open about, what you will not be open about, what you will permit, what you will not. There must be limits.

To that end, the new relationships you create with openness and social technologies need structure. Remember, you are building rela-tionships that have not existed before. Most of us understand the rules and etiquette of social interaction; for example, when meeting a stranger for the first time at a dinner party, we follow certain proto-cols and don't ask about the new acquaintance's politics or income— or ask for a loan of $500. But in these new open relationships, the power shift is such that we are not quite sure how we should be acting, and it sometimes feels like we are looking in on some alien world with its own language and social mores.

So it goes with the new relationships you craft with empowered customers and employees. If you hand over power, how will you know that someone will be responsible with that power? If you open up and put your trust in someone, what kind of accountability do you expect there to be?

These agreements don't happen in a vacuum. You have to make the time and effort to define the rules for these new relationships, setting expectations and clearly communicating them so that trust can develop over time. Open leadership requires that you create structure, process, and discipline around openness when there is none, so that people know what to expect and how to behave in a new open environment. Don't be shy—go ahead and make the rules, involving your employees and customers along the way. Think of it as one of your first openness initiatives—writing what I call the "sandbox covenant" that will govern *how* you will enter into these new relationships.

DEFINING YOUR ORGANIZATION'S SANDBOX

One way to think about openness is to use a playground sandbox metaphor. On the one hand, there are clearly defined boundaries to the sandbox, and within those boundaries, it's a safe place to play. On the other hand, the sandbox still has rules: no throwing sand at other players, no taking someone's truck unless you have permission. Let's start first with building the sandbox itself.

The first step is to define the walls of the sandbox—how big it will be, and what activities do and do not belong there. A good starting point is to look at the Openness Audit that you did at the end of Chapter Two. Where are you comfortable today in terms of what people can and can't do? Where do you anticipate you will need to be more open, and what limits will you put on it? You can go through and decide what the rules will be for each of the ten openness elements around information sharing and decision making. You are laying the groundwork for how you will operate, for your organization and for yourself.

Each company will have a different sized sandbox, depending on how open they want to be. You can also imagine that different teams will have bigger or smaller sandboxes depending on what they are trying to accomplish and the roles that people play inside of that team. Some companies have very, very big sandboxes. When

Microsoft first embraced blogging, for example, they decided to let any employee blog. They had an informal blogging policy that consisted of just two things: "Remember the confidentiality agreement you signed when you became employed here," and "Be smart." Microsoft said, in effect, "We hired you because you're smart, because you're a thinking rational person." They trusted people to use their best judgment when it came to knowing what to blog and what not to blog. As a result of hiring great people and trusting them, Microsoft can have a huge sandbox.

Zappos is another company with a giant sandbox—they *don't have* an explicit social media policy. Instead, they put new hires through a rigorous training program so that they are imbued with the company's core values concerning customer service, and they also learn how to properly use social media. As a result, Zappos not only openly encourages employees to engage via social media but also aggregates and highlights employee Twitter updates at twitter.zappos.com.

Both Microsoft and Zappos have the confidence to be able to let go and know that things will get done and that, for the most part, bad things won't happen. The evidence is clear that this approach works—in the past year, the number of public incidents involving employees at companies with very open social media policies (including Sun, Intel, and IBM) is a whopping . . . zero.

But most organizations don't feel they can trust employees to use social media at all in the workplace. A survey by Robert Half Technology of 1,400 CIOs of U.S. companies reported that 54 percent of them block the use of social media sites like Facebook, Twitter, LinkedIn, and MySpace in the workplace.[1] Another 19 percent allow access only for business purposes, 16 percent allow limited personal use, and only 10 percent allow full access during work hours. The concern: that employees will spend time on these sites rather than doing their work. In other words, these organizations feel they can't trust employees to do their jobs or their managers to monitor productivity. For these organizations, the sandbox is nonexistent, and leaders may feel they are "in control" of the situation simply by banning the activity.

This is the wrong approach, especially with access to these sites now nearly ubiquitous on mobile devices. Moreover, outright bans give executives and managers an excuse to not have to deal with social media use in the workplace. But deal with it they must, because employee use of these sites happens on mobile phones at work and at home in the evenings. And what they do as employees, and what they discuss online as it pertains to work, is of utmost importance.

So I believe that *every* company needs to develop and put in place a sandbox covenant—some type of openness or social media policy—even if this is, as is the case with Zappos, that the organization will *not* have a policy and will rely on existing company norms, values, and processes to provide safeguards. And even if your organization insists on blocking access to these sites, you still need to define the sandbox in terms of what employees are expected to do or not do in social media.

Don't be concerned if you construct your sandbox to be fairly small and limited—be realistic about how much openness you and your organization can take on at first. But be prepared to revise the sandbox size over time—as trust builds with successful open engagement, everyone will feel more comfortable growing the sandbox.

USING COVENANTS TO BUILD TRUST

I'd like to turn now to why I use "covenants" instead of policies and contracts. Covenants are promises that people make with each other, which differ from traditional corporate policies and procedures that *dictate* how things will operate within organizations. The philosophy behind covenants is more suited to openness strategies, because the promises, bargains, and contracts reflect a real trade-off and transfer of power and responsibility. When leaders open up and give up control they trust that employees will do what they promise, that customers will respond and engage in a civil manner.

A key part of a covenant is accountability, spelling out what happens if either party doesn't keep their side of the bargain. In the case of employees, if they don't act responsibly with the new freedom, it will be taken away. Or if customers act inappropriately and offend other members of the community, they will be kicked out. And employees and customers can also hold *leaders* accountable if they haven't acted in a way they have promised. For example, if an executive promises to share good and bad news with all employees, he better do so or face being called out by disappointed workers.

THE CONTRADICTION OF STRUCTURING OPENNESS

On the surface, it appears to be a contradiction that I'm advocating, in a sense, the control of openness. But rather than thinking of this as limiting openness, think of it as providing the guardrails within which being open can take place. Unless you clearly define what the limitations are—and *every* organization and person has limits to how open they can and want to be—people will not have the trust and confidence to *be open* in the first place. How are they to know that it's OK to talk with customers directly in a discussion forum? When can a manager approach an employee about their private, individual social media activities that may be casting the company in a negative light?

In the end, your sandbox covenants describe in detail the kind of relationship you want to have with your employees and customers. So the purpose of the covenants should be first and foremost to encourage a more open relationship, crafted and written with the purpose of enabling the new relationship to develop. As an open leader, it is up to you to lay the groundwork, the foundations for these relationships. Otherwise, few people are going to stick out their necks and begin.

Let's get concrete with sandbox covenants—I typically see two types of covenants in place with organizations: (1) social media guidelines for employees and (2) customer-facing guidelines, such as community participation or comment guidelines, as well as disclosure policies and codes of conduct designed to build trust with an audience. I'll go through each type and include for each one a specific action plan on how to get started. Let's begin with social media guidelines for employees, which I believe every organization needs to have.

CREATING SOCIAL MEDIA GUIDELINES FOR EMPLOYEES

A recent survey by Deloitte found that only 22 percent of companies have any type of social media guideline or policy in place.[2] Without any sort of guidelines, employees and their managers will be at a loss as to what is allowed and what isn't. And when situations come up, managers should all be able to recognize them as a problem (or not) and turn to the guidelines for advice on potential next steps. Otherwise, managers and executives will be left figuring out how to respond on the fly, reacting in the moment rather than in a way that's well thought out and consistent with an overall strategy.

I've collected hundreds of social media policies and guidelines and read through most of them (you can see a directory of them at open-leadership.com). It's encouraging to see the thought that goes into them—and also amusing to see how much copying and pasting goes on! In addition, I've advised several companies in their creation of social media guidelines, and I've found that the following elements are essential components (see Figure 5.1). We'll discuss each of these major points in turn.

INTRODUCTION: SETTING THE STAGE

It's important to start off with the right tone—which is why I strongly suggest that your guidelines start with a statement of encouragement and support. The first thing your social media guidelines should offer is an acknowledgment that the organization is excited about social technologies and wants employees to be more open to customers and other stakeholders through the use of social technologies. Here's an example:

> HP recognizes the unique value of social media sites and supports employees' responsible use of these increasingly popular

Figure 5.1. Social Media Guidelines Checklist

Introduction
- Encouragement and support—why social technologies are important
- When the guidelines apply
  - Personal use of social technologies when it's related to the organization
  - Using social technologies in an official capacity

Guidelines
- Identity transparency
  - When you do or don't identify yourself as an employee
  - Definitely when discussing organization-related topics
  - Potential conflict of interests that others should know about
- Responsibility
  - Take responsibility for your own words; don't post anonymously
  - Separate your words from your employer's with a disclaimer
  - Respect—for clients, fellow employees, and competitors
  - Don't let it interfere with your work
- Confidentiality
  - Remember the confidentiality agreement you signed
  - Respect the privacy of clients and peers
  - Highlight places where confidentiality might slip
  - List what is OK to share, what isn't
- Common sense and judgment
  - Make it clear there will be areas where common sense is needed
  - Ask if unsure

Best practices for social media practitioners
- Tone
  - Have a personality, develop a voice
  - Err on the side of caution; don't post when angry or upset
- Quality
  - Spelling and grammar
  - Add value
- Trust-building
  - Respond to people
  - Speak in your area of expertise
  - Link out a lot
  - Admit mistakes

Oversight and consequences
- When the organization will make requests
- Process to follow for managers
- Escalation and resolution process

Additional resources
- HR, press, and legal contacts for managers and employees
- Training

communication and learning tools. Active engagement in the blogosphere and social media sites allows HP employees to interact directly, openly, and in real-time with customers, prospects, business partners and the general public. This highly personalized information and idea exchange reflects the collaborative, customer-centered approach that defines our way of doing business.

Effective engagement in social media can help create and deepen interest in our company, our products and our services. It can enable us to learn about and respond more nimbly to urgent issues and concerns. It can help establish HP and its employees as "thought leaders" in today's dynamic technology universe.[3]

THE PURPOSE OF GUIDELINES

It's also important to explain when and for whom the policy applies. Explain why the organization needs social media guidelines and in particular when it applies to a person's *personal* use of social media. This may be distinctly different from the use of social technologies in an official capacity, in which case you may want to provide additional guidelines and best practices along with specific training. Razorfish does an excellent job of this in their employee guidelines, giving several concrete scenarios on when the guidelines apply and when they do not.[4] Also keep in mind the managers and executives who may be turning to the guidelines to determine whether or not something is allowed; make sure that it's easy to reference, has many examples, and includes common scenarios. Here, as an example, Mayo Clinic explains the purpose of their guidelines:

> The main thing Mayo employees need to remember about blogs and social networking sites is that the same basic policies apply in these spaces as in other areas of their lives. The purpose of these guidelines is to help employees understand how Mayo policies apply to these newer technologies for communication, so you can participate with confidence not only on this blog, but in other social media platforms.[5]

GUIDELINES: PROVIDING GUARDRAILS FOR ENGAGEMENT

This is the meat of your document, the detailed guidelines that set out your expectations for what people will and won't do. There are several components; I'll describe each in detail and also provide short examples for each area.

Identity transparency means revealing who you are and who you work for, in case there are any potential conflicts of interest. What differs from company to company is *when* this applies. Some organizations request that you always state this when discussing anything related to your organization's products or services or even related topics. Others require identification only when there is potential conflict of interest, which can be hard to define. For example, if I work for Procter & Gamble, should I disclose my affiliation if I comment about what type of diaper I use on my kids, even if I am not working in the Pampers division? It comes down to this—would it make a difference if the audience knew?

Honda ran afoul of this in the fall of 2009 when it launched the Accord Crossover on Facebook, where it received several negative comments about the new model's appearance. One person defended the new model, writing, "Interesting design. I would get this car in a heartbeat." He was immediately called out because he didn't identify himself as a Honda employee, even though it was his honest personal opinion and he was not acting as a Honda spokesperson.[6] Honda quickly removed his post and wrote an explanation, but it only added fuel to the growing fire.[7]

Here is an example of how Kodak requests that employees identify themselves:

> Even when you are talking as an individual, people may perceive you to be talking on behalf of Kodak. If you blog or discuss photography, printing or other topics related to a Kodak business, be upfront and explain that you work for Kodak; however, if you aren't an official company spokesperson, add a disclaimer to the effect: "The opinions

114

and positions expressed are my own and don't necessarily reflect those of Eastman Kodak Company."[8]

Responsibility means that you will be personally responsible for your personal social media activities online, and if you *are* writing about company-related topics, you will act in accordance with company values and expectations. This may include adding a statement, as noted earlier, that says your comments are your own and that you are not speaking on behalf of your organization. It may also include notifying managers of any significant social media presences or activities that may affect the company, engaging in a respectful and polite manner that reflects well on the company, and also ensuring that these activities do not interfere with getting work done. The level of responsibility can vary significantly from company to company, depending upon how open or restrictive the organization is about activities. Here is an example from Kaiser Permanente:

> Take responsibility: You are personally responsible for your post. Blogs, wikis and other forms of online discourse are individual interactions, not corporate communications. Kaiser Permanente staff and physicians are personally responsible for their posts. Be mindful that what you write will be public for a long time.
>
> One of Kaiser Permanente's core values is "trust and personal responsibility in all relationships." As a company, Kaiser Permanente trusts—and expects—its workforce to exercise personal responsibility whenever they blog or participate in any social media medium.[9]

Confidentiality means you will not disclose confidential company information. A simple reference back to your organization's confidentiality policy may be all that's needed. But the problem is, there's a tremendous amount of gray area—for example, it's clear you shouldn't talk about future earnings, but when is it OK to share new product ideas with key clients? Every organization has a specific concern about confidential information getting out, be it product features, client information, intellectual property, or employee gossip. You may want to specifically list the different types of information that are particularly vulnerable to inadvertent sharing. I turn again to Kaiser Permanente, which as a health care provider has specific concerns about patient confidentiality and compliance with legal requirements. Here's how they address it in their social media policy:

> Member/Patient Confidentiality. Employees may not use or disclose any member/patient identifiable information of any kind on any social media without the express written permission of the member/patient. Even if an individual is not identified by name within the information you wish to use or disclose, if there is a reasonable basis to believe that the person could still be identified from that information, then its use or disclosure could constitute a violation of the Health Insurance Portability and Accountability Act (HIPAA) and Kaiser Permanente policy.[10]

The result: Kaiser Permanente has several doctors actively blogging and using Twitter, often to engage with their patients directly.[11] With clear training on how they can abide by HIPAA requirements, the organization's management feels comfortable and confident that these medical professionals will engage safely.

Using judgment and common sense is probably the most important guideline to include. You appeal to people to use their training and experience to distinguish between the OK and the not OK—and to seek out advice when they are unsure. Many policies acknowledge that there is no way they can comprehensively capture all scenarios, so they appeal to people's general intelligence and capability. In the same vein, there may be instances when common sense isn't followed or poor judgment is exercised, resulting in an undesirable outcome. In many ways, this is a "catch-all" guideline that anticipates that there will be unforeseen situations that face employees and managers alike. Some examples include:

Common sense is the best guide if you decide to post information in any way relating to Cisco.[12]

Your video will be reviewed and rejected if it violates the guidelines and rules of common sense and decency. Do not put the Air Force in a situation that may result in account termination.[13]

BEST PRACTICES AND HOW-TOS SET EXPECTATIONS

Many organizations also include best practices in their guidelines on how to engage in social media, for both personal and professional purposes. To avoid confusion, it's best to delineate whether these are suggestions to be used in personal, unofficial activities or standards that are being set for official engagement. At times, the line between official and unofficial depends on whether a manager gets involved—and it's not always in the most positive context! Hence, listing best practices does double duty—setting out the standard quality of what the organization considers best practices, and providing a template for when a manager needs to engage if guidelines aren't being followed.

Tone is a highly personal best practice, incorporating not only what I call a "voice" that's unique to each person and organization but also what is called for in the context of the situation. One best practice is to have what many organizations encourage, "To have a personality"—meaning the person steps out from the shadow of the organization.

At the same time, there is a negative aspect of tone, in that sometimes people will speak out when they are upset or angry and post something in the heat of the moment. Many guidelines encourage employees to take a moment, including language like what Intel has in its guidelines: "If you're about to publish something that makes you even the slightest bit uncomfortable, don't shrug it off and hit 'send.' Take a minute to review these guidelines and try to figure out what's bothering you, then fix it."[14]

Quality: It's also important to pay attention to details and ensure *quality*. Basics such as spell check and use of proper grammar are

117

important. There's also the actual quality of the content being created—for example, not overpublishing inconsequential updates on Twitter or blog posts to the point where quality suffers and people start to ignore you!

Quality also means making sure that the information being shared adds value and doesn't waste people's time. The problem is, there is an element of judgment involved in determining what "value" means. IBM's social media guidelines put it eloquently:

> If it helps you, your coworkers, our clients or our partners to do their jobs and solve problems; if it helps to improve knowledge or skills; if it contributes directly or indirectly to the improvement of IBM's products, processes and policies; if it builds a sense of community; or if it helps to promote IBM's Values, then it is adding value. Though not directly business-related, background information you choose to share about yourself, such as information about your family or personal interests, may be useful in helping establish a relationship between you and your readers, but it is entirely your choice whether to share this information.[15]

Trust building: probably the most important set of best practices is in this area. These are the activities and behaviors that your organization identifies as the best ways to build a deep relationship with your audience and customers. They can include responding quickly to questions and comments from people; for example, "Reply to comments in a timely manner, when a response is appropriate." Include reminders to link frequently to people outside of the organization, which DePaul University expresses as follows: "Cite and link to your sources whenever possible; after all, that's how you build community."[16]

And the hardest best practice of all—*admitting that you've made a mistake.* It's always hard to admit when you're wrong, and doubly so with social technologies because of its public nature. Hence there is a need to call this out strongly and clearly in the best practices area, if it is indeed your intention to do this (we'll discuss best practices of how to handle failure in Chapter Nine). DePaul University again has a great way of stating this best practice: "If you make an error, correct it quickly and visibly. This will earn you respect in the online community."

OVERSIGHT AND CONSEQUENCES: WHEN MANAGEMENT GETS INVOLVED

Another important part of the guidelines is setting the expectations for what will happen if things don't go according to plan and the organization needs to step in, especially when it involves someone's personal online activities. Organizations walk a fine line when getting involved, so they need to clarify not only when they will do this, but also the process they will use.

One of most basic scenarios is when someone writes something inappropriate and it comes to the attention of that person's direct manager. The first thing a manager will likely do is read the guidelines to see whether any policies have not been followed. The guidelines should provide a process; for example, that the manager have a discussion with the direct report or seek guidance from somebody in human resources or the legal department.

If training and education around the guidelines are robust, employees being approached should understand the context of the conversation and not be blindsided when someone comes to talk to them. If the transgression is severe enough, such as gross negligence or misconduct, the organization may have to take further action, including and up to dismissal, if warranted. That's why some companies include information in the guidelines regarding this—to clarify upfront what is at stake. Dell includes the following in its guidelines: "Dell employees or company representatives who fail to comply with this policy will be subject to discipline, up to and including termination of employment from Dell. In addition, depending upon the nature of the policy violation or the online channel content, participants may also be subject to civil and/or criminal penalties."[17]

ADDITIONAL RESOURCES

Finally, the guidelines should include additional resources, such as contacts in public relations if there is a reaction taking place outside the company as a result of an employee's activities. And if employees have questions about the guidelines, they may need to have a resource other than their direct manager to ask questions confidentially without risk of retribution. Training resources, best practices guidelines, and in-house experts could also be listed in the guidelines. And ideally, there will also be a place where suggestions on how to improve the guidelines can be sent, as well as information about how future revisions will be handled.

ACTION PLAN: CREATING YOUR SOCIAL MEDIA GUIDELINES

That's a quick overview of what goes into general guidelines—the hard part is getting everyone in the organization aligned around a specific document, especially your legal team, which may not be as well versed as you would like on the benefits and risks of social technologies. Here is a general action plan on how to get started with this process:

1. Start with the openness audit you conducted at the end of Chapter Two and your open strategy goals from Chapter Three. Use these as the starting point in discussions with your legal team, so they understand what you are trying to accomplish and how open you want the organization to be.

2. Identify the biggest hopes and the biggest fears you face as an organization in achieving these goals. Include key stakeholders who will be involved in achieving your goal, as they will be the ones most likely to encounter guideline issues.

3. Collect real examples to illustrate guideline elements. Include both good and bad practices, as well as examples of gray areas where judgment and common sense should be exercised. The best policies come to life when they are put into the context of everyday operations.

4. Keep the guidelines practical by mapping out scenarios on how they will be used. They should work well in training and education as well as in oversight and escalation. Apply the guidelines to real scenarios to see how well they hold up under scrutiny.

5. Agree ahead of time on the writing and guideline decision process: who will be involved, who has final say, how you will go about involving other stakeholders, and how revisions will be handled. Have a clear review and feedback process for future edits, especially when and how you will review the policy in light of changing marketplaces and technologies.

AN EXAMPLE OF EMPLOYEE GUIDELINES IN ACTION

Back in 1997, IBM recommended that its employees get on the Internet—at a time when many companies were doing their best to keep their employees away from it. In 2005, IBM led the way again as one of the first companies to put in place blogging guidelines. To write the guidelines, IBM put up some initial tenets on an internal wiki and let all employees know that they were free to come and help write the guidelines. The guidelines were reviewed by the legal and human resource departments and adopted with very minor changes.

Over the ensuing four years the policy has been revised—via the same wiki-based process—and has evolved primarily to include all types of social technologies, not just blogs. A comparison of the 2005 and 2009 versions of the guidelines shows that the core guidelines remain largely unchanged, despite the rapid change and adoption of social technologies.[18] That's because I believe IBM's guidelines are centered on the kind of relationship they are trying to encourage employees to have with the outside world, rather than the use of specific technologies.

You'll know you've done a good job on the guidelines if people look at it and are encouraged to engage with others outside the company walls. And you'll know you have a great policy when employees create gray area scenarios and discuss how the organization would deal with pushing the openness envelope. That kind of healthy debate, in which employees push and pull against the sandbox walls for greater, deeper engagement, is where you want to be.

INVITING CUSTOMERS INTO A COVENANT

It is one thing to lay out enforceable guidelines for employees—it is something entirely different to do so for customers. But I think you do need to lay out the ground rules that dictate how you will interact with customers and vice versa. If you give customers a platform, you implicitly trust that the vast majority will act responsibly and respectfully when they write on your Facebook wall or participate in discussion forums that you offer on your site. But you can anticipate the problems that inevitably arise—something goes wrong, a customer is dissatisfied with something, and you end up with a negative review or comment on your site.

Sam Decker, the chief marketing officer at Bazaarvoice, a company that works with about six hundred brands to encourage user-generated content, says the company has had to build its business by overcoming this fear of greater openness with customers. "It's easy to be protective and to avoid critical comment and uncertainty," says Sam. "Everything in the marketplace, everything in Wall Street rewards predictability. So it is a fearful thing from the perspective of corporate America to do something unpredictable, allow whatever customers want to say right next to your brand, right next to your product." Interestingly, people turn out to be quite predictable when it comes to writing reviews—Bazaarvoice found that reviews are largely positive, with 80 percent of product reviews getting 4s or 5s (with 5 being the most positive score). Moreover, the average rating on a product is 4.3 out of 5 across Bazaarvoice's clients.

As uncomfortable as negative comments are, their presence can give the conversation a ring of authenticity—no group of customers is ever 100 percent completely happy with a product or service! And with the tendency for reviews to be positive—yet balanced—customers have the opportunity to get the real scoop from other customers (rather than from the company). It's getting to the point where if you're trying to sell something, customers expect to be able to find peer reviews. Again, Decker commented to me, "If your brand doesn't have user-generated content about it, people aren't learning about it. They're not considering it."

But there are times when a comment by a customer is not just negative, but unacceptable because it is defamatory, obscene, or simply off-topic—fundamentally, it doesn't match the level of conduct you want displayed in a public forum. When does it make sense to delete a comment or even bar someone from participating because they are a troublemaker, versus letting a negative comment stand because, although you don't agree with it, it reflects an opinion, is respectfully put, and furthers the relationship of the community at large? This can be a tough call for even the most experienced open organizations.

Comments in discussion groups and especially on blogs are a recurring area of concern for organizations. In its community guidelines, Wells Fargo lays out specifically what they will do, explaining, "To ensure exchanges that are productive, informative, respectful of diverse viewpoints and lawful, we will review all comments and we will NOT post comments that are or include . . ." at which point they go on to describe in detail comments that are Off Topic, Spam, Personal Attacks, Illegal, Offensive Language, and Private or Confidential Information. Ed Terpening, Wells Fargo's VP of social media, explained to me that in general, they don't need to exercise this very often, and that overall, negative comments form a minority of the opinions submitted.[19]

Intel also includes details on its moderation policy in order to ensure what it calls "balanced online dialogue." They cleverly include this clause:

> Whether content is pre-moderated or community moderated, follow these three principles: the Good, the Bad, but not the Ugly. If the content is positive or negative and in context to the conversation, then we approve the content, regardless of whether it's favorable or unfavorable to Intel. But if the content is ugly, offensive, denigrating and completely out of context, then we reject the content.[20]

Overall, organizations are leery of exercising their right to delete comments or to ban someone completely because they are being a nuisance. But I believe that organizations should clearly and firmly draw the line, because that ensures that productive conversations and relationship building can take place. Think of it this way—what would you do if someone came into a conference room in your building where you are hosting a meeting and started ranting, raving, and generally causing a disturbance? You'd try to reason with the person, but if the behavior persisted, you would call security and have that person escorted politely but firmly out of the room—and likely out of the building. When it comes to your online presence, it's important to let your customers know when you will step in and safeguard the environment—making it clear that you are willing to hear dissenting views but not at the expense of civil discourse.

CODES OF CONDUCT AND DISCLOSURE POLICIES

It's important for organizations to lay out the rules of engagement and make clear the responsibilities of each side. An excellent example of this is "The Company-Customer Pact" that GetSatisfaction has published, which calls for shared responsibility between the parties (see Exhibit 5.1).[21] In this way, the Pact is operating as a sandbox covenant, whereby each side promises to abide by a certain code of conduct.

Exhibit 5.1. The Company-Customer Pact

We, customers and companies alike, need to trust the people with whom we do business. Customers expect honest, straightforward interactions where their voices are heard, before, during, and between purchases. Companies work to inspire customer satisfaction and brand loyalty by constantly improving the products and services they offer.

It is evident that we all have a crucial stake—and responsibility—in transforming the adversarial tone that all too often dominates the customer experience. If we work together and share the responsibility of furthering effective conversation, we can build mutually respectful long-term relationships.

By adopting these five practical values, we can together realize a meaningful shift in our business relationships.

	Companies	Customers
1) Be Human	Use a respectful, conversational voice. Avoid scripts and corporate doublespeak.	Be understanding. Show the respect and kindness that you'd like shown to you.
2) Be Accessible	Cultivate a public dialogue with customers and demonstrate your responsiveness and willingness to be held accountable.	Share issues directly with the company or in a place where the company has a chance to respond.
3) Be Authentic	Encourage employees to use their real names and offer a personal touch.	Use your real identity and foster a long-term reputation with the company.
4) Be Patient	Some problems take longer to fix than expected, so do your best to set clear expectations for how you will address issues.	Give companies the information and time required to adequately address issues.

(Continued)

125

Exhibit 5.1. The Company-Customer Pact (*Continued*)

5) Be Productive	Do your best to keep the conversation going. Demonstrate good intentions by speaking candidly with customers as you work toward a solution.	Be ready to continue conversations you begin. Give companies the benefit of the doubt while they work toward a solution.

Available at http://getsatisfaction.com/ccpact.

Codes of conduct and disclosure policies serve one purpose—to develop trust. Chris Pratley, one of the first bloggers at Microsoft, experienced this: "When I first started writing, there were people commenting on my blogs, saying, 'I don't believe you, you must be a marketing guy. You must be a guy who is a front for something.' And I would write back, saying, 'Really, that surprised me. What made you think that? Ask me anything and I'll answer honestly.'" Over a period of time, Pratley was able to convince people to trust him, partly because he let negative comments stand, and also because he responded to people quickly and politely, even when they didn't agree with him.

The benefit of having a code of conduct and disclosure policy is that it may help shorten the time it takes to build that level of trust, because it makes clear to both your employees and your audience how you expect people in your organization to behave. At the core, you are explaining what kind of relationship you want to have with your audience. If they have never encountered you being open before, how are they to know what to expect? By taking the first step in clearly describing what *you* will bring to the sandbox covenant, you are setting the foundation for a relationship.

For example, HP's Blogging Code of Conduct lays out what they will do, starting with a simple, strong statement: "We will strive to have open and honest dialogues with our readers."[22] Exhibit 5.2 presents another example, from Hill & Knowlton, a public relations firm that wants to make sure of how and when it speaks on behalf

Exhibit 5.2. Hill & Knowlton's Social Media Principles

Personal use of social media

If you could be identified as a Hill & Knowlton employee or use company resources for your personal use of social media, please consider the following:

- Your clients, manager, reports and peers may read what you write. Criticizing them could result in the company losing business or even you losing your job.
- Think of what you write in the same way as things you might say to a journalist, or conversations you might have with people you don't know. If you wouldn't say it in those situations, don't say it online.
- Never disclose any information that is confidential or proprietary to our clients, Hill & Knowlton, WPP, or any third party that has disclosed information to us (e.g. journalists, suppliers, etc.), even if you think it is secure. Your existing employment agreement in any case prohibits this.
- There are many things that we cannot mention as part of a publicly owned company. Talking about our revenue, future plans, or the WPP share price could get you and the company in legal trouble, even if it is just your own personal view, and whether or not you directly identify yourself as an employee of Hill & Knowlton.
- Your personal use of social media at work should be appropriate for your role. If you are in doubt, discuss with your line manager or refer to your employment agreement.
- If you explicitly identify yourself as a Hill & Knowlton employee, you should make it clear that the views you express are yours alone. You may want to use the following form of words on your blog, Web site or profile:

These views are my own and do not necessarily reflect the views of my employer.

Professional use of social media on behalf of Hill & Knowlton and clients

When it comes to using social media professionally (i.e. as part of a pitch, client campaign or when representing Hill & Knowlton), please follow these basic principles:

(Continued)

127

Exhibit 5.2. Hill & Knowlton's
Social Media Principles (*Continued*)

- Understand the rules, beliefs and desires of the online communities you communicate with.
- Don't engage with social or consumer-generated media on behalf of a client without their knowledge, permission and guidance from the Hill & Knowlton consultant leading the engagement, or if it contravenes a client's own policies.
- Understand your clients' policies and abide by them. Where there is irresolvable conflict, Hill & Knowlton's principles prevail.
- Disclose who you are and who you work for (both agency and client).
- Be honest and don't pretend to be someone or something you are not.
- Respect the privacy and contact preferences of each individual you interact with, where available.

Where practical, link to our principles in your opening communications (http://www.hillandknowlton.com/principles).

of clients.[23] There are more excellent examples and a Disclosure Best Practices Toolkit available from the Social Media Business Council.[24]

DEALING WITH THE LEGAL DEPARTMENT

Johnson & Johnson, a major pharmaceutical and health care product company, was understandably concerned about allowing the public to freely comment on the firm's sites. What should J&J do if someone reported an adverse reaction to one of its regulated products? What if someone wrote about a beneficial side effect—an off-label use—and urged others to use the medication? "Allowing a conversation about an unapproved use of one of our regulated products could result in us running afoul of the FDA's guidelines on promotion," explained Marc Monseau, director of social media for Johnson & Johnson.

When the company decided to dip into social media and start their first blog in 2006, Margaret Gurowitz, a member of the corporate communications department, stepped up to the plate because she was confident she could address and allay those concerns. A self-professed history buff, Gurowitz proposed a blog called "Kilmer House" that would focus on the history of the 120-year-old company.[25] Gurowitz pointed out that a blog about history would be a low-risk way for Johnson & Johnson to start participating in social media because most of the things she would be writing about happened a hundred years ago. Regardless, she worked very closely with the legal and regulatory group to understand their concerns, and she got corporate approvals to move forward, including a signoff from the CEO.

The key was having policies and processes in place. Says Monseau, "Margaret put in a comments policy that not only would the comments be reviewed before they would be posted, but we tried to make it very clear only certain comments would be allowed—those that did not pertain to the products we sold." They also set up a process so that if someone did submit a comment that included an adverse event report, they used channels that were already set up to funnel such comments that came in from the main Web site. The clinical affairs group would then follow up or report on that adverse effect, in line with legal requirements.

A year later, Monseau approached the same legal teams to start the JNJ BTW blog, which discusses current issues at Johnson & Johnson.[26] Having already experienced public comment with the Kilmer House blog, the legal team and senior executives had greater confidence taking on current issues. Robert Halper, director of video communications at Johnson & Johnson, then jumped into the world of online video. Applying some of the approaches taken by Margaret and Marc, Rob worked with the legal department to establish a whole new set of processes to create a YouTube channel featuring educational videos but also allowing open (but moderated) commenting. Monseau explained, "It's about taking baby steps that not only provide experience, but also make such projects less troubling to others in the organization—thereby enabling others to take on more aggressive projects. Rob, Margaret, and I have found that by taking these steps within Johnson & Johnson we have created a roadmap for others to follow."

I've worked with many concerned legal departments and have found that the key is to connect with them early in the process and educate them on the benefits of greater openness—otherwise, they see only the all-too-real risks of engaging in an open manner. Using the sandbox covenant analogy draws them into the discussion, by asking their advice on how to define the sandbox walls, rather than dismissing it altogether. Finally, by identifying the top worst-case scenarios and putting in place mitigation and contingency policies, you can often address and alleviate many legal and executive concerns.

ACTION PLAN: CREATING YOUR COMMUNITY GUIDELINES

If companies like Johnson & Johnson and Wells Fargo, who are in highly regulated industries, can have open engagement with their audiences, you can too. The key again is to start with the kind of relationship that you want with your external audience; the kind of processes you put in place will reflect this. Here's a step-by-step plan for getting started with your community guidelines.

1. As with your social media guidelines for employees, start with the openness audit and open strategy goals from Chapters Two and Three. With your goals in hand, have an initial discussion with your legal team, making sure they understand the benefits of what you are trying to do.

2. Outline which behaviors and actions you will accept and which you won't. This includes what it means to be "negative" when expressing a different, legitimate viewpoint, and what it means to be disrespectful. Clearly define all the actions that you deem unacceptable.

3. Create a review process and also a way to communicate any concerns you may have with someone who is violating your community guidelines. Thoroughly train the people who will be involved in that process.

4. Set up processes and workflows so that you can handle customer service or other nonrelated comments in a timely and respectful way. It wouldn't do for someone who has a customer service issue to not be contacted quickly. (We'll discuss more about changing workflows in Chapter Six.)

5. Understand and clearly state your responsibilities as an organization and as employees of that organization. This may include a code of conduct or a disclosure policy. Make sure that relevant employees who are acting as spokespeople have adequate training and education on these guidelines.

6. Last, get constant feedback from your audience and revise your guidelines with their feedback.

SOME LAST WORDS OF ADVICE

I've set out some specific action plans for creating social media guidelines for your employees as well as for your external audiences. But before moving on, I have a few last words of advice concerning the whole concept of setting up rules and processes for control. I take inspiration from how Netflix approaches processes, in that the company identifies "good" processes that help people get more done and "bad" processes that seek to prevent recoverable mistakes.[27] Netflix believes in creative environments versus manufacturing environments—it thinks that preventing errors can actually inhibit excellent work. So it actively tries to get rid of "bad" rules that get in the way of excellence.

The company did exactly that when it got rid of its vacation policy. Until 2004, it had the standard number of vacation days that each employee could take. But the reality is that everyone worked evenings, checked email at odd hours, and also took time off in the afternoons for personal time. Netflix wasn't tracking how many hours people worked, so why did it make sense to track how many days they weren't working? It didn't. To quote from Netflix, "Just as we don't have a 9–5 day policy, we don't need a vacation policy." So Netflix doesn't have a vacation policy or tracking in place.

But Netflix didn't just snap its fingers and put this policy in place. It first had to have a strong culture that seeks out and supports what it calls "stunning colleagues." It pays more to make sure that these people come to Netflix—and stay. With high performers, Netflix doesn't need to worry about how many days of vacation they take—they may take more vacation days in the end, but it makes up for all of the extra hours they put in.

I share this because the sandbox covenant that you put in place has to be consistent and congruent with the kind of relationship you have with your employees and your audience. If they are not ready for openness, if you are not ready for openness, then you will have to make your sandbox covenants tighter and more closely defined to have a good working relationship. But I encourage you to start, even if it's starting small, to build the foundation for even bigger and better relationships in the future.

We'll now move on to Chapter Six, where I'll discuss the operational details of how to orchestrate your openness strategy.

6

ORCHESTRATING YOUR OPEN STRATEGY

You've decided on your goal and figured out how to craft the right sandbox covenants so that people know where they stand. Now it's time to pull it all together. This chapter is about how you orchestrate openness across the entire organization. Openness by definition means that there will be bridges built between traditionally isolated departments and silos—and some people may not be all that happy about this. People are comfortable in their well-defined positions; then, suddenly, openness changes the rules and requires that they work together in concert toward a common goal.

This change doesn't happen overnight, nor will it happen on its own. You will need an overall action plan that lays out the details for the open strategy and goals that you developed in Chapter Three—essentially, the score that you will use to conduct and lead your organization. You may be starting from scratch, in which case this chapter will act as your initial roadmap. But if, like many companies, yours has already dabbled with openness and social media initiatives, this chapter is also for you, but you may be using it more for course corrections. I'm going to lay out the map's main highways and include a checklist at the end of the chapter that will help you as a leader make sure that all of the elements of a well-orchestrated open strategy are in place.

Your detailed plan should include the following five elements:

- Create robust socialgraphic profiles of your customers and employees
- Identify points where workflow and stakeholders are affected
- Determine the best organizational structure
- Assign roles and responsibilities
- Design appropriate training and incentive plans

Let's get started with conducting a formal customer and organizational audit.

CREATE THE SOCIALGRAPHIC PROFILE

If you want to have a relationship with someone, it's helpful to know something about them! You've got your openness audit and your goals, but what do you *really* know about the people you want to have a relationship with? You've heard of demographics and psychographics, and you probably also are familiar with behavioral profiles that can be built around a person's online activities. Socialgraphics takes this one step further and looks at the whole social landscape in which your audience is active.

There are three elements of socialgraphics:

- *Social audit.* Where are your customers going online socially, what do they do there, and what topics do they discuss? Social monitoring tools like Radian6 are integrating with Web analytics vendors like Webtrends and CRM tools like Salesforce.com to provide a more complete picture of your customers; they can also map behaviors and activities. The same can be done to a lesser extent with your employees, if you are already using collaboration tools and suites. For example, where do your customers go today to discuss topics related to your business? What sites and services do your employees use—both internally and externally—to connect with each other and with customers?

• *Engagement audit.* Using the engagement pyramid discussed in Chapter Three, you should understand how deeply engaged your customers and employees are with particular topics, brands, and companies. Having an idea of how different segments engage more or less will be crucial to identifying your first tactical steps. For example, if you know that many of your employees are already engaged in sharing behaviors, it may take only a small nudge or incentive to get them to share internally and support a new strategic initiative.

• *Influence audit.* Finally, you need to understand who has influence— and also who influences whom. For example, if you have a customer who is highly networked and influential, you will want to prioritize any requests that come from that person. Likewise, if you know that a new prospect has a strong connection to other customers, you may look at buying patterns to infer what products the new person may be interested in.[1] Social relationship data is becoming more readily available, coming from vendors like Rapleaf, Lotame, and Media-6Degrees, which allow you to explore and tap into the social graph of a person.

By mapping the basic socialgraphics of your audience, you'll have a fundamental baseline of where your customers and employees are today. Without this knowledge, you'll be starting your journey without a full map, and you can quickly get lost trying to figure out where your audience is and what kind of relationship they currently have with each other—and with you. I'm frequently asked how to go about creating a socialgraphics profile. There are three basic approaches that you can use:

- *Monitoring.* There are many different monitoring services available, ranging from traditional press-like clipping services that just monitor mentions to deeply analytical services that draw from multiple sources. This is a rapidly evolving service area, with even giants like Microsoft jumping into the fray. To stay on top of it, be specific about the most important behaviors and trends you are tracking, rather than trying to get a comprehensive 360-degree view of a particular audience or individual.
- *Custom survey.* Monitoring picks up only behavior; it doesn't do a good job of linking it to other profile items such as deeper demographics or psychographics. Narrow down your target and understand not only what they are doing, but also *why* they are visiting sites, the content they read, and, just as important, what sources they trust and have influence over their decisions.
- *Market observations.* To conduct detailed engagement and influence audits, you need to supplement your monitoring and survey work with direct observations of how engaged your audience becomes and, of great importance, what causes them to increase their engagement. Do friends make a difference, or is it a new interface design that increases the number of commenters on a site?

With the socialgraphics map in hand, you can take your open strategy goals and begin to operationalize them within your organization. Now let's examine how your open strategy will affect existing operations.

IDENTIFY KEY WORKFLOWS AND STAKEHOLDERS

One of the first actions you need to take is mapping out the workflows, processes, and stakeholders that will be affected by your open strategy goal. This is the foundation of your action plan—what happens first, second, third when you start engaging with people externally and internally. You need to anticipate how requests need to be handled and to clearly communicate that to the people who will have to take action.

I'll be discussing three types of workflows: (1) triage of real-time requests, (2) crisis management, and (3) internal communications. Let's start with triaging inbound requests.

TRIAGE

When someone interacts with another person and discusses your company, what do you do about it? It depends on the location and context, the nature of the comment itself, and also your interest in engaging. Spelling out each of these permutations will help you figure out when it makes sense to engage—and when it makes sense not to.

As an example, let's take a look at the workflow process that the United States Air Force (USAF) published about how it handles online comments (see Figure 6.1).[2] This workflow applies to any comment that someone in the public affairs department may come across on line, be it in a discussion forum or blog on a USAF site or on a third-party site with no affiliation with the USAF. What I like about this is that it is consistent with the logic of the sandbox covenant laid out in Chapter Five, in which clear expectations are being defined on how USAF personnel will interact with people. But there are also clear guidelines on how to respond—and on *who* should respond. For example, if someone is a "Rager," then the instruction is to not respond, monitor only, and "notify HQ" (the phone number and email are conveniently listed on this page as well).

At this point, you may be thinking that this is a tremendous amount of work, having to map out and consider the various processes, scenarios, and permutations that could occur. However, given the risk associated with being open, and also the uncertainty, I believe it is incumbent on you to take the initiative to anticipate these triage points, and to be committed to refining your workflow maps over time. If you can't anticipate the questions, demands,

Figure 6.1. A Simplified View of How the U.S. Air Force Handles Blog Comments

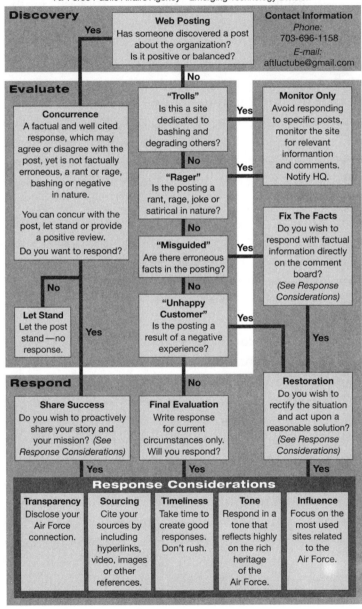

Air Force Web Posting Response Assessment V.2
Air Force Public Affairs Agency - Emerging Technology Division

Discovery

Yes

Web Posting
Has someone discovered a post about the organization?
Is it positive or balanced?

Contact Information
Phone:
703-696-1158
E-mail:
aftluctube@gmail.com

No

Evaluate

Concurrence
A factual and well cited response, which may agree or disagree with the post, yet is not factually erroneous, a rant or rage, bashing or negative in nature.

You can concur with the post, let stand or provide a positive review.
Do you want to respond?

"Trolls"
Is this a site dedicated to bashing and degrading others?

Yes

Monitor Only
Avoid responding to specific posts, monitor the site for relevant informantion and comments.
Notify HQ.

No

Yes

"Rager"
Is the posting a rant, rage, joke or satirical in nature?

No

"Misguided"
Are there erroneous facts in the posting?

Yes

Fix The Facts
Do you wish to respond with factual information directly on the comment board?
(See Response Considerations)

No

No

"Unhappy Customer"
Is the posting a result of a negative experience?

Yes

Let Stand
Let the post stand—no response.

Yes

Yes

Respond

No

Restoration
Do you wish to rectify the situation and act upon a reasonable solution?
(See Response Considerations)

Share Success
Do you wish to proactively share your story and your mission? *(See Response Considerations)*

Final Evaluation
Write response for current circumstances only.
Will you respond?

Yes

Yes

Yes

Response Considerations

Transparency	Sourcing	Timeliness	Tone	Influence
Disclose your Air Force connection.	Cite your sources by including hyperlinks, video, images or other references.	Take time to create good responses. Don't rush.	Respond in a tone that reflects highly on the rich heritage of the Air Force.	Focus on the most used sites related to the Air Force.

138

or responses now, it's inevitable that you'll have to deal with them later—when you don't have the luxury of time and foresight.

There are three types of workflow triage that you will need to map out, in particular because they likely affect how things are being done today:

• *Customer service request.* If your monitoring tools discover a dissatisfied customer, who's responsible for resolving the problem? In some organizations, the person monitoring Twitter conversations, like Frank Eliason at Comcast, is part of the customer service organization. But if it's someone from your corporate communications department who finds a problem, who do they call? That's why it's essential to have previously identified specific people who can respond to service problems.

• *Sales support.* Similarly, if someone has a question about a product they are considering, how does this get routed? Salesforce.com integrates Radian6 and Twitter into its services and can potentially create alerts that ping an account manager if a key customer shares a link related to the company or makes a relevant comment. This elevates "knowing your customer" to a completely new level.

• *Internal communications.* With better information flow and sharing taking place—sometimes outside the company firewall—internal communication departments at larger companies need to monitor and respond to employee comments. If somebody in human resources picks up on the fact that an employee is networking with other companies, the HR person may send a note to the employee's manager to check in and see how the employee is doing. Or if the CEO sends out regular messages via an internal blog, should the employees be required to read it when they sign into their computers? What if there are employees who don't have access to computers on a daily basis—how do they get access to online information?

There are themes common to all of these three situations. First, there's the identification of a social behavior; then a decision needs to be made whether to act on that information. Does it need a response or follow-up? There are understandably concerns of privacy and the risk of appearing like "Big Brother," constantly looking over the shoulders of your customers and employees. But the biggest concern that most companies have is the sheer volume of comments. Coca-Cola receives thousands of responses each time it posts an update on its Facebook page—their triage process is going to differ significantly from that of a company like Kohl's, which can manage to respond to half of the comments because of the much lower volume.

Second, it needs to be clear who will take action and what the range of actions could be. Better moderating and workflow tools are becoming available to help manage this. Visible Technologies has a full-featured monitoring and workflow offering to route all types of social content around a company, and other monitoring players like Radian6 and Microsoft's LookingGlass are adding workflow management. There are other specialized solutions as well, such as CoTweet and HootSuite, which specialize in managing Twitter conversations among multiple people and marking specific tweets for follow-up.

And last but more important, the actions that take place are frequently the responsibility of a department outside of communications or social media. That means other people with existing job descriptions and responsibilities, and other departments with limited resources and budgets, will need to take on additional responsibilities. By far, this is the biggest conundrum that open organizations face—when push comes to shove, work needs to get done, and on the surface, greater openness seems to just create more work!

The key is for everyone to understand that this is *valued* work— valued by the company and valued by the customer or employee. If your open strategy is clearly tied to your organization's strategic goals, it will be clear why it's important to address these inbound requests. Take, for example, how Johnson & Johnson deals with an adverse effect report—if somebody comments on the company's site that they used a product and got a rash, it is captured and routed through to the right departments and is processed normally like any other reporting.

At the core of the workflow mapping is this question—how will it affect the customer or employee experience and, in turn, your overall relationship? To make sure the experience is seamless, it's crucial to get alignment and agreement on how information and responsibilities will flow.

IDENTIFY THE STAKEHOLDERS MOST AFFECTED

As we discussed earlier, open strategies tend to open up previously isolated silos within organizations; and when established roles come into question and people start thinking about organizational changes, it can be very disruptive. Individuals may feel as if their understanding of their power base and of how they fit into an organization is being thrown under a moving truck. The psychological effect is especially strong for people in leadership positions, because it's *their* world that is being upended, their people, workflows, and budgets that are being called on to change.

Like most change, becoming more open is hard, and you need to take into account when and how key stakeholders will be affected. Understanding their positions is crucial. Take, for example, this scenario: somebody from the social media team shows up in the customer service department, saying, "Hey, I need you to handle these customer service issues I'm generating." Not only have these calls not been budgeted for, but you are also being asked to provide an even *higher* level of service because somebody outside the department has deemed these calls to be more important than regular inbound calls. And here's the kicker: there's no additional budget, which is why the social media person is standing in front of you. As you can imagine, this isn't the way to get things done! Yet I see this scenario being repeated over and over again, with new responsibilities getting tossed back and forth because no one wants to own them, no one wants to allocate budget to them.

Cisco faced this problem when it started pushing collaboration and decision making down into the organization with the mandate of developing new business lines—without, in most cases, any increase in budget. For example, Dave Holland, Cisco's treasurer at the time, co-led a board that looked at expanding Cisco's offering in sports and entertainment. The goal: serve the needs of team owners such as Lew Wolff, owner of the Oakland A's baseball team, who was eager to improve the fan experience while also increasing sponsorship revenues. By pulling together products and services from multiple departments and function areas, Holland was able to sign Wolff, followed by many other teams and stadiums around the United States as well as Europe.[3]

One key to Cisco's success is that the boards and councils are co-led, usually by people from different departments like sales and engineering. That way, for example, decisions to sell a new product don't move forward unless engineering agrees to build it, and vice versa. Holland admits that it was tough to pull this off: "The board didn't have a budget or ability to add resources. If we wanted to get something done, we had to convince the people in various functions that the opportunity was big enough for us to pursue." This natural negotiation of trade-offs reinforces that good decisions are made. If new opportunities are worth it, then other, less promising activities are stopped to make room for the new ideas.

The problem with most open initiatives, though, is that the structure for this kind of give and take doesn't exist in the organization, and commitments are made where stakeholders *want* to help achieve the goal, but in the end frequently fall short because of limited commitment. In addition to the direct challenges that workflows bring, stakeholders may feel threatened by changes in the way power flows around organizations. Traditionally, people who had titles and positions were the ones in power, but in the future the power will be with the people who can funnel and share information and have relationships across the organization. In particular, the people who are the most networked with each other are privy to exclusive information—moreover, because of their cross-department relationships, they will be able to act quickly and decisively. The same will be true for people who can articulate, express, and interpret what is happening outside the organization and convince the people within of their point of view.

Last, we should also consider broadening the definition of "stakeholder" to include suppliers, shareholders, vendors, local officials, government regulators, reporters, interested outsiders, and more. These could be environmental groups concerned about a company's position on pollution or human rights groups concerned about overseas child labor. One large corporation has told me privately that their external affairs people spend half of their time addressing questions from outside stakeholders, not from customers.

To conclude this section, I reiterate the need to share clearly the strategic goal of your open strategy and to make sure that stakeholders share in the commitment to that goal. The issue then becomes not who's going to get stuck with the hot potato—an internal focus—but how together you can best achieve the shared goal—an external focus. There is no magic sauce here; instead, good change management involves best practices that require goals to be clearly articulated and concerns addressed in a respectful, constructive manner.

ORGANIZATIONAL MODELS FOR OPENNESS

I briefly mentioned earlier how Cisco is organized for decision making using a system of multidisciplinary boards and councils. But most organizations can make only small structural changes quickly, and it's often a puzzle how best to organize for greater openness. One of the biggest problems is identifying who "owns" the openness or social media strategy. In our work at Altimeter Group, we've found that successful organizations adopt one of three models: (1) organic, (2) centralized, and (3) coordinated (see Figure 6.2). I'll go through each of the models in detail, but I want to emphasize that there is *no single best model*. The right model for you depends heavily on the level of openness in your organization, your goals, and how you are currently structured. In addition, your organizational model may change over time as your goals and internal structures change.

Figure 6.2. Three Organizational Models for Openness

	Organic	Centralized	Coordinated
Description	Individual efforts spring up when and where they find traction.	One person/group leads the efforts and sets the pace.	One group provides best practices, with execution at the edge.
Pros	Meets the needs of each department.	Can move quickly, try cutting edge efforts, small staff needed.	Spreads best practices broadly, consistent.
Cons	Inconsistent, likely no official funding, support. Multiple groups uncoordinated, fractured customer experience.	Slower to spread around the organization. May not appear authentic to community.	Competes for limited budgets and attention, not always cutting edge or fast-moving, requires top down buy-in.
Staffing	Driven by individual evangelists, who serve as experts, but not coordinators.	One strong evangelist leads the way, builds a central team over time.	Department-like investment at the corporate level.
Best suited for	New adopters with slim corporate staff and resources.	Strongly centralized, especially with corporate marketing/PR.	Distributed organizations, or advanced organizations ready to invest.
Examples	Humana, Microsoft	Starbucks, Ford	Red Cross, HP

ORGANIC

The *organic* model is very natural and allows openness to develop where it is most likely to grow and thrive. It typically develops without a lot of direction or control, sometimes in stealth mode without official permission or oversight. Somebody might say, "Hey, I think we should put up a blog," and she puts up a blog. Somebody else says, "I think we need a Facebook page for marketing purposes" and puts up a Facebook page. Somebody else says, "We need a discussion forum for customer support" and establishes a discussion forum.

It's very organic because it's built on the very specific needs of each group. Everybody is doing their own thing, but doing it in a way that makes sense for their individual departments and goals. Microsoft is a great example. It has a large population of bloggers inside the organization who are basically free to blog whatever they want, wherever they want. Managers don't really know who is blogging about what topics—and they are fine with that, because, as we discussed in the previous chapter, Microsoft's sandbox covenant is so broad.

Another example is Humana, a Fortune 100 company providing health insurance in the United States. An internal innovation center started experimenting with social media in the summer of 2008, and by January 2009 the company was ready to move forward. But rather than coordinate it from the innovation center, they decided to set up a virtual "town square" where each business unit and department could set up their own social media outpost. Greg Matthews, director of consumer innovation at Humana, recalls, "There was recognition that every piece of our business knows how to do its business best, and is going to be able to design a social media function that is best able to support that strategy. We didn't want this to have a top-down control structure." Representatives from each group meet monthly for a social media "chamber of commerce" to share best practices, but no additional funds are spent, nor is there any type of central review process.

The results have been impressive. The marketing department created a series of videos that answer common questions about health care insurance, which appear on a dedicated site as well as on YouTube.[4] Another example is a private community created by Humana Medicare for preretirees at realforme.com, offering people between fifty-five and sixty-five a place where they can get information and tap resources about retirement. And at the time this book was written, Humana Military had just launched its own Facebook page.[5] Again, all of this is done without any additional budget allocation from Humana's corporate coffers.

The disadvantages of the organic model are that you leave it to a department's self-interest to get social media in place, so it may not provide the organization with a concerted organized push and entry into the space. In addition, because the efforts are uncoordinated, you run the risk of having a partridge-in-a-pear-tree situation: five blogging systems, four communities, three discussion forums, two social networks, and one confused (and exasperated) CEO.

But I find that the lightweight nature of the organic organizational model is ideally suited for companies just beginning to venture into social media and openness, who want a flexible approach that taps into the enthusiasts and needs that already exist in the organization. It also works well for highly decentralized organizations with minimal corporate support and oversight. From this initial start, organization can evolve the organization model into one of the other models—most often, they move into a coordinated organization, which I discuss later in this chapter.

CENTRALIZED

More commonly, companies start out with a *centralized* effort, usually with the support of executive management who believe that the organization or department needs to be more open to customers and to embrace social media. There is typically a plan and strategy, and if any individuals deviate from the plan and try to start something on their own, they are gently encouraged to "stick with the plan" and work with the centralized group. One key characteristic of the centralized organization model is that there are typically only a few people running the strategy and making decisions, even though there may be tens or hundreds of people across the organization actually working on it. The key strategic decisions are made centrally, allowing these organizations to move quickly, decisively, and in a highly coordinated way. The disadvantage is that when it comes time to spread openness around the organization, people have gotten somewhat used to "social" being somebody else's responsibility.

Two companies with successful centralized organizations are Starbucks and Ford. At Starbucks, six people work on the social media initiatives as part of the online media group: two community managers who directly interact with people, plus four programmers and support people. As I discussed in Chapter Three, their first initiative was MyStarbucksIdea.com, where people can submit and vote on ideas to improve Starbucks. Most impressive was that they had fifty other people involved in vetting and responding to the ideas. Moreover, the Facebook and Twitter pages are also centrally run by one community manager. The result: at the time this book was written, the Starbucks Facebook page had over six million fans, making it the most popular brand sponsored page on Facebook, and the Starbucks Twitter page had over eight hundred thousand followers.[6]

At the center of these efforts was Alexandra Wheeler, the Starbucks director of digital strategy. While Starbucks CEO Howard Schultz was personally invested in engaging with customers, it was Wheeler who translated social media for nervous managers and employees, cajoling, prodding, and convincing everyone to take that first step. As the team has grown and comfort levels increased, Wheeler has transitioned herself and the team to being more proactive and spreading the effort. For example, Starbucks added international versions of the Facebook page, putting them into an "Around The World" tab accessible on the main page.[7] Each country has its own page, but all were set up and trained by Wheeler's team. "We provide the strategy and framework, as well as best practices that the U.S. team has discovered and learned. But then each country team localizes Facebook for themselves. There are lots of really interesting voices and subject matter experts that just need the right coaching, guidance, and structure."

What is just as interesting, though, is what *isn't* taking place—that is, there aren't legions of Starbucks employees in the stores engaging in social media. Think about it—there are thousands of twenty-something baristas in the prime of their social media usage working at Starbucks, but for the most part they are not engaging openly on behalf of the organization. Wheeler explained that she and her team want to put a system in place that is relevant for the baristas. "It's mainly about protecting them; giving them the right guardrails to extend their 'green apron' behaviors on social media," says Wheeler. Starbucks wants to ensure that the customer experience is consistent across Starbucks. Starbucks' hope is to eventually give employees the freedom to tweet and blog and befriend customers at the local level, but not until the right structures and training are in place to ensure a consistent customer experience.

At Ford, Scott Monty has been an unstoppable force of nature. He was hired by the executive team to jump-start the company's social media efforts, which consisted of exactly one YouTube channel before Monty arrived in the summer of 2008. Within just a few months, Ford had been named by Abrams Research as one of the top North American companies using social media.[8] A key driver of Ford's quick success was the commitment of the organization to allow Monty to do what he did best—not only to engage the outside community via Twitter and other channels, but also to work closely with various departments, especially by developing close ties with executives and the legal team. As part of the public relations team at Ford, Monty works closely with strategic initiatives around the company, such as the Ford Fiesta launch in the United States, as an advisor on their social media efforts. Much of the actual social media work is executed with the help of two outside agencies, Social Media Group and Ogilvy PR.

Ford's approach points to two of the most compelling reasons to strongly centralize efforts, especially around a highly capable person like Monty—speed and impact. With one strategic hire, Ford was able to launch its initiatives and create examples for the rest of the organization to emulate. Monty said, "We spent the first year focused on our home base in the U.S. But thanks to an internal clip sheet and through all of our appearances online, employees in other regions have started to model their own programs after what we've done or just pick up the phone and call me." Future plans include developing internal social media resources that every employee can access for training and guidelines.

COORDINATED

In a *coordinated* model, there is usually strong centralized direction—such as guidelines, policies, best practices, and maybe even preferred technology platforms for blogging and communities. But it's up to each department or person to staff, budget, and execute on initiatives. A coordinated approach is well suited for decentralized organizations that want to create greater synergies and collaboration between various efforts. But the coordinated model is also one that more mature organizations tend to gravitate toward, as they seek to spread best practices throughout the organization.

One organization that started out with a coordinated model is the American Red Cross, which we discussed in the Introduction. As part of a decentralized organization, the seven hundred chapters historically had always been able to do whatever they wanted—and the social media organization had to reflect that reality. Wendy Harman, the organization's social media manager, explained, "We had a sort of hub-and-spoke model from the beginning, although the spokes were totally separate from the hub!" So Harman created a handbook and guidelines and put it out publicly on the Web for everyone to see.[9] With a sandbox covenant in place, the chapters didn't have to get permission to be open—they were free to proceed as they normally would with other local chapter initiatives.[10]

Hewlett-Packard is another organization that started out with a coordinated organizational model. They launched their first blogs in 2005 and made sure that officially sanctioned blogs all had the same look and feel and appeared in the main navigation of hp.com, and that bloggers abided by the new social media policy and code of conduct.[11] But the content and moderation was all handled by each individual blogger—after some initial training, each person was free to write and respond as he or she thought best. Very quickly, blogs sprouted up all around the organization, ranging from providing support for HP printers to discussing data storage and warehousing.[12] The social media efforts have evolved to also encompass support forums, dedicated communities, and wikis. Supporting all of this is a "center of excellence" at the corporate level, bringing to bear resources ranging from best practices to cutting-edge research coming out of HP Labs.[13] At the core is the philosophy that the center and corporate efforts are there to support execution at the edge—that although there's a need to have a strongly coordinated approach, the people best able to interact with customers and employees are at the front lines themselves.

The two disadvantages of the coordinated model are that it can't move as quickly as the centralized model and best practices may not always be employed. But this may be fine, given your strategy, especially if you are focused on long-term, widespread adoption of social technologies throughout the organization.

CHOOSING AND TRANSITIONING ORGANIZATIONAL MODELS

I am frequently asked which organizational model is "the best," but I am loath to recommend any single one model for all organizations. Rather, I recommend that you consider how you are currently organized and balance that against your open strategy goals. For example, if you lack a strong corporate structure and instead have a highly distributed organization, you will want to consider either the organic or the coordinated model. The determining factor in choosing between these two is how much control and coordination you want and are able to exert over widespread efforts. In contrast, if you have a highly urgent goal to move quickly and you anticipate pushback from organizations, you may want to pursue a centralized organizational model, whereby you not only can create successful examples quickly but also will have the ear of the executive team in case you need them to break down barriers.

Last, you should plan to evolve your organizational model over time. Dell started with a highly centralized team centered in corporate communications and PR, reaching out to unhappy bloggers; the team eventually starting its own blog in the summer of 2007. With the full support of CEO Michael Dell, the team was able to quickly launch other initiatives. Now, with a firm foundation, the organization is moving into a coordinated model where it supports initiatives that arise throughout the organization—a necessary step if it hopes to scale its social media investments. As you saw in the examples of Starbucks and Ford, Dell too is planning to distribute the centralized efforts around the organization. Note that this can cause some significant unease with the centralized team members who are themselves used to a high level of control. The irony is that in your effort to open up your organization with a centralized organization model, you may end up simply command-and-controlling your way into the social media space. As long as you are aware of this tendency and can plan for it in advance, a centralized organizational model will naturally evolve into a coordinated model.

ASSIGNING ROLES AND RESPONSIBILITIES

After determining the organization model, the natural next step is to figure out who is going to be doing what. In most situations, there are three major responsibilities: laying out the strategy, building and maintaining the tools, and engaging with the community. The strategist is the person who sets the direction of the open initiative and makes sure that a strategic plan is in place, corralling executives behind it and securing resources as needed. This position requires excellent internal collaboration skills, as that person will be working closely with the legal team, figuring out workflows, and smoothing any ruffled feathers of stakeholders.

The second role is that of the builder or program manager—the person who actually decides on the technology, details the business model and workflow, and manages ongoing maintenance. Then there is the community manager, who facilitates and responds to the community, be that communicating with an external community or fostering internal employee collaboration. This person may be coordinating who is actually going to write the blogs or may be writing the blog itself. Moderation of comments and community forum, as well as updating Facebook and Twitter pages, also may fall to this person.

Scott Monty performed both of these roles for the first year and a half that he was at Ford, but this is highly unusual—and he also had assistance from outside agencies that helped with many of the monitoring, implementation, and moderation responsibilities. More typically, these roles are held by different people. For example, Wells Fargo's social media efforts and strategy are spearheaded by Ed Terpening, VP of social media marketing, who in 2006 helped create the first banking blog, "Guided by History." He gradually built up his team, which now includes three program managers who oversee the operations of each of their channels on YouTube, MySpace, Facebook, Twitter, and a virtual world, Stagecoach Island.[14] Two production people who handle the technical aspects round out the Wells Fargo social media team.

But I think it's most interesting that Wells Fargo has people at the business units functioning as the community managers. Terpening explained, "Wells Fargo runs a very thin corporate layer and believes in pushing execution to the people who are closest to the customer." For example, the Commercial Electronic Office (CEO) blog is written not by someone in corporate marketing, but by Marcus Yamame, who is on the CEO team. And Sateen Singh, who is an active contributor to the Wells Fargo Twitter page, works in the online banking division.

In some cases, organizations have brought in outside agencies to manage community engagement. Public relations agencies frequently take on this role as they evolve their services to include community response. Community platform providers like Lithium and LiveWorld also provide moderation services, even for communities that they don't host. And there are now dedicated community management agencies like Impact Interactions that are solely focused on moderating social content on behalf of brands like Cisco and AARP.

When does it make sense to outsource what would seem to be a critical strategic asset—the management of your customer relationships? First, if your organization is brand-new to engagement and you have a large, activist customer or employee base, you may want to have an experienced agency not only provide guidance but also do the actual community management. They know what it means to be community facilitators, have many best practices, and—from a customer service point of view—know how to soothe ruffled feathers. Second, you may be short-staffed and unable to fulfill the obligations of engaging your community. Third, there may be a short-term spike due to a marketing outreach that you anticipate will increase the need for engagement.

There are ways to ensure that not only your agency but also your employees serving as community managers are responding in an appropriate way. Style guides, workflow maps, and response standardization—all these details can be worked out and agreed on in advance. Tone and voice can also be determined and training provided so that responses are consistently delivered. Wells Fargo's Terpening admitted that they struggled with the issues of consistency and risk management, especially in the light of their engagement in a highly regulated industry. "While we have only light centralized control, it's a constant concern that we train and monitor how we engage with our customers." To that end, clear expectations, best practices, and rigorous scenario planning are your best bets for making sure things go smoothly.

THE NEED FOR TRAINING AND INCENTIVES

When it comes to openness and social technologies, the inclination is to think of training centered on the hard skills of using these new tools—how to use collaboration suites, how to connect with social networks and Twitter, how to blog. Some companies, like Humana, have social media training modules uploaded on their intranets, with titles like "Understanding LinkedIn in 15 Minutes," "Understanding Twitter in 15 Minutes," and more. Other organizations organize mentorships, whereby younger, more socially-savvy employees buddy up with a senior executive for weekly online training sessions.

But I believe a more important education and training initiative for you to consider—although also much more complex and difficult—is one for changing mind-sets and behaviors. One person could know how to use an internal Twitter but never use it because she sees no need for it. Another might know how to write an effective blog post but never do so because he does not see the value. How do you change that behavior?

It comes down to the incentives the organization puts in place. The organization rewards the behavior it wants through recognition, responsibility, or—as a last resort—money. It doesn't punish for non-tweeting or nonblogging (that *would* be counterproductive), but non-performers go unrewarded. When someone sees a benefit in being more open and sees a reward for doing so, behavior tends to change.

Take, for example, United Business Media (UBM), a global business media company based in London that publishes trade magazines and operates trade shows. The company has 6,500 employees in more than 30 countries organized into specialist teams that service publications for audiences ranging from doctors to game developers, from journalists to jewelry traders, and from farmers to pharmacists around the world. Chief information officer David Michael explained that they decided to install Jive, a community platform, to help smooth information sharing across these many disparate groups. I asked him how the company was training employees to use the new platform. Michael's response: "We're not."

He elaborated, "When we selected the system, it was really important to us that we pick something that didn't require hours and hours of training, because it was never ever going to work if we had to do that." The UBM headquarters in London has about a dozen people, "so we don't have any central trainers or anything like that." Moreover, the business units rarely have a full IT department, may not have HR, and certainly have nobody directly responsible for training.

But although the organization had no one to do the training, management knew they needed to have a rainmaker. Says Michael, "You can't have a party without a host to get it going." Rather than hire a trainer, UBM invested in a full-time community manager. That person has a global view of the corporation and the system, and his job was to identify pockets of users who weren't using the system and who were already collaborating in some other way. His job was to convince them that Jive was a way to improve their business process. Ultimately, by getting enough of these groups on the system and making their life easier, the word spread through UBM that a system was available for employees to use—and it was in fact quite easy to use.

"We now have lots of community managers around UBM," says Michael, "and they actually have the job title of UBM Wiki Community Manager, but it's not a full time job. It's sort of a side responsibility. They are really advocates. If it's necessary, we do a bit of training for somebody who wants to know how to use advanced features. But more than anything, Wiki Community Managers are advocates."

At some point you will want to provide incentives for your customers to engage with you as well. Although you can count on some level of natural engagement, you may also want to nudge the process along. It may be blindingly obvious to you how to engage, but to the consumers who buy and use your product, it may not be the most intuitive thing—after all, they aren't necessarily thinking about how to have a deeper relationship with you and your organization. When you are starting to become more open, you have to give handholds to your customers, teaching them how to be open with you.

Let's take, for example, the user experience on YouTube. Most people go to the site and simply watch videos; in other words, they are watchers. But you'll notice many opportunities to increase your engagement scattered around the site. First, YouTube makes it very simple to share the content—you can send it via email to someone you know, post it on a blog, or post an update on your favorite social network. And if you are signed into your YouTube account, the site can auto-populate the options with your email address, blog, or social network accounts to make sharing as easy as one click. In addition, you're encouraged to rate the video, add your comments, or even upload your own video as a response—thus escalating your status as a commenter. Finally, YouTube makes it easy to upload videos and even to make your own channel and become a producer. YouTube's goal isn't to have everyone become a producer, but they do make it easy for a person to engage more deeply with the site, without having to hide anything behind a link or click.

I think of deepening engagement in terms of dating. You don't rush into marriage from the very first date (or you shouldn't, at any rate). Think about the kind of relationship that you have today. Then imagine what you would like that relationship to be like three years from now. With that vision in mind, you can begin to figure out the roadmap of where and how quickly you want to bring a customer along, especially when you take into account their socialgraphics. For example, if your customers are primarily watchers in terms of their engagement with you, consider how can you turn them into sharers in the short term, and in the future, if appropriate, deepen the relationship so that they feel comfortable becoming commenters or even producers. Starting small should be your mantra, as any change in mind-set can come only over time and with your commitment to building the relationship.

ACTION PLAN: ORCHESTRATING YOUR OPEN STRATEGY

Once you have a good understanding of how you want to approach your audience and have formulated a strategy, the hard work begins: building competency, identifying workflows, and setting up organizational structures. One of the biggest roadblocks at this crucial point is good old internal politics. As I mentioned earlier in the chapter, your showing up uninvited to upend a department's process isn't going to be well received, so you need to have done your homework from Chapter Four and have readily at hand the benefits of being open. Some best practices I've gathered include the following:

- *Find an executive sponsor.* If you've crafted a strategy that's aligned with key corporate initiatives, you should have a natural executive sponsor who can help clear the way for you.
- *Make it everyone's problem, everyone's opportunity.* Take the time to figure out how to connect with a recalcitrant manager or department head. If you can align your initiative with one of their core objectives, you will have a much better chance of success.
- *Revamp incentives.* Take a close look at incentives—and not just those associated with money. Recognition and reputation play an important role both inside and outside the organization.

As you embark on executing your open strategy, keep in mind that as you run into the operational realities of orchestrating your strategy, you'll need to frequently refer back to your original openness audit and open strategy plan and adjust them as necessary. Being an open leader requires that you keep in mind that the strategy and tactics you employ are always

(Continued)

157

(Continued)

subject to the changes that the marketplace and your organization place before you.

In Figure 6.3, I've included a checklist of the items you need to think about in your open strategy from an operational standpoint. You can get more details for this list online at open-leadership.com, which includes many of the items we use at Altimeter Group with our clients.

Figure 6.3. The Open Strategy Plan Checklist

☐ Open Strategy Objective
  Learn, Dialog, Support, or Innovate
☐ Create a socialgraphics profile
  Social audit
  Engagement audit
  Influence audit
☐ Workflow
  Inbound comment triage
  Customer service request
  Marketing and sales support
  Internal communications
  Market research or product development
☐ Stakeholder impact
  Executives
  Other departments (legal, IT, support, products)
  Partners
  Investors
  Suppliers
  Press
  Customers
☐ Organizational model
  Organic, centralized, or coordinated
☐ Assign roles and responsibilities
  Strategist
  Community or program manager
  Agency role
☐ Training and incentives
  Quarterly reviews
  Rewards and contests
  Recognition

Now that you have an open strategy and plan in place, let's take a look at what it will take for you to personally lead the open organization. In Part III of the book, I'll take a look at what it means to be an open leader, starting with the mind-set that differentiates an open leader from traditional leaders.

OPEN LEADERSHIP: REDEFINING RELATIONSHIPS

OPEN LEADERSHIP: MIND-SETS AND TRAITS

A major theme throughout this book has been that leadership is about relationships, and because social technologies are changing relationships, leadership also needs to change. As I laid out in Chapter One, empowered customers and employees are loath to sit by the sidelines and accept business as usual. There are also systemic changes causing leadership to change—the recent economic recession has seen a marked decline in business confidence, causing company CEOs to promise greater transparency in operations and company financials in order to build customer and investor trust.

All of this leads to a critical juncture in leadership. Yet many of the executives I speak with refuse to acknowledge that any change is needed; they believe that in times of crisis and change, greater leadership from the top is needed. Thus they insist on sticking with their traditional command-and-control leadership style of limiting information sharing and decision making.

I wish them luck, because they will need it.

I have no problem with a command-and-control approach, as long as open leadership options have been examined, considered, and strategically rejected. What I strongly warn leaders against is the wholesale dismissal of a powerful new way of building relationships with your most engaged and potentially most valuable customers and employees, especially when simple elements of open leadership such as listening and learning are easy to adopt.

One of the biggest reasons why open leadership is feared and avoided is the concern that the leader will lose all semblance of control. As you saw in the previous chapters, especially Chapter Five about the use of sandbox covenants, I actually advocate a disciplined approach to an open strategy. In the same vein, open leadership requires forethought, planning, and structure. In fact, it requires that a leader be both open and in command.

Thus open leadership is not about simply being warm, fuzzy, authentic, transparent, or "real." It's more than simply sharing anecdotes from your personal life or tidbits from professional meetings. Rather, it's a mixture of mind-set, temperament, learned behaviors, and skills that build on and amplify good leadership skills. Leadership takes on a different dimension in a connected, networked world—that of being a catalyst for change both outside and inside the organization.

So how are you supposed to lead in this new world? To start, I'll explain how open leadership is defined by two specific mind-sets, and the leadership traits that accompany these mind-sets. I'll also provide an assessment tool to identify what kind of open leader you are—and to understand how open you need to be to accomplish your open strategy goals. Conducting the assessment on yourself as well as your top leaders can help you to understand your collective personal approaches to open leadership and thus to create a leadership plan for your overall strategy.

THE DIMENSIONS OF OPEN LEADERSHIP

In my research and interviews, there are two mind-sets that define and determine how open you are as a leader. The first is your view of people—in general, are you optimistic or pessimistic about people's intentions? No one is completely optimistic nor completely pessimistic—and, like an open strategy, this often depends on the situation at hand. But in general, open leaders believe in "win-win" situations, in which when people act in their self-interest it also turns out to be in the best interest of the organization. A pessimistic mind-set, in contrast, believes that greater openness, sharing, and collaboration cannot come to a good end—that there is an inherent give-and-take, and that the risk of giving up control is too great.

Optimism allows open leaders to be more open with information, both in sharing it with a greater audience and in gathering it from different sources. If a key component of your open strategy involves more open information sharing, then you will need to have leaders who are more optimistic than pessimistic in their mind-sets.

The second mind-set is your view of your successes: as either coming primarily from your efforts as an individual or stemming from the efforts of a team. A good leader always has elements of both views, but in tough times, where do you draw your strength from as a leader—yourself or the people around you? Open leaders recognize their limitations and are quick to collaborate with others, whereas individualistic leaders turn inward and rely first on their own strength and ability to prevail.

If your open strategy requires more distributed decision making, then having leaders who are comfortable with collaboration will be crucial. This is not to say that individualistic leaders can't be success-ful, but they are less likely to be able to use open strategies to tap into collaborative advantages such as speed and quality.

Let's first take a look at the optimistic mind-set, to better under-stand its origins and how it makes someone a more open and effec-tive leader.

THE OPTIMISTIC LEADER

I find people in general tend toward an optimistic or pessimistic view of others, which is largely shaped by previous experiences. Optimists tend to believe that most people want to do their best and want to be responsible, trustworthy, and honest—they have a high level of trust in people and extend that trust to a wider circle of people than their pessimistic counterparts. Optimists feel that, given the right opportunity, most people will grow in confidence, in ability, and in their own sense of self-worth. They likely have had many previous experiences in which their belief in someone paid off in a success.

In contrast, pessimists tend to believe that most people cannot be fully trusted because they are looking for an advantage to win, usually at the expense of someone else. As such, leaders with a pes-simistic mind-set have a hard time seeing how more open informa-tion sharing can be a positive thing, because they haven't personally experienced the benefits of such openness—in fact, they probably had just the opposite happen where they placed their trust in some-one who then disappointed or, worse, betrayed that trust. At times, the pessimism can border on paranoia, to the point that the leader trusts only a very small, tight circle of confidants.

I believe that optimistic leaders not only can embrace being open but also inspire and motivate people to become open leaders them-selves. Think back to your favorite, most inspiring manager. What were the qualities that made you want to follow that person? It prob-ably was not because she or he was the smartest person, or had the right degrees, or held a certain position in the organization. More likely, it was because that leader made you feel valued and inspired you to do more than you thought you could do. In the process, she helped you learn more about yourself.

Brian Dunn, the CEO of Best Buy, says he learned something about leadership when he was fourteen years old and working in a grocery store. One day the manager asked Dunn, "What do you think about this process we're using here in the front end to tell people to pick up their groceries?" It was a simple question, and Dunn says he gave an innocuous, nonspecific answer—sort of, "Everything's fine." The manager pulled him aside and said, "Now listen, I asked you about this 'cause I really care what you think. You're doing this every single day, and I want to know what you think about it." Dunn says today, "I know it seems simple, but just that notion of learning from people who are actually doing the work, and the encouragement he gave me to tell him exactly what I thought, really stayed with me, and it was a recurring thing throughout the time I worked for him."[1] That early experience colored Dunn's approach to leadership and inspired him to pursue an open strategy for the company that places tremendous power and responsibility in the hands of employees.

This is a recurring theme I heard from open leaders—that they valued the contributions of people throughout their organization and from customers. Thus when these same people gained power through their use of social technologies, it didn't threaten these open leaders—in fact, they welcomed these empowered people with open arms. What quality enables them to do this that is not shared by their pessimistic counterparts?

James Cornell, the chief marketing officer at Prudential Retirement, put it well: "An open leader has to be someone who has a very high degree of emotional intelligence. They listen very, very well, and they don't just speak their mind. This is someone who can use situational analysis and external perspectives to actually change their own point of view and opinion on a subject, including on topics that have been taken as historical assumptions." To Cornell, open leaders are optimistic about engaging because they believe the organization will be stronger because of it.

In my research, people used two words over and over again to describe what was unique about open leaders: *curiosity* and *humility*. Let's dig deeper into the concept of emotional intelligence by looking at these two specific character traits.

THE IMPORTANCE OF CURIOSITY

Open leaders are inherently curious about the world and have an insatiable need to constantly seek out opportunities to improve themselves and the world around them. They are curious about customers, about their employees, about suppliers, about industry trends, and about the wider world. Most intelligent leaders are open to what they don't know, but open leaders are driven by a deeper quest to learn constantly. And they look at social technologies as a unique way for them to extend that learning in a way that they never could before.

Take, for example, Dell and Starbucks, which are today led by their founders, Michael Dell and Howard Schultz. These leaders had as their core founding values the ability to connect closely with their customers. Dell historically had a direct-selling model, so it was natural for the company to use online tools. Dell started providing customer service on CompuServe back in the 1980s and then on the Web. Michael Dell jumped on selling on the Internet in 1995 when there was no proven ROI in such a distribution model—for him, it was a natural extension of the direct model. And when he returned as the CEO of the company in early 2007 after a three-year hiatus, one of the first things he did was to launch IdeaStorm.com, where people can submit ideas, then comment and vote on them.

Michael Dell shared the story of the early successes of IdeaStorm with Howard Schultz, the CEO of Starbucks. As the founder of Starbucks, Schultz used to go around and spend time in Seattle coffeehouses, learning what the customers liked and didn't like. Schultz and his leadership team were connected to what customers were experiencing and saying in those stores on a daily basis. While the company was small, it was relatively easy to maintain that kind of personal involvement with customers.

As Starbucks grew, however, the company couldn't grow in the same way it had in the early days—or could it? "We really lost touch with that listening culture," says Alexandra Wheeler, director of digital strategy at Starbucks. So when Schulz learned about IdeaStorm directly from Michael Dell, he saw it as a way to reconnect with customers. He launched MyStarbucksIdea.com, the corporation's first entrée into social media. The site "brought us back to the listening culture that Howard launched the company with," says Wheeler. It is a way to use technology to accomplish on an international scale what Schultz was able to do when he was visiting Seattle coffee shops and Starbucks was just a handful of stores.

In a sense, Dell and Starbucks were lucky in their transformation to open organizations. They were able to adopt social technologies faster and better than their industry peers because they already had core values and a history as an organization that predisposed them to greater openness. But more important, their leaders saw this as a way to extend a core part of their personal values of curiosity into the organization, and they saw the value of having a deep, close relationship with customers and employees.

THE IMPORTANCE OF HUMILITY

Being curious isn't enough to make people open leaders—you can be a constant learner but not necessarily want to change your view of the world. Humility is also needed, and as Jim Collins pointed out in his book *Good to Great,* it's a key characteristic of great leaders.[2] But in the context of open leadership, humility plays a special role—it allows open leaders to accept that their views on something may need to shift because of what their curious explorations expose. In a sense, humility gives them the self-awareness and confidence to admit when they are wrong or need help.

Take, for example, Kodak, a company that's had to completely reinvent itself, from its first incarnation as a consumer print film company to its present one as a mostly business-to-business imaging company. Jeffrey Hayzlett, Kodak's chief marketing officer, is a world-class marketer as well as a prolific blogger and user of Twitter.[3] He emphasizes that much of Kodak's successful turnaround came because of its ability to listen, even when that was tough. "An open leader has to be willing to take criticism and know when it's important or not. It's not for the weak, because you will be criticized. People will come at you directly, and you have to be comfortable with this, to be able to say in a respectful way, 'That's your assessment, and thank you for offering it.'"

But Hayzlett also stresses that humility requires a high level of self-awareness and confidence, to be able to recognize when help is needed. "It's a huge and powerful decision to say, 'I need help' as a leader, a recognition that you can't do it by yourself. It also sets the example for your team members to come forward and ask for help when they need it. What's interesting is how often open leaders are doing this now in public, tapping into the source of power that is their base of loyal customers and employees." When you are not afraid to show your weaknesses and discuss your failures, you can afford to be honest and take responsibility for them.

As a result of the confidence in the relationship, driven to a great degree by this sense of optimism, open leaders tend to share a great deal more information with people. They are confident that doing this will enhance and improve these relationships—and not weaken themselves or their organizations in the process. Open leaders invest in the relationship by sharing more about themselves, what they are thinking, feeling, and doing, but they are also circumspect in what they share—they have an innate sense of what is appropriate for a situation and what is not. They also have the proper sandbox covenants in place so that responsibility is clearly laid out; for example, "Don't share the confidential information I'm sharing with you."

Let's move on now to the second mind-set: having a collaborative approach to getting things done.

THE COLLABORATIVE LEADER

The second core mind-set of an open leader is a disposition toward collaboration. The problem is that as a society we do not value, teach, or encourage collaboration—it's simply not part of most leaders' DNA until fairly late in their careers. For the most part, students are graded on their individual achievement, and it often isn't until they reach the business world that they are required to work on a team. Even then, it's usually the contributions of individuals on a team that are evaluated and compensated. The result: the payoff for collaboration doesn't happen until well into a person's professional career, meaning that they don't get a chance to develop a truly collaborative mind-set until later.

That was the case with Barry Judge, the CMO of Best Buy. Throughout his career, he was very focused on personal achievement. He told me, "I am very ambitious, very competitive, and was an athlete. It was always about what I could personally do and what I could personally bring to the situation. I had to understand in my heart that ideas can be shaped and improved with other people providing input. I met with Joe Trippi from the Howard Dean campaign back in 2004, and he asked me, 'Do you think the five thousand smartest people work at Best Buy?' I said, 'No,' and it really clicked for me that it would be powerful if you could create an environment or a conversation where people can weigh in and provide input. It became this different way of thinking."

Judge and other Best Buy executives realized that if they could open up and manage collaboration at scale, they could unleash the power of one of their most important assets—165,000 employees who are electronics mega-geeks. But this didn't happen overnight—after all, you are changing the mind-set of not only executives but the whole organization. And it's also tough for highly individualistic leaders to grasp this new way of work. "It has taken us five years to get there," Judge said. "We had to be really encouraging, and yes, the decision making process can take a lot more time, because people don't say what you expect them to say. It takes coalition building and realizing that getting to the end is often a very circular process, the opposite of a straight line route. I think getting used to that is the hardest thing as a leader."

Person after person, leaders that I interviewed echoed this viewpoint—that collaboration was a hard skill for them to learn and that the practices that made them successful in the past were not necessarily the skills and mind-set that will allow them to be successful going forward. They learned that they had to include others in the process, because they can't assume that they know everything needed to be successful.

I believe this is the crux of open leadership—having the confidence to let go of total control, to be more open, and to still get things done. What you're letting go of, however, is your need to be *personally* involved in the decision making process, not necessarily all your rights to have any say. By setting up the right structures, you can feel comfortable that the right decisions are being made by the right people in the right way. Thus open leaders set a clear strategy and the parameters with sandbox covenants, ensuring that everyone is headed in the same direction.

Cristóbal Conde, SunGard's CEO, says, "It is very arrogant to think you can make better decisions than the thousands of people below you. This may be true if you have more information.[11] Conde went on to explain that with more open information sharing, most strategic decisions at SunGard are now made collaboratively. But he also recognizes that there are limits to collaboration. "In the last five years I have made one key strategic decision, which was to take the company private. But *I* had to make that decision, because it was so strategic and required a certain point of view that no one else could have." The leader's role today, Conde believes, is to make the handful of decisions that no one else can make and to maintain a collaboration system that can handle all other decisions that the organization needs to make. That way, the open leader can focus primarily on those tough, strategic decisions that require the leader's attention, rather than trying to have a hand in every decision that takes place.

As we saw in Chapter Three, Cisco has accomplished a dizzying number of initiatives because it has been able to leverage distributed decision making. But it works for Cisco because of the investment it has made in collaboration tools and culture. It has been a difficult road, though, and no one stated this more strongly than John Chambers, CEO of Cisco Systems. He observed that people tend to stay with something that has made them successful and to remain within a comfort zone. "The most difficult people to change," Chambers told me, "are usually the ones who have been the most successful in your organization, including me as CEO. Everybody has had to go through the same learning curve that I did, which is that I had to get comfortable with letting other people make decisions I used to make, realizing that if I give people access to the right information and challenge them the right way, they will make a better decision than I could."

Changing that mind-set has taken years—Chambers told me he started Cisco's evolution toward a more collaborative environment almost ten years ago. "In 2001, my team wasn't very comfortable with it. If you had voted in 2003, it would have been nineteen to one not to continue it. It needed command-and-control for dramatic change to get off the ground. By 2005, it reached the point where it was in the DNA of our top forty people. Today it's in the DNA of probably our top six hundred people—and the key is to get it to all sixty-five thousand employees."

Chamber emphasized that much of the advances Cisco has made in the past two years happened because of collaborative and social technologies it put in place, which allow people to communicate in a way that was not possible before. Blogs, Twitter, internal networks, podcasts, video, and much more all allow leaders to communicate with other people, but just as important, they allow people involved in the process to communicate *back*. Chambers said, "Without those technologies, not only available, but working in concert, we wouldn't be able to accomplish a lot of what we do today. I think the IT use of collaboration will move from being enabling the business strategy or vision to be so deeply embedded in the vision and strategy that you can't tell the difference."

One last thing to keep in mind is that open leadership is more than a specific role or title in the organization. Many of the people who are the best collaborators are those who have many different—and many different *kinds of*—connections. They know it's not enough to collaborate with just the colleagues on a team or up and down one level. They also collaborate with colleagues across different departments and with contacts at multiple levels inside the organization as well. And it's important to note that they also have deep collaborative relationships with people outside the organization.

Let's move on now to understand how the two open leadership mind-sets of optimism and collaboration combine to create archetypal leaders within the organization—because knowing what kind of leader you and other people are in the organization will be crucial to executing your open strategy.

THE OPEN LEADERSHIP ARCHETYPES

Just as there is a continuum of openness for organizations, with virtually none totally open or totally closed, there is also one for open leaders. Individuals fall into one of four categories, and understanding how open you are—or are not—can help you develop your own open leadership skills.

Leaders can be plotted along two dimensions, optimistic versus pessimistic, and collaborative versus independent, which I've already discussed. Certainly no one is totally paranoid (or if anyone is, ideally that person is not walking around on the loose) or entirely optimistic (we all have our down days). Similarly, no one is totally independent or totally collaborative. We all operate somewhere on these scales, and we may slide toward one end or the other side of the scales as a situation changes. Nevertheless, for the sake of clarity and to make my point, I've plotted these characteristics against each other to yield four specific Open Leadership archetypes: the Realist Optimist, the Worried Skeptic, the Cautious Tester, and the Transparent Evangelist (see Figure 7.1).

Figure 7.1. The Four Open Leadership Archetypes

	Pessimistic	Optimistic
Collaborative	Cautious Tester	Realist Optimist
Independent	Worried Skeptic	Transparent Evangelist

Keep in mind as you read that you can find leaders representing these archetypes at all levels in an organization, from team leader to division manager, from department head to president.

Within each of the following sections, I'll explain the characteristics of each type of leader and the roles each archetype typically plays within the organization.

The Realist Optimist is the most powerful and effective of the open leader archetypes, somebody who can see the benefits of being open but also understands the barriers. The Realist Optimist can work through the tough situations, has the collaborative mind-set and skills, and most important, knows how to overcome organizational obstructions by showing doubters the genuine benefits of being open and winning their trust. Realist Optimists will be the engine behind your open strategy, and they are not likely to be the people at the top of your organization.

For example, Wendy Harman, the social media manager at the American Red Cross, says that for a time after she arrived at the organization she could not get approvals to start a blog or to have a Flickr account to show the Red Cross volunteers at work helping firefighters, disaster workers, and blood donors. "So I just went ahead," she says. "I knew if the senior people could just see the effect they would like it." She used her personal credit card to buy a domain name, created several accounts, and set them up with her own money, because she knew she could never get approval until management saw the positive results. Fortunately, they did. When Harman's payment terms came to an end, she went to her supervisor to ask if she could now charge the expenses, such as they were, to Red Cross to continue her efforts on behalf of the organization. The response? "Yes, absolutely, without hesitation," Harman recalled. "There's no approval necessary anymore."

Realist Optimists have that rare combination of both optimism and collaboration so that they understand the context in which technologies—Facebook, Twitter, YouTube, and all the rest—have to be deployed. They embrace social technologies, but they also realize they have to work with people who are not as optimistic as they are. Consequently, they're somewhat restrained and temper their optimism. They are grounded in the reality of their organizations and have the willingness and the patience to work through the process to encourage long-lasting change.

They also have deep relationships with people throughout the organization—relationships through which they accomplish their jobs. They believe in the benefits of being open but also understand where they must apply their skills to promote transparency in the organization. Knowing the organization's success depends on their openness and collaboration, Realist Optimists understand where they stand in the organization and the role they need to take to lead it.

The Worried Skeptics are the exact opposite of Realist Optimists in that they are pessimistic and independent. These are people who by nature worry about all the things that can go wrong—and with good reason, because Worried Skeptics are usually the people at the top of the organization who get the calls from the press and board members. And with an independent mind-set, they believe that success comes from the strength and skills of individuals, and that belief starts with themselves. They place tremendous value on individuality. It's how they see themselves as successful and how they've risen to the top. As leaders they expect an individual to take command and to control events and consequences.

Worried Skeptics can be seen as gatekeepers. Because they are pessimistic, they see themselves as the hero with the finger in the dike who keeps a flood of bad things from happening in the organization. They are also skeptical about things that can be done with the new social media tools; after all, they achieved success without these tools, and they can't believe that people who don't have the same perspective and responsibilities could possibly understand or help. They look at Twitter and see nothing good coming out of it—because it's people with too much time on their hands talking about their lunch, their parking frustrations, their insomnia. They have heard about the hundreds of millions of people on Facebook, but upon setting up an account they did not find people like themselves, and they didn't see the appeal.

Worried Skeptics rely primarily on their own excellent analytical and intuitive skills to work through problems. They do not frequently practice open leadership skills such as having a dialog with key audiences, because they experience a heightened sense of risk and insecurity. Rather than opportunity, they see the landscape filled with landmines waiting to be tripped.

The Cautious Testers are different from Worried Skeptics in one major dimension. Although they are still pessimistic and see all around them the dangerous aspects of being more open, Cautious Testers understand the need to collaborate because they can see the benefits, to the organization and to themselves, of involving a greater circle of people.

Cautious Testers are willing to test options, plans, and new ideas, and to do so with other people—but their enthusiasm for trying new things is tempered by their pessimism. Their associates can talk to them about opportunities and benefits, and because of the relationships and trust that have been developed, they are willing to give something new or different or strange a chance. Cautious Testers also can temper their pessimism about individuals by carefully putting in place the sandbox covenants, expanding the boundaries only after developing a healthy, trusting relationship. But they seldom initiate the move on their own. They do so because individuals they trust have brought them along.

Like Worried Skeptics, Cautious Testers do not have much hands-on experience with social technologies and activities—but they do have some. They have just enough experience with collaboration, hands-off decision making, and trust that they are beginning to see the advantages of open leadership, but not quite ready to abandon their command-and-control practices; they have too much lingering fear of what could go wrong (something . . . anything . . . everything) to commit to full openness.

The Transparent Evangelists are both optimistic and individualistic. These people have been bitten by the technology bug. In my presentations I like to characterize them—a tongue-in-cheek picture—as wearing black turtlenecks or black T-shirts and black jeans, their hair spiked. They believe in the ability of new technologies to transform people and organizations and are constantly promoting them. They have personally experienced a transformation and derive tremendous personal satisfaction—and, yes, joy—from engaging with people through social technologies. They are transparent; you can read them; what you see is what you get; what you hear is what you get. They believe wholly in their message, which is "Technology is the answer. What's the question?"

But Transparent Evangelists are also independent in the way they think about and look at the technologies. They tend to see them in isolation from the organization and from their personal point of view: how they can use these technologies themselves. They don't truly understand how technology needs to be coordinated or collaborated inside the organization to make things happen effectively.

I often find frustrated Transparent Evangelists—the social media experts—inside organizations I visit. They are butting their heads against a wall of managerial skepticism, saying, "How come you just don't get it? We need to get up on Facebook. We need a company blog. We need to encourage customer reviews." But they're not making any progress, because they don't have a collaborative mind-set that asks and answers questions like these: How open does my organization need to be? How would the organization benefit from being open? What are the barriers to doing it? What are the benefits to customers? To management? To individual employees? Transparent Evangelists don't have the relationship capital and ability to go to the other three archetypes and be able to translate the opportunity they see, possibly quite realistically, in the marketplace.

Transparent Evangelists are confident in the openness creed, and they frequently and loudly issue the clarion call to be open. They believe an organization cannot be too open. But because they operate independently, they do not have a sense of how to work through or around organizational constraints to be effective.

Transparent Evangelists are similar to Worried Skeptics in the way they believe in themselves. They believe they are the ones who are right, and they are so committed to the cause of openness and transparency that they do not think through the implications of how being open could hurt the organization. This is, of course, the flip side of the Worried Skeptics. *They're* so nervous about the risks, they can't see the opportunities. But Transparent Evangelists and Worried Skeptics often express themselves the same way, in the same tone, and with the same fervor to convey their views of the world. They can't believe another point of view might be possible.

THE OPEN LEADERSHIP ASSESSMENT

As I've said, self-awareness is a key attribute of open leaders. I believe it's important to understand your mind-set as it pertains to how you approach being open, and also to do an assessment of key leaders within your organization as well. The reason: if having and implementing an open strategy is of importance to you, then you will need effective open leaders to lead the way. Moreover, you'll need to know whether someone does *not* share a similar mind-set when it comes to open information sharing and/or distributed decision making, as they could be a significant barrier to your implementing your strategy.

I encourage you to conduct a simple self-assessment of your open leadership mind-set to better understand where your biases lie. A short list of assessment questions appears in Figure 7.2, and a test is also

Figure 7.2. Open Leadership Self-Assessment

Below are contrasting statements about having pessimistic and optimistic mind-sets. Rate yourself on each pair as: **1** (agree strongly with left statement), **2** (agree somewhat with left statement), **3** (agree somewhat with right statement), **4** (agree strongly with right statement). Then add up your scores and divide the total by **8** to produce your average score.

More pessimistic ⟵————⟶ More optimistic		Score
People will be harmful if given the opportunity.	1 2 3 4	People will do the right thing when given the opportunity.	
People will be negative and try to cause harm with their comments.	1 2 3 4	People will be positive and constructive in their comments.	
We have more to lose by sharing information publically than we stand to gain.	1 2 3 4	We have more to gain by sharing information publically than we stand to loose.	
Employees can't be trusted with confidential information.	1 2 3 4	Employees can be trusted with confidential information.	
Employees should get only as much information as needed to do their jobs.	1 2 3 4	Employees should get as much information as possible to do their jobs.	
Front line employees and customers mostly complain.	1 2 3 4	I can learn a lot from front line employees and customers.	
When someone criticizes me, I take it personally.	1 2 3 4	When somone criticizes me, I use the opportunity to learn.	
Mistakes should be avoided at all costs.	1 2 3 4	When a mistake is made, it's an opportunity to learn.	
Average score		

You are pessimistic if your score is equal to or less than two.

You are optimistic if your score is greater than two.

Below are contrasting statements about having individualistic and collaborative mind-sets. Rate yourself on each pair as: **1 (agree strongly with left statement), 2 (agree somewhat with left statement), 3 (agree somewhat with right statement), 4 (agree strongly with right statement)**. Then add up your scores and divide the total by **8** to produce your average score.

More individualistic ←———————→ More collaborative		Score
I attribute much of my success to my ability to personally get the job done.	**1 2 3 4** I attribute much of my success to my ability to collaborate with other people.	
When times are tough, I depend mostly on myself.	**1 2 3 4** When times are tough, I depend on other people.	
Involving key stakeholders, and thus more people, will slow down decisions.	**1 2 3 4** Involving key stakeholders, and thus more people, will speed up decisions.	
Involving fewer, more knowledgeable people can improve the end result.	**1 2 3 4** Involving more people in a decision can improve the end result.	
When starting a new project, I think first what I have to do.	**1 2 3 4** When starting a new project, I think first who to involve.	
The judgment of an individual trumps the collective wisdom of the group.	**1 2 3 4** The collective wisdom of a group trumps the judgment of an indivdual.	
It's good to give decision-making authority to people who know what the whole organization is doing.	**1 2 3 4** It's good to push decision-making authority down to people who are closest to the customers.	
My knowledge and leadership is needed to make important decisions.	**1 2 3 4** Important decisions can be made without my direct involvement.	
Average score		

You are individualistic if your score is equal to or less than two.

You are collaborative if your score is greater than two.

available online at open-leadership.com. The questions gauge where you fall on the continuum of mind-sets:

1. Are you pessimistic or optimistic about how people use information and decision making power? For example, do you see Facebook as a time sink or a great way to connect with people in both personal and professional ways? What do you think the outcome would be if employees had greater access to information?
2. How do you tend to get things done? Do you tend to push things through as an individual? Or do you work easily with others, even with people with whom you have no natural connection?

With your results, you can figure out which archetype of open leader you are, as depicted in Figure 7.3. Be honest about your assessment—this is not about, say, trying to land in the upper right-hand corner and be a Realist Optimist, but about really understanding how you approach being open. If self-awareness is a key virtue of being an open leader, then being honest about your mind-set is a key initial step.

The goal of the self-assessment is to understand to what degree your open strategy for information sharing and decision making is being colored by your personal inclination or disinclination to be more open. Your employees and customers may be clamoring for greater openness, and your strategy is pointing you in the direction of sharing more information and decision making authority—but you may feel

Figure 7.3. Identifying Your Open Leader Archetype

	Pessimistic	Optimistic
Collaborative	**Cautious Tester** • Pessimistic (<2) • Collaborative (>2)	**Realist Optimist** • Optimistic (>2) • Collaborative (>2)
Independent	**Worried Skeptic** • Pessimistic (<2) • Independent (<2)	**Transparent Evangelist** • Optimistic (>2) • Independent (<2)

torn inside. In the same way, you may be a very open person but feel that your strategy simply isn't doing enough to achieve openness.

I believe that if your open strategy and open leadership styles are not congruent and consistent, you will have a very hard time executing the strategy effectively because you will not truly believe in it. For this reason, I believe it's also important to conduct the assessment with members of your leadership team, so that you are all aware of how each of you approaches being open. You will want to make sure that there are enough open leaders to be able to support being open.

The effort to understand and visibly make plain these mind-sets is not an attempt to label someone; more than anything, it aims to understand what skills and people are needed to support your open strategy. If you are being driven to adopt a broad open strategy because of market conditions—in much the same way that Ford has been—you may have to go outside the organization to find an open leader like Scott Monty to lead the change.

HOW THE ARCHETYPES SUPPORT EACH OTHER

One thing you can do to change the mind-sets and skills of your leadership team is to pair up different archetypes with each other, so that they can be purposely exposed to and learn from a different mind-set. For example, you may want to pair up Worried Skeptics and Cautious Testers, with the specific aim of having the Cautious Testers share the success they have had around collaboration. In addition, they can share how they are able to reconcile a pessimistic mind-set with collaboration through the use of small experiments that have built greater confidence, as well as the use of sandbox covenants to ensure clear guidelines and procedures.

One pairing that I have seen not work that well is putting a Transparent Evangelist together with a Worried Skeptic or a Cautious Tester. The problem: they are each squarely planted in the belief that their viewpoint—their optimistic or pessimistic view of the world—is "true," and they don't have the collaborative disposition and skills to be able to temper their individualistic tendencies. The result is that the Evangelist preaches the technology and how it can make you more open, when being open is the last thing the Worried Skeptic or even the Cautious Tester wants to be!

A better pairing is to have the Realist Optimists work with Worried Skeptics and Cautious Testers—and to have Transparent Evangelists close by to observe the process. The Realist Optimists have the internal respect and relationships to bring to bear against resistance, coupled with the optimism to believe that the Worried Skeptics and Cautious Testers *can learn* to be more comfortable with being open, especially when they understand the benefits. Realist Optimists have the patience of a saint, the willingness to give pessimists time to explore a new way of doing things, and the ability to encourage and support them throughout the process.

It's important for Transparent Evangelists to observe this process, as they will need to develop their collaborative skills, especially because they lack the innate mind-set to be collaborative in the first place. In the meantime, the Transparent Evangelists can play an important role in working with external stakeholders, especially customers and partners who are already eager to engage the organization. They can also help identify other optimistic open leaders in the organization, finding the other "zealots" who will help support your open strategy. In this way, the Transparent Evangelists become the frontline foot soldiers in implementing your open strategy, and they become ever more versatile and effective in doing this as they grow their collaboration skills.

Finally, let's discuss the important role that Realist Optimists play. As I mentioned earlier, the Realist Optimists are the linchpins of your open strategy. They are the ones who have the organizational knowledge and relationships to be the catalyst and change agent, and they are facile in their use and understanding of open technologies that enable these new relationships. These are rare individuals—people like Lionel Menchaca at Dell, Michele Azar at Best Buy, Wendy Harman at the American Red Cross, and Scott Monty at Ford. Menchaca and Azar were both longtime employees at their companies, whereas Harman and Monty were hired into their positions. What's interesting is that they were moved or hired into their positions by executives who themselves were not necessarily Realist Optimists but more typically Cautious Testers. These initial Realist Optimists went on to develop and nurture more open leaders—and, in effect, drive the open strategies at those companies alongside those Cautious Tester executives.

I bring this up because although you may be a Cautious Tester or a Worried Skeptic, you need to aware of this and thus be able to compensate by finding the Realist Optimists, as well as the Transparent Evangelists, who will be the executors of your open strategy. Even if you do not have the disposition to be an open leader, just the realization of and appreciation for being more open, and having an open strategy, is an important strategic step forward. Many of the executives I spoke with, like Barry Judge and John Chambers, were not open leaders at the start but slowly evolved their mind-sets and skills to that point.

ACTION PLAN: CHANGING YOUR OPEN LEADERSHIP MIND-SET

If the open strategy you developed requires that you and your organization's leadership be more open in your sharing or decision making, how prepared are you personally to do this? If you do not feel that confident about sharing, you'll need to take a look at the underlying reasons why this is the case—primarily, your pessimism about the outcomes. If you do not feel comfortable bringing people into the decision making process and being more collaborative, you'll need to start widening your circle of trust. Transforming mind-sets requires time, patience, and repeated small successes to build confidence. Here are some steps to get you started on building a more optimistic and collaborative mind-set:

(Continued)

(Continued)

- *Develop sandbox covenants that provide the guardrails for engagement.* When you share information or push down decision making, what are your expectations about what will be done with this power? What responsibilities do you want employees and customers to take on?

- *Partner with optimists and strong collaborators.* You probably know someone in your organization whom you regard as an optimist and open leader. Sit down with this person to understand his or her perspective and outlook on the world. What does this person do to ensure being in control while opening up? How does this person make openness work in your organization?

- *Examine your own background with people who know you well.* Your mind-set is developed through crucial personal experiences, so it would behoove you to talk with people who know you well on a personal level. Every person harbors some optimism, so turn to people whom you trust to help you find that starting point where you will feel comfortable engaging with people.

- *Start small to build trust.* It's hard to suspend a mind-set that's driven you throughout your professional career—it may feel completely unnatural to you and go against every fiber in your body. You can't suddenly announce, "From today forward I will be collaborative; I will be optimistic." It takes time to shift a mind-set, and it happens only with repeated successes. Take it one step at a time, so you can build confidence in sharing information and decision making with an ever-widening circle of people.

In the next chapter, we'll look at the specific skills and behaviors you need to develop as an open leader, both in yourself and in others throughout your organization. Traits and mind-sets are very hard to change; if you are naturally pessimistic or most comfortable as a loner, that's hard to overcome. Skills and behaviors, however, are more tactical; these are things that you can start practicing. Learn a new skill or consciously change your behavior, and over time your mind-set may start to change as well. So let's go on to Chapter Eight, in which we'll discuss how to nurture open leadership by encouraging specific skills and behaviors.

NURTURING OPEN LEADERSHIP

W hat does it mean to be a good leader? And, more important, how does one *become* a good leader? Hundreds of books have been written on this topic, and I'm not about to rewrite the wisdom that has come before me. Rather, in this chapter I'll discuss how one becomes a good *open* leader, because the new rules of relationships created by the advent of social technologies require that you develop new skills and behaviors that accentuate and support your own individual leadership style. I'll explain what it means to be "authentic" and "transparent," how you can use social technologies personally to be an effective leader, and also how to develop other open leaders using social technologies.

Let's get started by dissecting two of the most overused concepts when it comes to being open—authenticity and transparency.

THE TRUTH BEHIND AUTHENTICITY

To be a leader, you must first be a good person with intangibles like integrity, honesty, fairness, respect for people, a sense of humor, daring—in short, traits that, as described in Warren Bennis's classic *On Becoming a Leader*, get people to trust and follow you.[1] Hundreds of leadership books have been written to describe these characteristics, and I'm just adding to the chorus, but with a small twist. I turn to Marcus Aurelius, who said almost two thousand years ago, "Waste no more time arguing what a good man should be; just be one."

Most adults know what it means to have integrity, honesty, fairness, and more. A friend who teaches a business class in a men's prison tells me that, as one of his exercises, he asks these convicted felons to each write down three characteristics of someone they respect. He then lists their words on the blackboard. The results are the same session after session: the individuals these people respect are honest, trustworthy, fair, intelligent, reliable—evoking the Boy Scout law.

People understand what it means to be a person of good character, regardless of whether that person is the leader of a gang or a leader of a church. The qualities that inspire a gang to follow a leader are the same qualities that inspire a congregation to follow a charismatic pastor. The gang leader and the pastor may not share the same ends, but they share the same characteristics of leadership.

But in a world where relationships are influenced by social technologies, just having these qualities is no longer enough. Personal and organizational actions are scrutinized by anyone willing to pay attention; hence leadership—the good, the bad, and the sometimes very ugly parts—is quickly exposed. Leaders who are able to embrace the new culture of sharing and turn it to their advantage can amplify their good characteristics and actions, but it can be turned against them as well.

So in addition to characteristics like integrity, open leadership requires one over all others—authenticity. This word has lost much of its meaning because of its overuse and because we have such a hard time defining it. "Managing Authenticity: The Paradox Of

Great Leadership," an article that appeared in the *Harvard Business Review* in 2005, explains the root problem: "Authenticity is a quality that others must attribute to you. No leader can look into a mirror and say, 'I am authentic.' A person cannot be authentic on his or her own. Authenticity is largely defined by what other people see in you and, as such, can to a great extent be controlled by you."[2]

So all of the calls for you to "be authentic" are curiously correct—the paradox is that you *control* how authentic you want to appear, depending on the situation you find yourself in. As a result, you could come across as *inauthentic* if the information that you share and make visible is seen by the wrong audience. For example, you know me as an author, but I am also defined by my experiences growing up as a Chinese-American in Detroit, as a mother of two children, and as a Harvard-trained MBA woman in the business world. All of these elements blend together into my sense of self—but it doesn't mean that I show all aspects of it, all the time. Every so often, my work persona surfaces at a school meeting, and conversely, I slip in personal references at a business meeting. I hope that I do these things when it's appropriate, but those glimpses can easily come across as inauthentic or awkward if I reveal them at the wrong time, to the wrong audience.

Open leaders have the ability and skill to pull the relevant parts of their authentic selves into the conversation, to innately know which parts of their identity and personalities to show to whom, and when. Knowing when and what to "check at the door" is a highly prized skill for becoming accepted by a community—something that many women and minorities innately understand.[3] As such, open leaders need to learn how to manage their authenticity, especially in relation to the many varied audiences they may be reaching with social technologies. You've likely met people who are *too* authentic—so uncompromisingly true to themselves that it ends up hurting their ability to compromise and function within an organization. These people can't reach their potential because they lack the ability to moderate and manage their authenticity in a specific context.

The new culture of sharing created by social technologies makes this an even more urgent skill to develop—and because you may be new at "being authentic" in these channels, you may come across as not authentic enough or, worse, divulging too much information and thus coming across as inauthentic! No wonder leaders are hesitant to engage—not only are the stakes high, but the odds are low that you'll get the balance right, at least at first. So how do you get started being an "authentic" open leader?

First, you must remain true to your values and focus on what you want to accomplish. Take, for example, Chris Pratley, one of Microsoft's first bloggers, introduced in Chapter Five. He was the product lead for OneNote, and as you might expect, most people assumed he was a marketing front person, not really interested in a relationship. So before he even started, he had the imprimatur of not being authentic placed on him simply because of his association with a large company. But because he showed genuine respect and interest in developing a relationship—he would quickly respond to challenges, answer questions, and provide detailed information—people began to trust him. He demonstrated his integrity, trustworthiness, and honesty with each and every post and comment that he made.

The challenges to his integrity made him all the more determined to prove that he was trustworthy. Chris commented to me, "People would constantly say to me, 'Thank you for doing this, because the evidence is there that you really do care. You left the negative comments up, and you respond to everyone, even when they don't agree with you. And then you come back with more detail. You are clearly a real person who really cares about what your product is, and that comes through in what you write.'" Pratley became authentic to his audience, but it took persistence and determination on his part to get his audience to take him at his word. In this way, he was practicing one of the new rules of open leadership detailed at the end of Chapter One—to share constantly to build trust.

The second thing you can do to build your authenticity skills is to start small. That's exactly what Best Buy CMO Barry Judge did. He recalls that when his marketing team approached him about starting his own blog, "They made a powerful point about how I could go beyond the corporate office and speak directly to the people who were actually buying the product. That was a really powerful idea, but my first blog post was scary! I was so relieved when it was over—it was just two sentences to get started."[4] But he quickly got the hang of it. "You just had to dive in, figure out what to do, how to do it, and how it works for me. I quickly became aware that by doing it, what the power of being open was. It is through doing it that that came to light."

Judge's experience parallels what many other people experience the first time they engage with social technologies—you will be at a loss as to what to say and how to act, and the first time you click that "Publish" button, it may be terrifying—I know it was for me![5] But by tapping into the core of the person that you are—and just as important, centering your efforts on the people and audiences you want to reach—you'll soon find and develop your voice.

TRANSPARENCY IS NOT ABOUT SHOW-AND-TELL EVERYTHING

The other key skill you will need to develop is transparency. Executives like Brian Moynihan, the new CEO of Bank of America, understand the importance of transparency, saying "We . . . are changing the way we do business. We are committed to fairness and transparency."[6] Moynihan is acknowledging that after the transgressions of the past decade, organizations need to be more forthcoming about how they conduct business. Like authenticity, transparency is defined not by you the leader, but by the people you want to trust you and your organization. How much information do they need in order to follow you, to trust you with their money or business?

Let's dive deeper into what exactly transparency means. Rather than actually using the word "transparency," which implies complete openness and candor, I prefer to describe this skill as making information and processes "visible." You make visible your goals, and also the challenges, threats, and opportunities you face. For a given strategy, you give people updates and share the options under consideration, the challenges, and the results of a decision. Greater visibility incorporates primarily the "explaining" and "updating" types of openness defined in Chapter Two. And just as important, greater visibility can also come from *not* sharing, as long as it's accompanied by reasons why the leader cannot say more (for example, "We're in negotiations," "We're in a quiet period," or "We're being sued").

Harriet Green, the CEO of Premier Farnell, a distributor of electronic components, realized that greater transparency was needed at the company when she took over in 2006. One of the first things Green did was to implement a new strategy that moved most of the company's transactions online—which involved tracking and handling the inventory of hundreds of thousands of different types of electronic components around the world. Green realized that one barrier within the globally dispersed company was that people didn't know how everyone else was contributing to the strategy execution, so they couldn't coordinate or collaborate toward a common goal.

Green saw that a new generation of workers needed a different type of leadership style, and that greater transparency would lead to greater trust, empowerment, and thus higher performance. To enable that transparency, Green implemented a program called "eLife." Its centerpiece was SuccessFactors—a business execution software program that could visually depict every person's goal, to make visible what every single person in the company was responsible for, from the warehouse stocker to the CEO. By making accountability visible, Green removed the mystery and distraction of how each person was being evaluated and rewarded.

But eLife wasn't just about putting in a technology solution; it also involved a commitment on the part of Premier Farnell's leadership to encourage greater sharing and support of each person's initiatives and achievements. As was mentioned in Chapter Two, Green distributed inexpensive handheld video cameras to everyone to document and share best practices on an internal "OurTube" channel.

That transparency extended to the flow of information internally and externally as well. The company started an external community for engineers called Element 14, and Green herself began blogging internally on a regular basis.

She shared that it is sometimes tough to sustain these new communication channels. "After every meeting, after every session you have to be thinking about how you communicate with the organization. If you go quiet for a week, people start to think the worst. This form of open communication is very addictive. It generates enormous attention, and you can't do it in a halfhearted way. It has to be a commitment for life." Green realized that creating trust also required a significant commitment, one that could be made only because of her belief in the new role of transparency in leadership.

Green also shared that it took some time for her to get used to not only the nature of two-way communication, but also the *volume*.

> There are days when the 254th email on a particular subject comes in and you think, "Why did I go down this route? Wouldn't it have been a lot simpler just to have communicated by memo at the end of the quarter the results?" So it does generate a lot of activity, and you could argue that some of it is not entirely worthwhile. But I think, overall, it enhances our productivity. When you give people all this information and you emancipate them in this way, they are going to challenge you. I think that is right, but it is not always easy.

SUPPORTING OPEN LEADERSHIP WITH TECHNOLOGY

Green and other leaders have learned that they are capable of using social technologies to extend and support their leadership. As we saw in Part II of this book, open leaders will need to be very comfortable with using social technologies to implement an open strategy. This has to start at a personal level—how comfortable are *you* with these technologies yourself? You may be comfortable being authentic and transparent with the people within physical shouting distance, but that's not sufficient in this new environment. To develop new open relationships, you'll have to *scale* your authenticity and transparency.

But you may be looking at Facebook or Twitter and shaking your head—there's no way you could see yourself using those tools alongside your Generation Y employees! If this is the case for you, rather than focus on the technologies, go back to the core objectives you want to achieve with your open strategy—learning, dialog, support, and innovation—and figure out how you will *personally* use these tools to achieve these objectives.

Take for example, Bill Marriott, the CEO of hotel chain Marriott International, who has been blogging since January 2007.[7] At the age of seventy-eight, he's not exactly facile with the technology—he admits that he can't even type! So when he wants to write a blog post, a member of the Marriott communications staff records what he wants to say, transcribes it, and posts the text and audio file on his blog. Sometimes Marriott writes out by hand what he wants to say, sometimes he uses notes, and sometimes he speaks off the top of his head. "Being a technophobe like me adds a lot of steps, but I make it work," he says, "because I know that it's a great way to communicate with our customers and stakeholders in this day and age."[8]

What drives Marriott isn't the technology; it's his desire to have a new, different kind of relationship with the people he is leading. As you've seen from the preceding discussion, it's important to have a plan for when and how you will be open, authentic, and transparent, because you are making a commitment to a relationship with the people you are leading. In the same way that you develop an open strategy for your organization, you need to have a *personal* open strategy for yourself.

Take a moment and ask yourself the following questions to gauge how well you practice authenticity and transparency as an open leader, particularly your personal ability to use social technologies to this end. At the end of the chapter, there will be a more complete open leadership skills assessment tool, which you can also access at open-leadership.com.

- What are the values that underlie who I am as a person?
- What are the rules that govern what I will share, and with whom? How does this apply when I use technology to facilitate sharing?
- How well do I communicate my decisions and ideas? How comfortable am I doing this with social technologies that can scale conversations?
- How well do I encourage dialog and dissension around decisions? How can I use technology to facilitate that dialog?
- How comfortable am I admitting that I don't know something, have made a mistake, or need help? How comfortable am I doing this on open platforms?

Let's move on now from your own development as an open leader to looking at how you can foster and nurture open leadership in your organization.

OPEN LEADERS AS CATALYSTS

In an open organization, the open leader still sets the goals, the strategy, and the agenda—but with greater information sharing and distributed decision making, the leader's role in the organization changes in subtle but significant ways. The open leader needs to be a catalyst, the inspiration for people to pull together and accomplish things together. Everyone has to be aligned for the performance to come off successfully.

Being the catalyst is, as you know, a challenge, because you are asking a group of individuals to do things differently from what they've done in the past. This section looks at how open leaders as catalysts create and nurture an environment in which openness can prevail—how goals are set and communicated, how people are encouraged to be open leaders themselves, how they create a culture that encourages innovation and risk taking, and how they remove barriers. Let's look first at how open leaders set and communicate goals and in the process create even more open leaders.

CREATING SHARED GOALS AND A SHARED VISION

One common theme among the open leaders I interviewed was the importance of creating a strong sense of shared goals among all employees and communicating it broadly both inside and outside the organization. You'll recall from Chapter One that the Obama campaign was able to unify everyone with the same goal—get Obama elected—and then executed the strategy almost flawlessly with frontline involvement because everyone operated with the same set of core values. By making sure that the right values drove what people did, the campaign felt comfortable letting go of control and in the process unleashed a powerful source of energy—and cash.

Business, however, doesn't engender the same level of passion and commitment as a campaign does—witness the problems the Obama administration has had trying to wrangle a recalcitrant Congress to pass initiatives ranging from health care to stimulus packages. John Chambers, CEO of Cisco Systems, faces this problem every day— even though he is the CEO, he can't simply command-and-control his sixty-five thousand employees into a strategy. He discovered that everyone had a different way of understanding and expressing the corporate strategy. So Chambers set up a new strategy process that had at its center a clear vocabulary, values, and goals that drive every strategic discussion.

Chambers realized that he needed help communicating and creating the structure needed to instill the new way of thinking. For this task, he turned to Ron Ricci, VP of corporate positioning, who was able to take Chambers' ideas and create a new leadership and decision making process. At the center of the strategy is collaboration, which enabled Cisco to make distributed decision making a reality. Ricci explained to me why technology played such an important role: "Shared goals require trust. Trust requires behavior. And guess what technology does? It exposes behavior."

For example, if a department head is going to shift significant resources into a new initiative, it requires a tremendous amount of trust on the part of the other departments that are affected. Cisco invested heavily in remote collaboration tools like WebEx and its TelePresence video conferencing system, making it readily available to anyone who needed to use it. Why is this important? Ricci says, "When you make decisions that affect the value position of the business, there is nothing more important than for you to ask your business partner, 'Are we in this together?' And when that person nods enthusiastically, and you can look into that person's eyes and see sincerity, it's a big step to building trust. There are many productivity benefits as well, but the real benefit is greater trust."

Cisco's internal blogs and discussion forums provide further support for decisions and accountability for execution. Want to know what your partner has done lately on a project? Simple—just check the project's blog to get the latest update. There's less wondering what is happening, less time spent on checking up on implementation details, and more time spent thinking strategically about initiatives.

Leading the change to greater collaboration was Chambers himself. He shared that early on he was approached by younger employees who told him that he was defining collaboration too narrowly. He recalled, "They said that it should be all Web 2.0, and that I had to be pulling these technologies closer to me, and to lead by example in how to use them—including blogging." Chambers was concerned that blogging wouldn't be a good fit. "I can talk two hundred words a minute, but I didn't want to write a blog. I'm not a good speller, and it shows my grammatical mistakes." Instead of writing, they told him try a video blog. Reluctantly, he agreed to give a video blog two tries. "I did it the first time to communicate to our leadership team, and I wasn't even through with the first session and I knew they were right."[9]

Chambers set a personal example from the top of how to be an open leader. And like Bill Marriott, Chambers had to set aside his initial, natural reticence about using technology in order to accomplish his goal of not only communicating a strategy but living it as well. His advice: have members on your team who complement your weaknesses, allowing you to think—and act—out of the box.

DEVELOPING OPEN LEADERS

A key open leadership skill is developing other open leaders. Although not everyone has the background, personality, or desire to be a leader, I suspect more people have the capacity to lead than conventional wisdom would have us believe. You may find candidates in unexpected places, and sometimes you need to go outside of your organization to find them.

To nurture and grow open leaders requires rethinking the leadership pipeline. In their book *The Leadership Pipeline*, Ram Charan, Stephen Drotter, and James Noel point out that moving from being an individual contributor to being a manager can be difficult for many people because they are technicians who know how to do a specific job. "They have spent their time developing great skill at carrying out a given assignment rather than being in touch with the needs and expectations of their peers."[10] But with the advent of social technologies and the networked employee, that's rapidly changing. Charan et al. explain in their book that these kinds of connections typically develop at much higher levels of management, not at the individual contributor level. The advent of social technologies means that people at the front lines now have the relationships that enable them to move quickly and freely around the organization.

The new tools also mean individual contributors can exercise leadership *now*. They build their own relationships within the organization, offering help to their peers, making suggestions to other groups, asking for aid from outside contacts. This means you could be a leader just because people follow you—literally—on your blog, on Twitter, on your Facebook page, or elsewhere. Leadership is defined not by the position you hold but by the people who follow you. This means there are opportunities for individual workers to practice open leadership skills and experience leverage, collaboration, and influence earlier in their careers. The more positive relationships you have, the more power you have.

Open leadership, in short, is not something to be practiced only by the top echelons of the company. Rather, it's something that needs to occur at all levels in the organization, with team leaders and employees practicing it to a different degree and in a different way than executives. A John Chambers or a Bill Marriott can speak for the corporation as the CEO, but with the power of social technologies on the rise, anyone, any employee or customer, could be just as powerful a voice for your organization.

Finding Your Open Leaders

I'm often asked where to find these individuals—the would-be open leaders in the organization—and how to unleash them. In *The Starfish and the Spider*, Ori Brafman and Rod A. Beckstrom describe how a catalyst with the vision pairs up with a champion who becomes the front person for the strategy.[11] It's important to understand your roles as the catalyst—the person who brings together the vision and sets the strategy—versus the champion who goes out and executes the vision.

At Best Buy, Michele Azar—VP of Best Buy for Business—is such a catalyst. As an open leader, Azar recognized in 2007 that Best Buy was sitting on top of a huge asset—its thousands of enthusiastic electronics geeks who were using open approaches and social technologies. She had been personally involved in the past in transforming Best Buy, store by store, and she immediately recognized the power and speed of empowering employees using both the Web as a platform and social technologies. She talked her way into a new job on the BestBuy.com team and started creating an open strategy for the company.[12]

Along the way, she identified what she came to call her "zealots" around the company. Like Brafman and Beckstrom, these individuals are driven by a cause—they have a vision that burns in their brains, something they just have to build. They are true believers in a cause, which in Best Buy's case meant getting close to other employees, or customers, or both. They recruit people to their cause, and they are optimists because they think things can get done. Azar observed, "If you have zealots, they will talk about the thing that they are passionate about, and that thing for us was their intense focus on customer relationships centered on electronics. What makes them successful is that they talk about things that come naturally to them; they are authentic because they know intimately, inside and outside, the products or services that they want to talk about. And they are genuine about wanting to build relationships and helping customers find relationships that just work."

Best Buy realized that it is important to find and empower these open leaders because they would be the engine driving forward the company's open strategy. I encourage organizations to look for the following traits when identifying your open leaders—they may not have the traditional skills of a leader, but they have the following mind-sets and skills that are essential for open leadership:

PASSION FOR THE VISION. When you share your vision and strategy, they are the ones who reach out to you and ask "How can I help?" They grasp the idea at a personal level and are willing to pour their entire heart and soul into the strategy. In some ways, their passion may be unnerving, as it may be even stronger than *your* own passion for the vision!

FOCUS ON RELATIONSHIPS. It's not enough to simply be behind the vision—these people also need to be just as passionate about building and fostering relationships with employees and/or customers. You probably already know who these people are—they are the ones who consistently advocate for the organization to look at opportunities and problems from the customer's viewpoint.

HACKER MENTALITY. Your zealots are not satisfied with the status quo, and even if they successfully get change made, they are still not satisfied. They believe at their core that everything can and should be "hacked" and made better.

I want to elucidate what I mean by "hacker"—it is not that I advocate the illegal security breaches of computer networks or software. Rather,

I mean someone with the passion to improve an existing system—and zealots have the same collaborative sense as Realist Optimists of how to do this within the confines of an organization. Facebook looks for exactly this type of person. Lori Goler, VP of human resources at Facebook, shared that one of the characteristics they look for in candidates is the ability to build. "We call them builders and hackers. How do you challenge the status quo? How do you think about doing things differently? They are entrepreneurs themselves. Hackers are going to find a new way around something."

LEADING OPEN LEADERS

Nurturing zealots raises a fundamental question—how do you manage them? How do you, as an open leader, foster and encourage open leadership in others, especially if they don't want themselves to be necessarily *led* in a traditional way? I believe there are four fundamental behaviors that open leaders display:

1. Hiring, training, and promoting the right people
2. Creating a culture that supports being open
3. Removing barriers to being open
4. Encouraging risk taking and speeding recovery from failure

Let's begin with how open leaders hire, train, and promote differently from traditional leaders.

HIRING OPEN LEADERS

You may be lucky, like Best Buy's Michele Azar, and have a plethora of zealots already in your company. But if you don't, or if you're eager to make sure that you *do* hire people with greater open leadership potential, then you need to take a close look at how you recruit and hire. A good example of how a company is changing its recruitment methods is Sodexo, a food and facilities management company that is the twenty-second largest employer in the world with operations in 80 countries and 350,000 employees—a third in the United States alone.

Its product is its people, who manage support services in many different industries: health care, schools, corporations, and more.

With that many employees in an industry notorious for high turnover and with a name that is not a household word, Sodexo has a major recruiting challenge. I talked with Kerry Noone, marketing communications manager for Sodexo USA's Talent Acquisition Group; she shared that the company recognized that social technologies could help improve Sodexo's hiring process. But Sodexo doesn't just dabble in social technologies—they are all over it. They have a presence on Facebook, LinkedIn, YouTube, and Twitter, and a blog; all together, these have more than tripled traffic to the Sodexo career page.[13] And they have online communities for different groups, such as veterans, reservists and National Guard, and even Sodexo alumni.

The result: They increased the number of candidates applying by 25 percent and also increased by 50 percent the number of diverse (female and minority) candidates. The main goal of all this activity, says Kerry, is to reach out and create personal relationships with people who are interested in working for Sodexo. "That is part of our employment brand. We are telling our candidates and people who are interested what it is like to work for Sodexo—real stories coming from real people."

Now if you're a young person just starting out and looking for a job, which would you gravitate toward: a company that blocks and shuns social technologies, or a company like Sodexo that embraces them as a way to build initial relationships? Finding open leaders starts from the moment someone starts thinking about working for you, whether it's a referral from a friend or the mention of your company on someone's Facebook page. If you're not present and conversational, the future open leaders of your organization are going to pass you by.

Training Your Company's Open Leaders

In my research, I also asked many companies how they train and develop their leaders, especially in areas of being open. One of the best—and most extreme—examples of hiring and training that's designed to find and develop the right people is that of Zappos.

All new Zappos call center employees—key to a business that sells shoes and clothing online and over the phone—receive four weeks of training. At the training's conclusion, Zappos offers all the new hires $2,000, plus pay for their time spent in training (at $11 an hour), to quit. Zappos CEO Tony Hsieh began the practice in 2005 because it weeded out people who were there just for the paycheck. Zappos instead wanted those workers who were passionate about their jobs, ready to be zealots of customer service.

Recently, Zappos launched an even more comprehensive curriculum to develop leadership skills. The first course, intended for employees who have worked at Zappos for two years or less, involves more than two hundred hours of class time (during work hours) and mandates that students read nine business books. Topics include Sarbanes-Oxley compliance and Twitter use—two topics that on the surface seem contradictory. Advanced students can take classes in public speaking and financial planning. "The vision is that three years from now, almost all our hires will be entry-level people," Hsieh says. "We'll provide them with training and mentorship, so that within five to seven years, they can become senior leaders within the company."[14]

Zappos put in place a leadership pipeline that fosters and nurtures open leadership skills at the front lines—employees are empowered to make customer service–related decisions without having to ask for permission. These leaders feel comfortable from the start playing the role of a catalyst and fostering open leadership skills and behaviors, because they themselves practiced these skills on the front lines. It remains to be seen whether Zappos will be successful at developing an entire company staffed with open leaders, but the prospect and the audacity of what they are trying to achieve should be an inspiration and aspiration for other companies to emulate.

CREATING A CULTURE THAT SUPPORTS BEING OPEN

One of the biggest concerns I hear from leaders is that their company cultures keep them from being more open. I'll discuss how to transform a company culture in greater detail in Chapter Ten, but there are some things you can do immediately within your own team or organization to create a supportive environment for open information sharing and decision making.

One of the most important is the recognition and incentives you use to reward open behavior. The best systems are self-reinforcing, meaning that positive actions result in rewards that directly encourage you to do more. For example, David Michael, the chief information officer at United Business Media (UBM), told me that the London-based company wanted to improve internal efficiency. When UBM held periodic summit meetings among its sixteen divisions, CEOs inevitably discovered that someone was trying to solve a problem that somebody else around the table had already solved. They realized that if they—and their subordinates—worked together, they could probably solve problems twice as fast as each could working alone.

That insight led UBM to install Jive software to support collaboration, which I discussed in Chapter Six. But software, on its own, does not solve any problems. The company found that executives were not the right people to be encouraging the 6,500 employees to use the new tool. Michael recalled that they realized it would have to be a grassroots movement, whereby the people at the front lines could directly see the benefits of participating.

So the company set up what it called "Wiki Wins": if someone used the internal wiki to solve a problem, they posted it in the Wiki Wins area. People had the incentive to post because that area of the wiki received a great deal of internal publicity, particularly from the group CEO. It thus became a self-reinforcing exercise. Michael explained, "If I'm in charge of commissions for freelance writers, and somebody in China helps me do it and, as a result, I save tens of thousands of dollars, I'm incentivized to post it on Wiki Wins." The system is mostly self-governing, so as successes take place, they bubble up, and everyone in UBM can see the success and a real benefit to collaborating.

But what does it take for UBM employees to take time out from their busy schedules to help another employee in another country?

First, there is the self-serving recognition of "paying it forward": someday you may want to partake of this resource yourself, so you support it in the short term. But another, more compelling reason is that people understand a higher purpose and a call for participation, a sense that they are helping the organization achieve its goal and that they have a valued contribution to make. In many ways, the trickle-down effect of open leadership is that this sense of ownership of the vision and strategy seeps into the furthest reaches of the organization.

Stephen Elop, president of Microsoft's business solutions group, which makes products like Microsoft Office, was a rare top executive hire into Microsoft in 2008. As someone coming into one of Microsoft's biggest business units, Elop realized the importance of broadly communicating the organization's strategy around interoperability—many people inside and outside the company just didn't believe Microsoft was interested in forging these new relationships. But Elop repeated the interoperability vision over and over again for anyone who was willing to listen. His shared his logic with me, saying, "If everyone of the thousands and thousands of people working in related spaces at Microsoft understands a fair portion of the strategy, then it will be the case that each individual in the course of their day-to-day work, they will make hundreds of tiny little decisions that aggregate up into what Microsoft delivers or how it engages with its customers. Every one of those decisions will just be ever so slightly biased in favor of that strategy, of that openness, of that interoperability that we want to drive."

To that end, you, as the catalyst for open leadership, must carry the mantle and burden of setting that vision and communicating it over and over again. This becomes the core of the culture that you foster, in which being open is a central theme. The incentives and recognitions, the examples that you personally set, and the success stories that are told again and again and become part of your organization's lore—all are the way you slowly create a culture of openness.

REMOVING BARRIERS TO BEING OPEN

Think about all the barriers that stand in the way of being open. It includes system problems like incompatible databases and bureaucratic problems like restrictive company policies. But the biggest barrier will probably come from the functional managers one or two levels above the front line. They are driven by efficiency and compensated by meeting quarterly production goals. When they are asked to dedicate 20 percent of a subordinate's time to a collaboration initiative—while the team goals remain the same—it's hard for them not to see that 20 percent as a drain on the team's effort. In addition, these managers may feel threatened by the power that employees accumulate as they build more and more relationships around the organization and cut the managers out of the information flow. If you are an empowered employee that the boss fears, how do you help the manager feel more secure? Or if you are the executive trying to help that manager become more open, how do you break through that person's fear? In my experience, a fearful boss is a miserable boss—arbitrary, petty, and vindictive. How do you encourage the manager to be open, especially in the context of a large organization that may itself not be open?

First, your objective is not to make them zealots, but to get them to simply understand and appreciate the objectives and to step out of the way. To do that, you must lay out the concrete benefits, many of which I outlined in Chapter Four. Ask them to take on *one* way of being open—for example, listening to customers who are using new technologies—because it clearly helps the team achieve one of its short-term goals. The more that you can align the open activities with clear benefits, the more successful you will be in reducing the fears of the manager.

In other cases, the manager may already be familiar with social technologies, but enough so that they don't see the benefits of being open. Already, the networking, communication, and collaboration skills of most managers today are improving—72 percent of management respondents in a recent survey reported that they personally visit social media sites at least weekly.[15] But a closer look at the data shows that they do so primarily for defensive and reactive reasons—most use social technologies to see what customers are saying (52 percent), to monitor competitors' use of social media (47 percent), and to see what current employees are sharing (36 percent). As a group, business leaders are mostly absent from the networked conversation, be it in the public sphere or internally.

In such cases, the manager may be most concerned about losing control because of the open dialog that is taking place, especially with customers. In such situations, involve the manager in setting up the sandbox covenants covered in Chapter Five to provide guardrails for participation. Overall, reducing the fear and anxiety of middle managers requires that you collaborate and educate them so that they buy in to the vision and benefits of being open. If this requires that you slow down your efforts temporarily to make sure that key people are brought along, it may be worth it.

Convincing the Curmudgeon

Just as every company has open leaders, every company has at least one curmudgeon: the resident naysayer and self-appointed keeper of the "way we do things around here" playbook.[16] If you're able to convince this person to understand and support open leadership, you'll have a powerful advocate on your side. But if you don't, you'll have a thorn constantly questioning the wisdom of being more open. Here are some common objections that The Curmudgeon poses, and how to respond:

- *"This is a fad and a waste of time."* Curmudgeons don't really understand how social technologies work, or how open information sharing or decision making can make a difference. The key is to make it real for them—do some research on personal pet peeves, or an area of interest to them that is being positively affected by being more open. This could be, for example, connecting them with an online community of duck hunters, or showing conversations with real customers that teach them something they didn't know. Or it may be connecting them with old friends or executives at other companies who are now using these tools. The key is to quickly bring this down to a personal level, where they can experience the power of being open and connected directly.

• *"There's no ROI in it."* Curmudgeons are likely to be senior enough in the organization that the corporate strategy is of great personal importance. Demonstrate to them how open leadership and the open strategy will advance strategic goals. Moreover, appeal to their experience in forming broad relationships and their recognition that it's hard to quantify the value of those relationships. Then demonstrate how open leadership can strengthen and deepen those relationships—especially with key partners and customers—and also inspire employees.

• *"It's way too risky."* This objection is likely the hardest to overcome. As a good open leader, you will put in place the necessary sandbox covenants and engage in scenario planning and contingency planning, all in the name of reducing risk. But the very nature of being open requires trust, and if The Curmudgeon fundamentally doesn't trust other people, it's a tough thing to change. Your only hope is to find some fissure, some crack in that wall of distrust that makes The Curmudgeon willing to take the risk. It may be small. It may be infinitesimally small. But take it, as it will be a start. Once you identify a chink in that wall of distrust, be sure to keep chipping away at it!

Appealing as it may be to think that everyone can be open, inevitably there will be situations in which there is a disconnect between a person's ability to be an open leader and the organization's need for openness. In such cases, you need to be prepared to part ways—which is especially difficult if that person was a high performer in the pre–open strategy world.

Cisco found itself in several of these difficult situations. John Chambers explained in a *New York Times* interview that collaboration changed Cisco, commenting "If people are not collaborative, if they aren't naturally inclined toward collaboration and teamwork, if they are uncomfortable with using technology to make that happen both within Cisco and in their own life, they're probably not going to fit in here."[17] Over the past few years, Cisco was forced to let valuable people and executives go, because it found that some people just would not be collaborative. Even though they may have tried, these people just did not feel comfortable with the amount of sharing and collaboration required in their new roles.

My hope is that you'll be able to find a role for many different types of leaders in your organization, even those who may take a longer time to warm up to the idea of being open. But if you find yourself in a situation in which someone simply cannot find a way to be open in the way that you need your team to be, I hope you will have the courage to have that tough conversation about that person's future role. It's part of being an open leader—being able to have those honest conversations so that the person and your organization will be more successful in the long run.

ENCOURAGING RISK TAKING AND SPEEDING RECOVERY FROM FAILURE

I'll cover this last skill briefly because I discuss it in much greater detail in the next chapter. An inherent behavior of open leaders is to encourage responsible risk taking. It's consistent with fostering the hacker mentality of your zealots, and it also encourages greater innovation from both within and outside the company. But with risk taking come the inevitable failures, and open leaders must prepare their organizations for those as well—in particular, how to deal with and recover from failure.

This begins, again, with the core trait and mind-set of humility that I discussed in Chapter Seven. The way that you personally deal with your own failures and shortcomings sets the tone and example for how the rest of your team or organization acts as well. There is no shame in admitting a mistake or a failing—there's shame only in not learning from it. Open leaders understand that other people make mistakes, and they use the occasion as a teaching moment rather than to place blame and punish.

ACTION PLAN: THE OPEN LEADERSHIP SKILLS ASSESSMENT

Although the traits of good leaders are universal, there are new skills and behaviors that open leaders must learn and master to be effective. In particular, open leaders must act as a catalyst to creating greater openness in organization, in ways that differ significantly from traditional leadership. I summarize some of those differences in Figure 8.1.

As you consider how to develop your open leadership skills, as well as the skills of your organization, ask yourself the following questions:

- Where is open leadership needed most urgently in your organization?
- Where is open leadership already naturally happening?
- Who are the most promising open leader candidates in your organization? How will you identify, train, and nurture them?
- How can you make it easier for open leaders to find and support each other?
- What kind of support is needed to nurture your open leaders?
- What barriers and friction need to be removed?
- How will you personally model open leadership?

And last, but more important, how ready are you to be an open leader yourself? How good are your open leadership skills and behaviors *today,* and do you need to improve on them or compensate for weaknesses through others? In Figure 8.2, I highlight some of the most important skills you will need to have, both in terms of overall leadership capabilities and also in terms of using social technology as a tool to extend your open leadership throughout the organization and marketplace. You can also go online to open-leadership.com to take a complete assessment there and also compare your results with others.

Figure 8.1. How Open Leadership Differs from Traditional Leadership

Traditional Leadership as a Role	Open Leadership as a Catalyst
Spends limited time thinking about how to be authentic and transparent.	Actively manages authenticity and transparency to form relationships.
Sets a strategy and commands control through the leadership chain.	Sets a strategy and engenders commitment with a common shared vision.
Uses communications to message the vision and strategy.	Uses networks to spread the vision and strategy.
Believes leadership is a rare, precious trait.	Believes leadership potential resides in every person.
Engages primarily in the executive suite.	Engages at all levels, outside as well as inside the organization.
Develops trust with transactions.	Inspires trust with engagement.
Controls information tightly for fear of leakage.	Develops a culture of trusted information sharing.
Writes rules for conformity and consistency.	Writes rules for risk taking.

OPEN LEADERSHIP

Figure 8.2. Open Leadership Skills Assessment Test

Score yourself on a scale from 1 ("I find this hard to do") to 5 ("I can do this very well *and* I actively practice this regularly").

Demonstrate authenticity	Score				
I seek out and listen to different points of view.	1	2	3	4	5
I make myself available to people at all levels of the organization.	1	2	3	4	5
I use social technologies effectively to communicate.	1	2	3	4	5
I actively manage how I am authentic.	1	2	3	4	5
Average	1	2	3	4	5
Practice Transparency	Score				
I take the time to explain how decisions are being made.	1	2	3	4	5
I reach out to customers frequently via social technologies, wherever they may be.	1	2	3	4	5
I encourage people to share information.	1	2	3	4	5
I update people regularly using social technologies.	1	2	3	4	5
I publicly admit when I am wrong.	1	2	3	4	5
Average	1	2	3	4	5

Develop and Encourage Open Leadership	Score
I identify and actively nurture potential open leaders at all levels of the organization.	1 2 3 4 5
I train and encourage people to use open leadership skills.	1 2 3 4 5
I encourage the use of social technologies throughout the organization.	1 2 3 4 5
I create a support network for open leaders.	1 2 3 4 5
I ask "What did I/we learn?" when things fail.	1 2 3 4 5
Average	1 2 3 4 5

Now let's move on to Chapter Nine, where we'll discuss something that makes most people cringe—failure.

THE FAILURE
IMPERATIVE

In my work with organizations, one big barrier to being open has been a systemic and cultural aversion to failure. When I start discussing the likelihood that things will go wrong when being open and using social technologies, I often see people squirming uncomfortably in their seats. So you're probably reading this chapter with a sense of discomfort—after all, nobody really likes to talk about failure.

But I'm convinced that a key part of being an open leader is the ability to effectively deal with failure, because even with the best structures and planning in place, things go wrong. By mastering failure, you create an environment in which risk taking is encouraged and recovery from failure becomes a skill that everyone in the organization possesses. Essentially, I'm talking about your ability to create a culture in which people have such trust in each other that they know they can safely take risks.

How you, as an open leader, deal with failure is just as important as how well you deal with success. Can you be open to and accept the fact that people will make mistakes? That products will fail in the market? That decisions will have unexpected—and sometimes unhappy—consequences? If you feel you cannot be open to mistakes and failures, think of the consequences of this closed mind-set. Your colleagues will be afraid to step out or to speak up, and that goes against the very core of being open.

Open leadership is about building a new kind of relationship with your employees, customers, and partners. In any relationship, things go wrong, mistakes are made, ups are followed by downs. The strength of a relationship is not how perfect it is but how resiliently it deals with the unavoidable downs. And with the advent of social technologies, there are new ways to form those bonds and relationships—but also more potential, as we've seen, to amplify mistakes.

In essence, this chapter is about the last of the new rules I discussed at the end of Chapter One—the ability to forgive failure in order to build trust, but also the need to create trust so that people know that mistakes will be forgiven. I'll discuss the importance of acknowledging failure so that you and your organization can learn and improve from it. I'll then lay out the skills, behaviors, and systems that an open leader must have to create a trusting, resilient organization capable of quickly recovering and learning from its failures. As Winston Churchill once said, "Success is the ability to go from one failure to another with no loss of enthusiasm." My goal is that by the end of the chapter you'll have a roadmap that will help you build the trusting culture you need to be an effective open leader.

BUILDING THE TRUST THAT COMES FROM FAILURE

Every summer, I go to a camp with my family where a highlight is the ropes challenge course. One of my favorite activities is The Leap of Faith. I climb up a redwood tree, about forty feet high in the air, clamber onto a precarious little platform, and look out at a trapeze about ten feet away. The idea is to fling yourself off the platform and catch the trapeze with your bare hands. I am wearing a hardhat and a harness tied to a rope for safety, but the only thing to keep me from falling and smashing my face into the dirt below is my family holding onto the other end of the rope. There's my husband, brothers, and kids, some of whom can barely grasp the rope. Palms sweaty, heart pumping, I gather up my courage, put my trust in them, and launch off the platform, aiming for the trapeze. And I always miss.

The point is, the only reason I'm able to take this risk is that I trust that my family is there to break my fall. And each summer it gets a little easier to climb that tree and fling myself off the platform—I'm getting accustomed to the risk, and it gives me hope that this might be the year when I finally can grab onto that trapeze.

In your organization, how important is it for people to be risk takers, to be innovators? If initiative and innovation are key to your future success, then you need to take a long hard look at how you personally create trust and approach failure, because it will be reflected back in the culture that you create. As I discussed in earlier chapters, to be an open leader you need to have the self-awareness and humility to know your limits and, similarly, to know the role that failure has played in your success.

In my interview with John Chambers, the CEO of Cisco, he shared that he often asks prospective employees about results. "I never get hard work confused with success. So I walk you through your successes, and what you did right. I also ask you to tell me about your failures. And that's when people make a tremendous mistake. All of us have had mistakes and failures, yet it's surprising how many people say, 'Well, I can't think of one.' That person immediately loses credibility with me. It's an important ability to be very candid on what mistakes they've made, and then the question is, what would you do differently this time?"

Chambers' comments reinforce that the ability to recognize and learn from failure is important. In fact, the best leaders prepare themselves and their organizations for failure, and make sure that there are ways that everyone, including themselves, can learn from these experiences so that they are not wasted.

GOOGLE'S AMAZING FAILURE MACHINE

One organization that is really good at failure is Google. Known as one of the most innovative companies in the world, Google understands that to be successful at innovating, they have to have lots and lots of failures as well.[1] Google has a motto: "Fail fast, fail smart." And one thing Google has done especially well is to deal with the leadership challenge of picking up the pieces after a failure.

For example, *Fortune* magazine tells the story of Sheryl Sandberg, a then thirty-seven-year-old vice president in charge of Google's automated advertising system. She committed an error that cost Google several million dollars. All that she said about the mistake was, "Bad decision, moved too quickly, no controls in place, wasted some money." When she realized the magnitude of what she'd done, she went to inform Larry Page, Google's cofounder and unofficial thought leader. "God, I feel really bad about this," Sandberg told Page, who accepted her apology. As she turned to leave, Page added: "I'm so glad you made this mistake. Because I want to run a company where we are moving too quickly and doing too much—not being too cautious and doing too little. If we don't have any of these mistakes, we're just not taking enough risk."[2]

I talked to Chris DiBona, the open source and public sector manager at Google, about failure and how the organization deals with it. "I fail a lot, so I can help you with that," he said, only half joking. He told me about one project he worked on that was launched inside the company as a test—a service Google could use internally as well as one it hoped to bring to market. "Frankly, the usage just wasn't what we were expecting. It ended up simply not working out. People just didn't need what we were creating." Google realized that releasing the service to the public would have been a waste of time and money. Once that became clear, says DiBona, it took a few weeks to shut it down—a project on which engineers had worked for almost two years. The engineers were obviously not happy to be shut down. "It can stink to fail. It can just stink," says DiBona.

What happened next?

"I felt way worse than pretty much anyone else in the company about canceling the project," recalled DiBona. "But nobody held it against any of the engineers. In fact, my boss, Alfred Spector, said, 'Listen, we should do what we can and give these guys a ton of flexibility to find projects they really want to work on that are either launched or launching so they continue to respect Google, and know that Google wants them to stay, backing up our commitment to people with resources and opportunities.'"

Google, says DiBona, does more than tolerate failure grudgingly—it actively creates a support system for people so that they feel comfortable failing. But more important, they are able to identify and separate the personal competencies of people from the failings of a particular project, allowing good people to take risks again. The engineers who kept their jobs now have a lot more confidence to try new things. "In our whole hiring and recruiting process, we emphasize points like this. We make sure the word is out so people come in knowing they can try things, that failure can be okay."

With its culture, Google creates the trust necessary for risk taking and demonstrates that support regularly through its actions. Granted, this level of tolerance for failure will be different for every organization, as each company has its own risk tolerance profile. The key is to figure out how much risk you will tolerate as a leader and how much your organization can handle, then to make sure that the two are aligned.

There are four actions that an open leader can take to ensure that the organization is resilient in the face of failure and able to learn and grow from challenges:

1. Acknowledge that failure happens.
2. Encourage dialog to foster trust.
3. Separate the person from the failure.
4. Learn from your mistakes.

I'll delve deeper into each of these in the following pages.

ACKNOWLEDGE THAT FAILURE HAPPENS

Failure is inevitable. Things go wrong. For example, you may lose clients or individuals make mistakes. People associated with the failure may begin looking for other jobs, or anticipate a transfer to a far-flung office. In the past, organizations tended to hide their failures, certainly from the public. Today it's much more difficult to hide failures—the employees and customers involved may Tweet and blog about it, and you have no way to turn it off. Not only must you guide your organization through the failure, but you are likely to have to do it in public for the world to see. Openly acknowledging a failure is a crucial part of openness. The key is to keep everyone focused on the larger goal, not the temporary setback. The greatest generals do not win every single battle, but they are able to rally the troops, analyze what went wrong, and make adjustments for the next battle.

Acknowledging failure publicly, though, can be very, very tough for many organizations. But doing so quickly and moving forward to resolve the problem is essential to driving trust with your customers. Facebook faced just such a problem in early 2009, after the site changed its Terms of Service (TOS) on February 4. For more than a week, nobody noticed. But on February 15, The Consumerist Web site posted their analysis of the new TOS, headlined, "Facebook's New Terms of Service: 'We Can Do Whatever We Want With Your Content Forever,'" spurring a backlash of protest.[3] The problem: the new TOS seemed to grant Facebook an irrevocable right to content created by users, even if users canceled their accounts and wanted nothing more to do with the site.

222

Almost immediately, Facebook responded with clarifying comments, including a blog post written on February 16 by Facebook CEO Mark Zuckerberg, all trying to explain the logic behind the new TOS. Zuckerberg even admitted at the end of his post, "It's difficult terrain to navigate and we're going to make some missteps, but as the leading service for sharing information we take these issues and our responsibility to help resolve them very seriously."[4] But the new TOS remained in place, and the explanation did little to abate the growing uproar and media coverage.

The next day, February 17 at 10:17 P.M., Zuckerberg wrote another post that reverted the TOS to the original one, writing,

> Over the past couple of days, we received a lot of questions and comments about the changes and what they mean for people and their information. Based on this feedback, we have decided to return to our previous terms of use while we resolve the issues that people have raised . . . Going forward, we've decided to take a new approach towards developing our terms . . . Since this will be the governing document that we'll all live by, Facebook users will have a lot of input in crafting these terms . . . If you'd like to get involved in crafting our new terms, you can start posting your questions, comments and requests in the group we've created—Facebook Bill of Rights and Responsibilities.[5]

Facebook clearly acknowledged that they had made a mistake, but they didn't just apologize—they moved forward not only by explaining how they would address the problem (revert the TOS to an earlier version) but also by creating a process for developing the new TOS with input from Facebook users. As I detailed in Chapter Two, Facebook's open culture allows them to move rapidly and to try new things—but it also gives tremendous power to users, which Facebook must in turn respect. Looking back at the TOS debacle as well as other failures, Lori Goler, VP of human resources at Facebook, commented, "In all of these mistakes, we look for the learning opportunity or the teaching moment, and then take it as an opportunity for innovation. TOS happened. We came out and apologized. Then we came up with an entirely new paradigm for the way we think about our relationship with users that I think has gone a lot farther than most other companies would be comfortable going."

All this goes back to the new rules I discussed in Chapter One. Open leaders respect that today an organization's customers, clients, prospects, partners, and others have power to share information. You can look at it as a way to expose failures, and fear it. But effective open leaders will also see it as a way to strengthen the relationships that will be needed to recover and move on from those failures.

Now that you understand why it's important to acknowledge that failure happens, let's move on to what to do about it and, in particular, how to build a culture of trust that enables people to be risk takers in the first place.

ENCOURAGE DIALOG TO FOSTER TRUST

Have you ever been in this situation? You attend a meeting where everyone avoids talking about "the problem." It can be anything, but it's the elephant in the room that no one wants to name—so it never gets dealt with. But right afterward, when the meeting adjourns, everyone begins talking about it privately. Kodak's CMO Jeffrey Hayzlett recalls his experience: "You can see the elephant in the room. We should deal with it in the room in the first place. When people do deal with it, it makes relationships much more powerful because you have the transparency to have that discussion."

Kodak is an interesting corporation because its long-time core business, photographic film, is rapidly disappearing. Fortunately for Kodak, the market shift did not happen overnight, and management has had time to move into digital photography and digital printing. They had to buy companies, integrate them, and continue to rev up their innovation engine. In undertaking such a massive shift, Hayzlett explained, many things weren't working right. "We didn't have the trust, and frankly you just can't go out and have a coaching program" to correct this.

So Kodak's leadership created with a core set of values they wanted the organization to exemplify: Focus, Accountability, Simplicity, and Trust, known by the acronym FAST. CEO Antonio Perez focused in particular on the last element of trust, an outgrowth of what he called "healthy debate." Hayzlett recalled, "If we got nothing out of FAST, other than that we made mistakes quicker, we would be further ahead." Kodak realized that healthy debate and an honest exchange between people would be the foundation for trust in the relationships they wanted to build. They needed to be able to have vehement disagreements, resolve them, and still be able to work together.

To support that honest dialog, Kodak put in place an internal social network as a way for people to get to know each other. Employees use the network as a way to develop relationships internally, and at the time this book was written, the plan was to open it up to customers so that they could get to know Kodak people better as well. This is especially important for Kodak's burgeoning new business-to-business relationships with hundreds of thousands of customers: with a simple click, customers can see profiles of their account manager, customer service team, and technicians and begin a dialog with them.

SEPARATE THE PERSON FROM THE FAILURE

One key thing Kodak did by spurring that debate was to separate what people did from the specifics of the failure. Rather than simply say or imply, "You failed, so you can't be any good," Kodak communicated to people "*You* didn't fail, the project did. So what can we learn from this to do better next time?" Hayzlett shared his framework for understanding the three elements required for trust: sincerity, competency, and reliability. These have always been necessary, but social technologies adds new dimensions to each of these elements.

Sincerity. By this is meant that you are saying what you genuinely feel or believe based on eye contact, body language, tone of voice, and past experience. You are not dishonest or hypocritical. Although in many social media situations we lack the eye contact and body language of an in-person encounter, tools such as Cisco's TelePresence enable individuals to see each other for more than once-a-year meetings. But when you engage in a regular dialog, respond to questions, help with problems, and offer useful tips, it goes a long way to convince a customer that you are sincere (aka authentic) in your desire to have a relationship. They can see in your blogs, in your videos, in your interactions with them that you are sincere in your desire to help.

One can, of course, be sincerely mistaken. People who believe they have been abducted by space aliens may be perfectly sincere. But that's not enough to warrant acceptance of the person's statement as describing a verifiable reality. In addition, I often see the issue of sincerity raised when somebody endorses or condemns a product; for example, in a blog or Twitter post. Does the blogger really love the product or is the person being paid? Conversely, did the tweeter truly have a bad experience or is that person really a competitor pretending to be a customer? Just as we as individuals in everyday life are usually able to ascertain the veracity of a person's comments, we are quickly acquiring this skill to differentiate between what is real and sincere online and what isn't.

Competency. This next element concerns your ability to do something and, more important, whether people *believe* you have the ability to do what you say you can do successfully or efficiently. Thus your actions speak for your ability—for example, you display your expertise publicly in your blog postings, in forums, in your reviews of books, music, products, services, and so on. Or you have given good advice to people over and over in a support forum, so they're going to trust the advice you give. Or they know that the products you have created in the past have worked really well. You have demonstrated that you can build a reliable car, an effective search engine, an elegant laptop, so they're going to trust the new products you develop are pretty good too. Also, other people in ratings and reviews vouch that you are able do what they need you to do.

Reliability. You are consistently good in quality or performance both in routine circumstances as well as in hostile or unexpected situations. Customers know they can depend on you. They can trust you to be there when they need you. When you say you will do something, you do it, and if you cannot do it in a timely way you tell them and give them a compelling reason why you cannot meet their expectations.

Breaking trust happens when one or more of these three elements are *not* present. It does not necessarily mean that a person who has failed is morally depraved or wicked—it may simply mean the person is sincere and competent but not reliable. For example, a child may be perfectly sincere in saying he will bring his jacket home from school. You know he is quite competent to do so because he's done it in the past. But he's not reliable; sometimes the jacket comes home, sometimes it doesn't. Because he's your child, and because a forgotten jacket is not a serious lapse, you don't fire him. Instead, you put in place a system to ensure that the jacket usually comes home with him. Similarly, if failures tend to repeat themselves in your organization, what structures can you put in place to prevent them in the future?

In the same vein, someone can be sincere and reliable but not competent. A dyslexic child may spell sugar "suger" every single time she writes the word. You know she's sincere in wanting to spell sugar correctly, but she reliably spells it wrong, so her competency is quite low. She is going to fail to spell sugar every time, so you look for ways to improve that competency. If you have an employee who lacks the skill to do the job and fails as a result, you may need to determine whether you have prematurely advanced that person without the proper training. The logical follow-up would be to give that person the proper training to increase the competency that's needed to do the task.

Finally, some people are reliable and competent but not sincere. This usually surfaces as passive-aggressive behavior in the organization. They are capable of doing the work, and they are, in their way, reliable when they do it. But they may say they will do something, they may agree with the plan, but they do not perform and follow through, because it's not in their interest to do so. For example, an IT manager may commit to some programming for a corporate project, but go back to the office and, rather than pull the best person from another project, assign it to whoever happens to be free. The result: the work gets done, but it's not of the quality that people expected.

This last point about passive-aggressive behavior is especially tough in collaborative environments like Cisco's, which is why that organization spends a significant amount of time making sure people are aligned around shared goals. Ron Richie, VP of company positioning at Cisco, says that although he and coworkers rarely have disagreements, "when we do, one of the things that is important is that it is not *personal.* One of the keys of the culture of shared goals is that you have to be able to disagree on the substance of the issue without it being personal." Ron and his coworker may have dramatically different viewpoints about what to do, but at the end of the meeting, if the coworker's idea is bigger than Ron's idea, and the group agrees on it, Ron has to accept that the decision is not personal. And then he has to agree to back the idea fully and, most important, *be held accountable.*

Having regular dialog facilitated by social technologies allows the open leaders at Cisco and Kodak to have personal relationships with people throughout the company and, increasingly, with partners and customers as well. That allows them to identify the problems, address them, and still retain the relationship. If passive-aggressive behavior is a problem in your organization, make sure that you have the full commitment of repeat offenders before letting them return to their desks—and follow up with measurable expectations that are clearly laid out.

Let's move on to the imperative of learning from your mistakes—not just to avoid repeating them, but also to make your organization stronger.

LEARN FROM YOUR MISTAKES

A friend of mine worked for a nationally branded coffee roaster. Several years ago, the firm introduced a special coffee blend for the western U.S. market. The tagline was "Black as Night, Hot as Fire." Because at the time Westerners preferred their coffee light and relatively weak, the product flamed out completely. Three years later, when my friend was involved with another brand introduction, he wanted to research the earlier brand's experience. It was like doing research in a paranoid totalitarian state. Management had not only killed the product and the campaign but also destroyed virtually all evidence that the brand ever existed. What a shame—in its fear of failure, the corporation lost any opportunity to learn from the fiasco.

As a study of contrast, take a look at how Walmart was able to learn from its failures. It was the fall of 2007, and from the perspective of many social media watchers, Walmart's social media efforts were a disaster. In 2006, Walmart launched its own social network, "The Hub," in a futile attempt to challenge then-leader MySpace. The Hub lasted only ten weeks, mostly because the site used actors and models to populate content and continually pushed visitors to buy Walmart merchandise.[6] Then in September 2006, a folksy blog about a couple traveling across the country in a recreational vehicle and staying in Walmart parking lots was revealed to be supported by Walmart.[7] Significant media coverage of the broken trust followed.

But wait, there's more. Walmart came back in the fall of 2007 with a Facebook Group focused on back-to-school shopping.[8] Although well executed, the Facebook group was focused on fashion, whereas Walmart was known for low price, so there was a disconnect with the targeted college audience. Worse, Facebook members started protesting Walmart's labor practices via comments and turned the site against the company.

It looked like Walmart simply didn't get social technologies and never would.

But behind the scenes, there was a steely determination on the part of the company to engage with customers via social technologies, in much the same way that the company engaged with customers in their stores. With every setback, it learned something new and took it to heart. It learned that it needed to be consistent with their corporate mission of helping families save money. It also realized that there were significant detractors with concerns that would be difficult to address in an open forum, so it had to navigate social media carefully in order to have a truly open dialog with people without having the conversation hijacked by detractors.

So in December 2007 Walmart launched its CheckOutBlog.com, with Walmart employees like Susan Chronister, a buyer in the movie category, writing the posts. The site was a hit, as it shared the perspective of what the Walmart buyers were thinking as they selected merchandise for the stores. That was quickly followed by the addition of ratings and reviews from Bazaarvoice, and in December 2008 by the launch of the elevenmoms.com blog, written by a collection of mommy bloggers sharing tips on how to save money. Walmart was undaunted by its previous setbacks and not only as determined as ever to figure out a way to engage, but also willing to try many new things, even as it struggled to figure out what works. The result: although not active in all social media channels, Walmart is well on its way to mastering social technologies. As of the writing of this book, its Facebook members number more than half a million and it has dozens of employee Twitter accounts tweeting to customers.[9]

What is your organization's ability to learn from mistakes? Are you like the coffee company, sweeping failures into musty dark corners, hoping that by ignoring that they happened, you will help your organization quickly move onward? Or do you face failure head on, as Walmart did, focused by a common vision to learn from the experience so that you can achieve your goal? In the next section, I'll explain how you can focus your energy on recovering from failure so that it becomes second nature to you and your organization.

STRUCTURE YOUR RISK-TAKING AND FAILURE SYSTEMS

Let's get down to the nitty-gritty of how to create the structure and discipline that will give you and your organization the resilience you need to deal with failure. There are four processes and skills that you can build into your organization:

- Conducting post-mortems
- Preparing with worst-case scenarios
- Building in responsiveness
- Preparing yourself for the personal cost of failure

CONDUCTING POST-MORTEMS

Whereas Walmart learned from a series of failures, Johnson & Johnson experienced a large public failure that proved to be an excellent learning experience. In the fall of 2008, McNeil Consumer Healthcare posted a commercial on its motrin.com Web site in which a young mother says:[10]

> Wearing your baby seems to be in fashion. I mean, in theory it's a great idea. There's the front baby carrier, sling, schwing, wrap, pouch. And who knows what else they've come up with . . . But what about me? Do moms that wear their babies cry more than those who don't? I sure do! These things put a ton of strain on your back, your neck, your shoulders. Did I mention your back? I mean, I'll put up with the pain because it's a good kind of pain; it's for my kid. Plus, it totally makes me look like an official mom. And so if I look tired and crazy, people will understand why.

For six weeks, the ad appeared on the site with hardly a comment. But on Friday night, November 15, 2008, one baby sling–wearing mom took offence—to her, Motrin seemed to be saying that mothers who carried their babies in a sling did so just to be fashionable, akin to suffering a little to wear spike heels. As homemakerbarbi wrote: "I love my front carrier, and don't appreciate being told I look 'crazy' for baby-wearing. Bad job this time, Motrin."[11]

Within hours of the first tweet appearing on that Friday night, the ad and the hashtag "#motrinmom" became the most tweeted subject on Twitter. On Saturday, someone posted a nine-minute video on YouTube—screen shots of the outraged tweets interspersed with photos of moms carrying babies in slings.[12] The maelstrom continued to swirl throughout the weekend, and the tenor changed from outrage at Motrin to bemusement—bemusement about the lack of Motrin's response. Wasn't the company listening to what these outraged moms were saying about its product? Were those behind the ad *clueless*?

In fact, Motrin was caught off guard. When I asked about the Motrin Moms movement, Marc Monseau, director of social media for Johnson & Johnson, the parent company of Motrin's manufacturer McNeil Consumer Healthcare, told me that he was personally monitoring for mentions of Johnson & Johnson, but not all of the hundreds of sub-brands within the company. He recalled, "I only became aware of it when I received a call from a friend on Sunday who said, 'Have you seen what's being said about Motrin?' Once the brand team saw what was being said about the baby wearing, the organization really sprang into action very quickly. They pulled together and made some quick decisions."

Once alerted to the problem, Motrin immediately took the ad off its Web site, and Kathy Widmer, who at the time was VP of marketing at McNeil, wrote on the JNJBTW blog: "It was meant to engender sympathy and appreciation for all that parents do for their kids. We certainly didn't mean to offend moms through our advertising . . . On behalf of McNeil, I'm sorry if you found this advertisement insulting. We are in the process of removing it from our Web site . . . we have learned through this process—in particular, the importance of paying close attention to the conversations that are taking place online."[13] Kathy also reached out to some of the key mommy bloggers and started engaging with people on Twitter.

The event underscored the need for companies to listen to what is being said about their brands and businesses online. Monseau says, "Organizations need to be prepared for these kinds of situations so that if something like that happens that they can move much more rapidly . . . companies need to move in matters of minutes rather than hours or hours rather than days. In more traditional organizations where it can take up to twelve hours to come back to a traditional media request, you now need to make that much more streamlined."

But more important, engaging with social technology has become the concern of every division within Johnson & Johnson, and at a minimum, they are all beginning to monitor discussions themselves rather than relying on Monseau's corporate communications group. "There are more and more businesses taking a hard look at what they need to structure, to create a program, and at least beginning to listen to the conversation. The Motrin Moms situation really reinforced the importance of starting to really listen and to observe more carefully."

I hope that your organization doesn't need to go through a damaging experience like Motrin Moms to see the light, and that you will consider adopting a more proactive open strategy. But if your organization does encounter rough waters, consider how you will recover. The next section is about how to do that—creating a structure and system that promotes risk taking and learning from failures.

PREPARING WITH WORST-CASE SCENARIOS

If your organization is inherently fearful of failure, you may have to slowly and in stepwise fashion adjust the mind-set so that failure is at least anticipated and planned for, if not outright embraced. One way to do this is with worst-case scenario planning, in which you brainstorm all of the things that could possibly go wrong, get them out on the table, and put in place mitigation and contingency plans to reduce risk and anxiety.

This is exactly what Ford did to launch the Fiesta in the United States in 2009, which I discussed briefly in Chapter Four. You may recall that Ford gave a hundred new cars to ordinary citizens for six months, asking them to chronicle their experiences in social media. On the surface, Ford seemed to be inviting problems—what would happen if somebody crashed? What if somebody got injured? To prepare, Ford did all sorts of scenario planning and war gaming, mapping out all the possibilities they could imagine, and planned the response: who should be involved, who could be told, when, how. All of which paid off one Friday afternoon in May when one of the "agents" in Brooklyn reported his Fiesta was missing.

The car was a hot pink with polka dots, and only a fraction of the ninety-nine others in the United States looked the same, so it wasn't terribly difficult to identify, but because the police didn't have a record of towing it, they reported it stolen. The cars did contain a GPS tracking system, but it was not working well, and the last report had the car somewhere in southern Connecticut.

"We basically put out an APB on Twitter," recalled Scott Monty, Ford's global digital and multimedia communications manager. "Anybody in southern Connecticut on I-95 heading north, if you see a hot pink Fiesta with polka dots, let us know." On Saturday morning, the Fiesta was spotted in Georgetown, in Washington, D.C., but it turned out that it belonged to a different Fiesta agent who was graduating from Georgetown University that weekend. Monty immediately wrote on Twitter, "You'd better put her car back before she gets out of her ceremony."

Back in Brooklyn, the agent who had lost the car thought back to where he'd parked it, went to the New York impound lot on a hunch, and hoisted a friend up on his shoulders; his friend spotted the hot pink Fiesta in the middle of the yard. It turned out that the cars all had Michigan manufacturing license plates, so the towed

Fiesta wasn't in the lot it was supposed to be in. Ford was able to convince the New York City police that the agent was permitted to pay his parking ticket and redeem the car.

Although certainly not a typical "worst-case scenario," what could have turned out to be more than a minor inconvenience ended up not being a big deal at all, mostly because of Ford's preparation effort. They had prepared many different types of scenarios and were ready to respond very quickly through social media if necessary. But more than just being prepared for problems, the planning had one major effect—it gave Ford's management team confidence that if anything *did* go wrong, the team had thought through the consequences in a responsible manner, responses were thought through, and the risks were sufficiently minimized.

BUILDING IN RESPONSIVENESS

One of the benefits of Best Buy's employee-led innovation was a little monitoring program called Spy that allowed it to monitor mentions about the company.[14] CMO Barry Judge liked it so much that he had it installed as a rolling display on a large TV in his and CEO Brian Dunn's offices. It gave Judge and Dunn real-time access to unfiltered conversations, something that would have been difficult or impossible in the past.

Having the program highly visible meant that Judge could see what was happening, and one day in September 2008 what he saw was not good—something had ignited a firestorm. The giant electronics retailer intended to test a new rewards card program for its best customers. Rather than send it to 1,000 people in a test, however, the vendor had mistakenly sent the offer to 6.8 million customer email addresses. The message congratulated people for being a VIP and said that they qualified for the new Black reward card.[15] Best Buy's offer was followed almost immediately by an email that said, "Today, you may have inadvertently and inaccurately received the below message during an initial email testing process. We sincerely apologize for any inconvenience or confusion." Scores of the newly unqualified recipients immediately began to tweet furiously.

Judge swung into action and quickly started responding to people. On his blog he wrote, ". . . we screwed up the execution which makes me feel sick about the customer trust that we have impacted. I was going to say 'potentially impacted' but it is pretty hard to see how we look good on this, I know because I tried this line out on my boss."[16] His public response was human, direct, and sincere—the antithesis of the carefully crafted corporate statement one usually hears from a senior executive in response to a screwup. But more important, he looked for guidance, writing, "I feel like this dialogue is just a start. I encourage you to give me your POV on how we are dealing with this situation. I am learning fast and I thank those who are participating." Indeed, Judge continued to have a dialog with people about the Reward Zone mistake, from responding to comments in his blog post (which I encourage you to go and read at the link in the endnotes) to replying to upset customers on Twitter (which he had just started using a few weeks before).

What struck me is that Judge views social media as a constant opportunity to engage. He commented to me that he wants "to make it as easy as possible for people to complain." Rather than see this as a negative, he views each complaint as an opportunity to hear about all the daily mistakes and failures at Best Buy, in an effort not only to resolve those problems but also to make Best Buy better in the long run.

In a similar way, Stephen Elop, president of Microsoft's business solutions group, makes sure that he is creating a culture that sustains a positive attitude toward failures. He told me, "One of the points I make to people is to escalate bad news quickly, rapidly. If you think you are on the verge of failure, get help. Get it out on the table faster than you would have ever thought possible. The whole idea of 'never go to your boss without a solution to a problem' is nonsense. Take the problem in earlier, sooner, higher in the organization. Otherwise, you are wasting time and denying the organization at large the ability to bring the entire resources of the organization to help solve the problem.

If you come to me at the end and say we have completely failed and we are out of time, there is nothing I can do to help. So part of dealing with failure is making it OK to escalate earlier, sooner, faster, more aggressively."

Elop shared that a formative experience for his philosophy was working previously for a company that described itself as a "risk-taking organization," implying that it was willing to take risks, and therefore willing to fail. But a balancing value was "we are accepting of *new* mistakes." So Elop's first reaction when someone comes into his office with a problem, with a failure, is "What can I do to help?"—reducing the fear that someone would have in revealing problems. But once the crisis is over, Elop makes sure to close the loop, ensuring accountability by also asking "What have we learned?" By systematically putting this simple practice in place, Elop personally sets the tone for risk taking in his organization.

PREPARING FOR THE PERSONAL COSTS OF FAILURE

Every organization's leader has always worried about risk and failure—and should. It comes with the job description. But my impression is that personal failure has never been so exposed as it is with social media. If you fail, you can't hide it. You can't bury it as easily as you could in the past. We must therefore have a whole different attitude about failing—about trying something that doesn't work, but just as important, how you address your failure.

This happened to my colleague, Jeremiah Owyang, when he wrote a blog post discussing rumors of layoffs at technology company Mzinga and added, "I strongly recommend that any Mzinga clients or prospects stall any additional movement till they brief me next Monday."[17] He was criticized in subsequent comments and in many blog posts about abusing his position a leading thought leader and analyst in the space. One telling comment on his blog read, "I consider this absolute rumor-mongering. Posting unverified FUD onto the Internet AS AN ANALYST is irresponsible . . . This . . . seems to be intended to raise your profile."

Owyang quickly realized his mistake and posted an apology.[18] "Although I had the best intentions, I posted without complete enough information, which was a mistake on my part . . . I know that I have influence in the space and need to make sure that I do so responsibly . . . The comments are open, and I will continue to read and absorb all of the thoughtful and tough feedback, I'm listening."

I spoke with Owyang shortly after the incident. I could see that he was deeply chastened, but also very grateful for the people who reached out to him and gave him support and advice. Recalling the incident several months later, he described what he had learned: "You can put all of the policies and triages in place, but you don't know what it's like until you've experienced a major social assault. People will jump on the bandwagon and try to be hurtful, but you have to realize that those people don't matter. The friends to pay attention to are the people who reach out to you when you're down. The even better friends tell you what you did wrong and what you can do better next time."

Owyang encourages organizations to hire people with what he calls "scar tissue"—people who have been in the trenches of social media and have experienced the ups and downs. Because every time you put yourself out there, expose yourself, you become vulnerable, and it's a leap of faith that your network and community will be there to cushion the fall. Do yourself a favor and find yourself people with that scar tissue so that you won't have to walk the dark streets of failure on your own. They have been there, they understand what it's like, and they'll give you the support that you need to get out there again.

ACTION PLAN: PREPARING YOUR FAILURE PLAN

When it comes to using social technologies, I can guarantee you that at some point you will fail. Some of you will fail spectacularly, like some of the people you've seen in this book. But most of you will make less spectacular mistakes along the way, disappointing colleagues and customers with your inadvertent missteps and awkwardness. You will need to extend yourself, to be uncomfortable because you are moving into uncharted territory where you don't know the terrain, you don't know the rules, and, most important, you haven't developed confidence in your capabilities. But you must do this if you hope to develop these new relationships. These strong, positive relationships do not come overnight. Not in real life, not in our personal lives, and not in business. To engage in these social technologies at all requires a level of trust that when you open up, you will be well received.

So how do you take that first step? As I've said before, make it a small step. The key is to make the failure acceptable so that you aren't afraid to fail. Take small risks at the beginning, ones that your organization can tolerate, so that it can get comfortable with lots and lots of failures. But in addition, here are some other concrete ways to build resilience and recovery into you and your organization so that you feel comfortable taking risks:

- **AUDIT THE LAST FEW FAILURES YOU AND YOUR ORGANIZATION EXPERIENCED.** What went wrong? What could you do better? One recommendation I heard was that in a postmortem review, only a quarter of the time should be spent on discovering what went wrong, a quarter of the time on discussing what you learned, and the majority of the time on what the organization *will do next.*

(Continued)

(*Continued*)

- **KEEP A FAILURE FILE.** Just as you likely keep a file of your success, kudos, and letters of thanks, create a file of your failures—include what you learned and also the personal notes of encouragement and support. Refer to this file from time to time, as you will take pride in having overcome the failures, learn from your past missteps, and find comfort in the words of your friends. Ralph Heath writes in "Celebrating Failure" how he is "riveted" by the stories in his failure folder, observing, "I am more proud for having stepped up in the attempt to succeed than I am in my accomplishments."[19]

- **IDENTIFY RISK-TAKING TRAINING NEEDS.** Just as in sports and in life, you need to build up resilience over time—it doesn't come naturally. That's also the case with risk taking and failure recovery—you and your employees will need training and support on how to do this. Identify where you are weak; for example, if elephants so populate the room that they hamper conversation, focus on strengthening authentic communication skills. If managers routinely penalize people who make mistakes, consider coaching classes for executives.

- **BUILD FAILURE INTO YOUR PLANNING AND OPERATING PROCESSES.** Include worst-case scenario planning, and how you will use social media to respond to it, as a routine part of day-to-day planning, making it second nature to anticipate and prepare for failure. The corollary is putting in place the contingency plans to be able to deal with problems when they arise.

- **CREATE SUPPORT NETWORKS FOR THE INEVITABLE FAILURES.** As you saw earlier, failure can be a lonely place, so when someone fails in a visible way in your organization, make sure that there are mentors and peers who have been through similar experiences available and ready to provide support.

- **HAVE A BOTTLE OF YOUR FAVORITE ANTACID TABLETS ON HAND.** I say this half in jest, because you never truly conquer failure—you can only manage your response to it. That said, I think the most important asset you can bring is a strong stomach, and failing that, a big bottle of antacid. Dealing with failure gets easier over time, with the right resources, processes, and training, but that stomach-churning feeling never goes away completely. In fact, you will know that you are doing things just about right if there's a slightly queasy feeling in your stomach that comes with taking a risk, but you can also take comfort in knowing that you and your organization will be OK in the long run because of the preparations you have made. Failures are never easy, but I hope you weather your fair share of them well on the road to greater openness and success.

In the next chapter, we'll look at the journey that several companies have taken on the road to being open, and how their leaders were able to transform entrenched company cultures into flexible, responsive, and open organizations.

HOW OPENNESS TRANSFORMS ORGANIZATIONS

At this point, I hope you have a better understanding of what it means to be an open leader and how openness can benefit your organization. But as you ponder the prospect of being more open, you may be thinking that there is *no way* you could see your organization becoming more open. There are just too many obstacles, entrenched values, and cherished rituals to allow for change. What I'm talking about is that immovable mass called the *company culture* that likely stands in the way of being open.

T. E. Deal and A. A. Kennedy's classic *Corporate Cultures* defined organizational culture as "the way things get done around here," a reflection of the "specific collection of values and norms that are shared by people and groups in an organization and that control the way they interact with each other and with stakeholders outside the organization."[1]

Leaders establish these values not by what they say, but by the actions they reward and the behavior they punish. As Ralph Waldo Emerson wrote, "Every great institution is the lengthened shadow of a single man. His character determines the character of the organization." If the organization's leader sees no value in openness or sees more risk than benefit in it, the organization will not be open, regardless of internal agitation or competitive pressures.

I am going to assume, however, that if you have come this far with me, you *do* see both the value in and the need for greater openness. In fact, you may believe that in order for your organization to achieve audacious goals, the culture of the organization must evolve and be transformed, and so must your leadership. The hard part is how you drive greater openness, which, paradoxically, requires a great deal of centralized authority and command-and-control. Essentially, how do you control the process of becoming a more open organization?

In this chapter, I describe how a handful of organizations—Best Buy, Dell, Cisco, Procter & Gamble, the State Bank of India, and the U.S. Department of State—are driving transformation and change, opening up their cultures. These are huge organizations with, in some cases, centuries of tradition behind them, and just the thought of trying to transform those cultures is daunting. But in every case, courageous individuals are taking on the mantle of open leadership because they see it as the best way to achieve their transformation goal. They don't adopt openness for the sake of openness—instead, they apply it pragmatically and skillfully.

The purpose of this chapter is to tie together the ideas I've explored in the preceding pages, ranging from open strategy formulation to the nuances of open leadership, so that you can envision how you will lead your organization through a transformation. Take note of how the values and norms of each individual open leader, as well as the existing culture, formed the basis for the transformation. Note how each organization restructured itself to be able to support and sustain openness. You'll see that four major themes emerge, which I explore in each of the case studies.

- *Values drive the vision.* There's nothing like a pressing deadline to focus the mind, and in many of the case studies the company faced a brutal market situation that demanded a new approach. For others, an overarching vision of what needed to be done strategically formed the underpinning of the open transformation process. After slipping in market share for decades, the State Bank of India made it a priority to regain the old glory of its past and become a market leader again. And Cisco's collaboration successes stem from the company's ability to set aside personal agendas to pursue shared goals.
- *Leaders set the tone and example for others to follow.* In every case, a leader carves out the path for being open by personally exemplifying openness in action. Best Buy's leadership embraced being open and systematically broke down obstacles that kept frontline employees from participating, including continually stressing the need for experimentation and acceptance of taking risks.
- *Extending the old culture into the new.* If culture is made up of norms and values, then all of these organizations had to create new processes to define how new relationships would work. For example, Procter & Gamble's "grow from within" culture had to be modified to accept that innovations could come from outside the company, but they also used the opportunity to highlight and focus the company on what it did best: developing and pushing products into markets.
- *Systems and structure sustain the transformation.* Supporting the new culture are new incentive and recognition systems, as well as revamped processes and procedures that govern interactions both internal and external to the organization. Dell's continued success and the State Department's initial entry into social media are the direct result of their thinking carefully about how systems, ranging from sandbox covenants to the deployment of collaboration tools, create the values and norms that define the foundations of culture.

So if you believe that you and your organization need to upend your culture with openness to achieve business goals, read on to learn how these organizations are making it happen.

STATE BANK OF INDIA: MAKING THE ELEPHANT DANCE

The State Bank of India (SBI) is the second largest bank in the world, with over two hundred thousand employees in ten thousand branches, and operations in thirty-two countries. Founded in 1806, it's over two hundred years old and has a long, proud history—which also means that changing traditions and processes will be tough. On top of that, as a government-owned entity, employees are given guaranteed employment for life, so any type of restructuring or transformation had to include every employee, with no possibility of layoffs.

By 2006, SBI found itself confronting a number of problems. It was losing market share in both deposits and loans to liberalized and deregulated competitors, the share dropping from 35 percent in the early 1970s to around 15 percent. It was still growing, but significantly more slowly than competitors. Its outdated processes and the intensifying competition were taking their toll, as competitors closed in on SBI's market position. And SBI was no longer the first choice of young and affluent customers, who characterized the bank as old and staid.[2]

Into this sad state of affairs walked Om Bhatt, who was appointed chairman of SBI in 2006. An employee of the bank since 1972, he remembered the glory days and believed that the bank could return to its previous state of leadership. "I know that this organization in the past was highly respected in India," Bhatt told me. "There was a great deal of pride in the organization, and knowing the people, I felt that we could do it again. But I knew that unless I could communicate with every employee what was in my head and in my heart, they would not understand, and we would not be aligned. Even if I gave them detailed instructions on what to do, they wouldn't follow them unless their heart and soul was aligned with me."

So Bhatt set out on an ambitious program to transform the organization, with open information sharing and distributed decision making as the centerpieces. He started with the senior leadership of the bank, taking them on a five-day offsite where the first thing he did was to show them, of all things, the movie *The Legend of Bagger Vance*, about a golfer who had lost his swing. The movie acted as a metaphor for further discussion about how the bank could get its "swing" back, with the added benefit that it was based on the *Bhagavad Gita*, a sacred Hindu story about selfless service.[3] Bhatt was able to draw connections between the bank's situation and the movie, and also draw on deep cultural Indian values to bring hope to his executive team. Bhatt recalled the conversation: "The thought was that setbacks happen to all types of people, but they are able to get their swing back. There was no reason why the bank couldn't get its swing back as well."

The next day, Bhatt gave a "state of the bank" presentation that laid out the bank's dire situation, and he did not spare the executive team, which was largely responsible for running the bank over the previous decade. But rather than cast blame, Bhatt asked for help. He recalled, "Any of these gentlemen could have been sitting in my chair, so I asked them to work with me as equals and recognize that I could not do my job without their ideas and conviction. My openness and transparency about the situation and the admission of my limits touched a chord in most of them."

From there, Bhatt crafted a strategy for the rejuvenation of the bank, detailing fourteen different initiatives. But Bhatt and his team realized that the plan would be worthless unless they could secure the support of the employees. The bank developed a program called Parivartan ("transformation" in Hindi) to candidly inform employees about the state of the bank. Although it took seven months to develop the program, Parivartan was rolled out in just one hundred days to 138,000 employees. An entire bank branch was closed so that all of the employees could attend the training together as a team, rather than as individuals. Why the need for speed? Bhatt realized that if he did it slowly, skeptics could undermine his efforts.

Moreover, Bhatt had only a four-year term as chairman, and he was already well into his second year. The response was immediate; Bhatt recalled, "The employees all asked us, 'Why didn't you tell us this before?' They were grateful that we told them the truth about how bad things were."

In addition to establishing the need for change, Parivartan also acted as a call to duty among all employees. During the sessions, directors encouraged and gathered feedback from the employees. Some employees vented their anger at the managers, many complained about customers or management, and a few tentatively offered suggestions. Bhatt personally met with two thousand assistant general managers, with the longest session running over ten hours. During the discussions, he would mostly listen and take notes, and at the end provide some feedback. Bhatt recalled for me, "My goal was to make them feel that this was *their* organization, that the organization needs *them*. So I would ask them, 'Why are you not doing anything about these problems? What is it that stops you from doing something about it? Is it the lack of knowledge? Is it that you don't have the time, the courage, or the conviction? You are telling me, the chairman, that customer service is a problem. But I can't solve it. I can't tell *you* how to solve it.' My point to them is that *you* are the most important person in the organization."

Bhatt realized that in order for this transformation to succeed, he would have to give each employee a sense of empowerment that had never existed before. He used open information sharing to jump-start things, followed up quickly with pushing down decision making authority to the frontlines. To further open the company, SBI set up special blogs for top management and other key officials to create informal communication channels with the rank and file. SBI redesigned its Internet site and made it more employee-friendly and informative. It established newsletters (*Colleague, NBG Bulletin, Customer Care, Wholesale Banking Bulletin,* and more) to disseminate information. It provided each employee with an SBI email ID to enhance communication with customers.

The result has been palpable. Parivartan caught the employees' imagination. Some described it as a tsunami that took the bank by storm; others praised it as an eye-opener and the best program they had attended in their entire career; some wondered why it hadn't happened ten years earlier. Bhatt says employees are "feeling a lot of pride now in the organization. They walk a little taller, work a bit harder, and contribute more. They don't ask for overtime, and they sit in the office late. They may not be able to help customers all the time. But at least they try."

But even more tangible are the business results. A study revealed a significant improvement (20 percent) in customer service and reorientation of employee attitudes and a 20 percent increase in customer satisfaction. More significantly, deposits grew 33.4 percent in 2009, net profit grew 36 percent, and net interest income grew 22.6 percent.[4] The bank increased market share to almost 20 percent and has won numerous industry awards, such as Bank of the Year in India, for its turnaround.

I was curious how Bhatt, who had spent his entire career with the bank, could have developed such a different point of view about how to empower employees, so I asked him where his optimistic view came from. He told me, "It was intuition, and it came from my own personal conviction and value system. I really believe that any person is capable of doing far more than what we normally do, that most of us deliver only a small fraction of what we are capable. I see that our two hundred thousand employees are capable of doing extraordinary things, but the question was how to enable them." What Bhatt did was possible because of his own personal value system that gave him the confidence to reach out and let go so that his employees could grab on.

Dr. Prasad Kaipa, a professor at the Indian School of Business in Hyderabad and an advisor to SBI, observed that Bhatt is not only optimistic about people, but also deeply philosophical, and he believes that goals can be achieved only with the support of many other people, especially during ambiguous and turbulent times. He observed, "Bhatt did not give up control. He let go of control." Kaipa further explained, "For Bhatt, it comes easily to look at igniting the genius inside people. It's a safe bet for him, but it looks risky for people who are ultra rational." It was very clear from my discussion with Bhatt that he was in control of the bank, and there was also a confidence that if he opened up, he would be able to retain control while empowering employees to take responsibility.

What impressed me most about SBI's transformation is how effectively Bhatt used open leadership to make change happen. As a leader, he clearly explained the challenge facing the bank—and also the way forward. He appealed to values widely recognized and highly regarded in Indian culture to connect people to the company's goals. He optimistically believed that people on the front lines could change their mind-sets for the better and, when empowered, would do the right thing. But he also held the same executives, managers, and employees accountable by putting in place clear goals, structure, and measurement.

CISCO: ORGANIC GROWTH OF COLLABORATION TAKES TIME

I've written in earlier chapters about Cisco's collaboration transformation, so I'll just reiterate some of the key points: John Chambers has made collaboration and distributed decision making the centerpiece of the company's operations, allowing Cisco to move at astonishing speed (see Chapter Two). Technology supports the collaboration, and Cisco has been meticulous at measuring the impact and benefits (Chapter Five). But collaboration is hard, especially for existing stakeholders, so Cisco made sure that its boards and councils included key decision makers who jointly led the team (Chapter Six). Behind all of this was the collaborative leadership of John Chambers (Chapter Seven), who used shared goals as a catalyst (Chapter Eight).

Obviously, I'm impressed by what Cisco has done to promote openness in its organization. But I want to take a closer look at how Chambers and his team changed the culture, because many executives look at what Cisco is trying to do with sixty-five thousand employees, then say wistfully, "I wish we could do that." But it isn't as simple as putting in place the structure of boards and councils, or promoting collaboration and shared goals. Ron Ricci, Cisco's VP of positioning, commented on what Cisco has been trying to do: "Over the last eight years, we have been on a journey to move from a culture of internal competition to a culture of shared goals. To do that, we had to examine what the values are that sustain us in the marketplace, and consider how we create a collaborative process that is organic to Cisco. We could never have brought anyone from the outside to develop the board and council model that we use, because it had to be organic to who we are."

It was surprising to see that it took *that* long for Cisco to get to where it is today, but also understandable. Chambers and Ricci both recounted the many times they had tried a new approach—sometimes getting it wrong, other times, by luck, getting it right: for example, stumbling upon the need to have *two* leaders for each board or council, or rolling out technology to support their collaboration goals. But more than anything, Chambers took the time to bring his new way of thinking to his executive leadership. Chambers told me, "It took me almost four years to get this belief across my top forty-two execs, so it was slow going. While I am an impatient person by nature, I was remarkably patient but also combined it with a sense of urgency and nudged people along the way."

To create the new culture, Chambers realized that Cisco had to develop a new reward system tied to the behavior he wanted to promote. That was done by establishing the shared goals that everyone is committed to—and rewarded by. "They were no longer an engineer or a salesperson or a manufacturing person or a lawyer," Chambers explained. "What mattered is how they thought as a team to achieve goals." But just as important, Chambers put in place the structure and discipline needed to be collaborative. "We needed to create a common culture in terms of this empowerment, and understand what it means and what it doesn't mean." So Chambers systematized participation of his top leadership in the collaborative groups. "We found that we had to give people access, not just to the same information [we] had, but we also had to let them experience the decision making part in different ways. Now I am moving our players around with tremendous speed and learning that allows them to make decisions much more effectively than ever before."

As I mentioned previously, John Chambers is effectively cloning his decision making process and judgment, institutionalizing a way of making decisions so that he doesn't have to be in the room to do it. With the structure, discipline, and process in place, Chambers, like Bhatt, was comfortable and confident about giving other people control. But there is no doubt that Chambers is very much in the driver's seat at Cisco, saying, "Make no mistake about it. In implementing collaboration teamwork, I was command-and-control. My job was to set out the vision, differentiate strategy, and then empower a team to make it happen." This is not to say that Cisco's approach is anywhere near perfect. But as Chambers continues to roll out his collaboration imperative to more and more executives and employees, this culture of collaboration will trickle its way down throughout the ranks.

The lesson I take away from Cisco's transformation, especially in contrast to urgency at SBI, is that the process can take time and patience. Chambers was able to leverage his secure position as CEO to figure out, primarily by trial and error, what being open meant at Cisco. And it wasn't until the technology came along to support collaboration that he was able to accelerate his efforts. As you contemplate the transformation you want to create, consider your time line and position within the company. Do you have the luxury of a secure position from which you can advocate transformation over a period of months and years? Because any transformation is going to take a long time and require that you find the unique formula of push-and-pull that works for your organization.

BEST BUY: RELEASING THE PASSION OF ZEALOTS

Stories often form the basis for culture, and Best Buy's story concerns a force of nature—literally. The company was founded in 1966 as an audio retailer called Sound of Music in Saint Paul, Minnesota. It grew to several stores in the Minneapolis-Saint Paul area, expanding into video equipment, went public in 1969, and was growing at a comfortable pace. Then in 1981, a tornado tore apart its Roseville, Minneapolis store. But rather than see it as a terrible loss, the company held a "tornado sale" of the rescued merchandise, labeling them the "best buy."

The impact of that tornado was tremendous—company leadership recognized the value of creative destruction and capitalizing quickly on opportunities. "What came out of the tornado was Best Buy," said Gary Koelling, director of emerging media technology. "Most of our senior leaders have roots in the store, so the story is core to how they approach day-to-day operations. Anything could destroy us, so let's rebuild ourselves on a regular basis, and leave enough slack in the system so that if an opportunity comes along, we can take advantage of it." Best Buy CEO Brian Dunn earned his leadership stripes in just such an environment, so it was very consistent with the company culture that when the opportunity came to leverage social technologies and become more open, Dunn and others leapt at the opportunity.

That opportunity presented itself when Michele Azar (whom I introduced in Chapter Eight), then a member of the merchandising team, attended the Web 2.0 Expo in the spring of 2007. "I saw the whole world transforming, and we were not even talking about it within our company," recalled Azar. "I was sitting on the conference floor, and I called the senior leader of our eCommerce team and said, 'I need to join your team.'" What Azar saw was the equivalent of a tornado headed toward Best Buy, and she wanted to make sure that the company stayed ahead of that oncoming storm.

Azar is a perfect example of the right person being in the right place at the right time. Previously, she was a VP in the customer centricity growth group, and she was trusted by many people around the company. Once on the Internet team, Azar wasted no time pulling together an open strategy for the company. One thing she had going for her was the strong entrepreneurial culture at Best Buy, one that stakes the future of the company on employee-led innovation. Azar proudly stated, "You can walk into a store and speak to a Blue Shirt and they will look you in the eye and say, 'I am responsible for growing this company at a local level.'"

But she realized that some significant barriers stood in the way of these same employees becoming more open. Best Buy had brought in many different thought leaders and social media experts (myself included), but except for a few individuals, the idea hadn't caught fire with employees. Azar realized there was a lot of friction in the system that prevented people from taking needed initiative, so she set up a plan to systematically address each of those obstacles.

The first step was to address the friction of hierarchy, especially the concern that executives and management weren't that interested in open engagement—or would actually put a stop to it. A set of open principles was written and broadly distributed around the company to get more people's heads around what it means to be open, answering concerns such as "I am scared; how do I act, how do I engage?"[5] Azar also brought in Peter Hirshberg from The Conversation Group to help depict the movement to open and make the case for change through a series of videos of people, both internal and external to Best Buy, talking about how they are open and use social technologies. Finally, she encouraged executives like then-CEO Brad Anderson and CMO Barry Judge to become more accessible; for example, responding to questions by frontline employees on Twitter or internal social networks.

The result: by not only hearing about the importance of being open but actually seeing their colleagues engaged in open dialog with senior executives, employees began to overcome their hesitancy to engage. Judge recalled one such interaction: "I was in a meeting with three hundred people and an employee raised his hand,

and based on what he was saying, I realized that I knew him very well from Twitter. Because he works in IT on BestBuy.com, I never would have met that guy if it hadn't been for Twitter. He wasn't in marketing, but he was more passionate and engaged about what we were doing in marketing than the marketing people were."

Azar's second step was to remove friction that impeded the use of data and technology by putting these things close to where people could actually use them. One major advance was the development of Remix, Best Buy's application programming interface (API) that allows anyone to tap into the company's entire online product catalog and create custom applications.[6] Remix was originally designed to engage third-party sites, but it had an unintended consequence— employees started creating applications as well. Azar explained, "An employee in Florida decided to build a better home theater recommendation tool with the API. He didn't need to schedule a meeting, didn't need to ask for permission, and didn't have to launch an official IT project to get access to the data. He just had access."

But the last and most important friction removed was the fear of failure. The easy access to the data and technology, as well as to executives and managers, meant that experiments were created and tested, and that feedback was given, very quickly. Ben Hedrington, who works on Bestbuy.com, connected with Azar early on and created innovations like Spy, which monitors mentions across social media. One day Hedrington showed a new tool called ConnectTweet, which could aggregate tweets from hundreds of Twitter accounts. His goal was to let "Best Buy employees speak on behalf of Best Buy on its Twitter accounts." Best Buy decided to take ConnectTweet to another level and invited customers to come and ask questions; the collective force of Best Buy would then try to answer. Twelpforce was born.

When it launched in July 2009, Twelpforce was positioned as a way to provide customer service from potentially thousands of Best Buy employees. John Bernier, the manager of Twelpforce, explained, "We tapped into those employees who are most passionate about this space and this way of communicating, and leveraged them to give people access to all the knowledge that we have stored within us." At the time this book went to press, 2,200 Best Buy employees were participating regularly on twitter.com/twelpforce.

Twelpforce was not without its risks and detractors. Barry Judge wrote in a blog post, "Twelpforce is obviously an experiment. A very public one. Twelpforce can be a catalyst to think very differently across our company about customer service. No longer is customer service a department but something that all of us can do."[7] Shortly, however, stories appeared in which employees were exposed as not providing correct advice, pushing their own points of view (which were not always professional), and sharing inappropriate personal information. But rather than pull Twelpforce or restrict access, Best Buy increased its training and gave direct feedback to people so that they would avoid those problems in the future.

The long-term benefit of Twelpforce remains to be seen, as employees begin to develop a following of their own. They may attract followers because they are experts on a particular product or topic or because they create a group of loyal followers who regularly come into the local physical store. By making possible a relationship with a Best Buy employee in the store, Best Buy is changing how it will conduct business in the future, one Blue Shirt at a time.

PROCTER & GAMBLE: STRUCTURING OPENNESS

At the beginning of 2000, P&G was stumbling. It had issued two profit warnings, revenue growth had slid to 3 percent to 4 percent a year, and seven of its ten largest brands were losing market share. In June 2000, the board of directors took an action unprecedented in its history: it fired the chairman and CEO and replaced him with A. G. Lafley (who retired in February 2010).

Lafley, who began his P&G career after earning a Harvard MBA, realized that P&G was introducing fewer and fewer successful new products, taking longer and longer between introductions, and spending more and more on research and development. The innovation machine was busted, yet as Lafley wrote in his book *The Game Changer,* coauthored with Ram Charan, "We knew that innovation would be the key to winning over the medium and long term . . . With this in mind, we looked at what we believed would be the key enablers or drivers of an innovation strategy; the drivers that would create an innovation-led operation and build an innovation culture; the drivers that would result in game-changing innovation that would touch more consumers and improve more lives."[8]

To repair P&G's innovation machine, Lafley put the consumer at the center of everything the company does, opened P&G up to outside ideas, and began thinking about innovation in new ways to do what had always been done. Lafley recognized that P&G was amazing at taking new ideas and bringing them to market—but that the engine inside of P&G couldn't keep up. Jeff Weedman, VP of global business development and the person primarily responsible for driving outside innovation at P&G, put it this way: "We have nine thousand great scientists at P&G, but our estimates are that there are about two million scientists outside of P&G who are doing work that is relevant to the company, and many of them are in countries we may not have considered, like China or Russia." If the company could connect with any and every source of innovation available—basically, becoming agnostic about the origin of the idea—they could then develop the scientists' creations through manufacturing, product design, packaging, branding, marketing, and distribution—the stuff P&G is really good at.

Thus was born the "Connect + Develop" program, which includes a portal at pgconnectdevelop.com. Opening up to the outside for the first time in its 173-year history was a significant cultural change and challenge because P&G had a strong "promote from within" philosophy. People traditionally joined P&G shortly out of school and stayed until retirement. New ideas had *always* come from people internally, and it could have been seen as a sign of failure to use an external idea. The challenge was to move the company from its disdain of "not invented here" products—a stubborn belief that no external idea could ever be good enough—to a "proudly found else-where" mind-set, by putting in place the right infrastructure and incentives. Lafley made it a virtue to find and adapt outside inno-vation, and set as an official strategic goal to source half of all new innovations externally within the next decade. But just as important, Lafley and other executives became role models themselves for the new attitude, constantly asking questions like, "Did you look out-side for ideas? Have you thought about partnerships?" And they also started using the ability to be open to the outside as a criterion for promotion, making it clear that the way to progress upward and be successful in the company was to exhibit these new open behaviors.

Lafley did something early on to exemplify this behavior himself. He showed up unannounced at a P&G alumni event in Chicago and started engaging these former employees in idea generation. Nathan Estruth, VP and general manager of P&G FutureWorks, recalled, "We had never really engaged openly with what is really one of our strongest assets, the alumni network of people who absolutely love this company and who will bend over backward to help us because they are still, in their hearts, P&Gers. We turned what could have been a weakness called insularity into a strength." It was Lafley's first foray into crafting outside partnerships, and by starting with a small, safe, and known group, he was able to bridge the transition for many nervous employees.

On the Connect + Develop Web site, there's opportunity for peo-ple to submit ideas (almost four thousand ideas were submitted in 2009). There's also a "needs list" of innovations that P&G is look-ing for (such as "All-day facial beauty without shine"). On the sur-face, this seems like a surefire way for competitors to figure out what P&G is trying to do! Chris Thoen, director of global open innova-tion office, agrees that this seems counterintuitive, but explained, "It's a two-way street. If we don't say what we are looking for, people are not going to come to us with potential solutions. So we had to become comfortable showing our needs in a way that we don't necessarily give away all our jewels and all our secrets, but provide enough information to potentially interested parties that they can come and provide solutions to us."

Lafley also made a wise move in finding internal P&G innovations that could be licensed to other companies and even to competitors. Jeff Weedman heads up this team; he established rules that internally protect ideas for a short time but then make them automatically licensable after a few years as a way to monetize innovations for those divisions. The best example of how a licensing deal can work to the researchers' benefit is P&G's agreement with Clorox, a direct competitor, which licensed the technology from P&G to make the GLAD Press'n Seal wrap. Not only did P&G license the technology, but it also took a 20 percent stake in the overall GLAD business. The technology was obviously valuable, but it was underutilized at P&G. The division that developed the technology gets to keep the licensing fees, which it can then turn around and use for more research and development.

To date, there are one thousand licensing deals in place; in approximately 40 percent of the technology deals from P&G are licensed out, and in about 60 percent the technology is licensed into the company. Deals with other companies generate over $500 million in annual sales for P&G, and $3 billion in other companies' sales are derived from P&G assets and intellectual property.[9] And more than half of P&G's products have a component that was sourced externally, up from less than 10 percent in 2001.

But Weedman, for one, believes that there's still a great deal of room for improvement. He said, "If you went to our Web site, it was in English, and it's shortsighted to think that to be innovative you have to communicate in English. P&G now has added Chinese and Japanese versions of the Connect + Develop site, and aims to have it soon be available in more languages."

A.G. Lafley and his team demonstrated insightful and courageous leadership in opening up P&G, and they did so by understanding and appealing to the strong, capable culture that already existed in the company. But rather than view that culture as insular and close-minded, they took the best of it—close-knit communications, global consistency, and shared values—and leveraged it with outside technologies and opportunities. If you face a strong existing culture, you'll have to think about ways to redirect and bend the best parts of it to your transformation goal, rather than trying to subsume it under a new fragile set of norms and values.

DELL: WHERE DIRECT DRIVES THE CULTURE

Let's look now at Dell Computer, whom I've mentioned several times throughout this book. In so many ways, Dell is now a poster child for being open and for the use of social technologies. But they weren't always this way. In fact, for a while in the summer of 2005, it was exactly the opposite—Dell was being pilloried for not "getting" that transparency and engagement mattered. Let's go back to the situation that summer that led to what is known as "Dell Hell."

The crisis erupted when journalism professor and popular blogger Jeff Jarvis attempted to get Dell to fix his new laptop. Jarvis had paid extra for on-site service, but Dell made him send the laptop back for repair anyway. When Dell returned it, it still didn't work properly. Jarvis complained to Dell through every avenue he could find, online and off, blogging every step of the way, and chronicling his descent into "Dell Hell."[10] Jarvis's blog postings attracted a flood of comments from other dissatisfied customers. Within a few days, mainstream media outlets had picked up the story, galvanizing the discontent into a full-blown crisis. A blogger wrote that he learned that Dell monitored blogs and forums but had a policy of "look, don't touch." Even if Dell employees noted the complaints, they never joined the online conversations, nor did they get in touch with the complainers.

I asked Manish Mehta, VP of social media and community at Dell, what had happened that summer—why hadn't Dell been willing to engage? Mehta explained that Dell had always believed in the direct model, and that "if you had an issue with Dell, you would contact Dell through an 800 number. So we falsely assumed that the existing communication channels supported talking to customers directly, and were going to be able to handle issues like Dell Hell that emerged. What we didn't recognize was that this was truly a unique medium."

This was Dell's "Aha!" moment, the realization that the company's traditional way of doing business had to change. In February 2006, Lionel Menchaca, a long-time public relations professional at Dell, started reaching out to bloggers who were writing about problems with their Dell machines. Supporting Lionel was a team of customer and technical support experts, capable of taking on any issues. Dell wasn't just going to engage people in social media; it was bringing its business operations into this new channel.

After four months of intense listening and resolving problems, Dell was ready to take another step into engagement with blogging. Menchaca, who became Dell's chief blogger, recalled, "It became very clear through that listening what the core issues we needed to address were. And most important, I knew that I could blog about whatever customers want to talk about, even if it is negative, because we had Michael's support."

Michael, of course, is Michael Dell, the founder of the company. Although he was not the CEO at the time, he was watching closely and offering continual support to these nascent open efforts. And that support was needed right from the start. The first few posts that appeared in July 2006 were very product focused, with managers talking about products like the XPS 700 gaming system. The problem was that just a week before, a Dell notebook had spontaneously erupted in flames at a conference in Osaka Japan.[11] So blog visitors didn't want to talk about the XPS 700; they wanted to know what was up with exploding Dell laptops!

Many people criticized Dell for its early blogging efforts, using it as more evidence that Dell just simply didn't understand how to be open, authentic, and transparent. Menchaca took the criticism to heart and started making changes immediately. But the watershed moment came with his post of July 13, 2006, entitled simply

261

"Flaming Notebook."[12] In the short, hundred-word post, Menchaca set the tone for a new type of relationship, one centered on dialog and information sharing. It turned out that the lithium ion batteries used in Dell notebooks—as well as most other notebooks made by other manufacturers—needed to be recalled. Menchaca used the blog to give updates about the battery recall, respond to questions in the comments, and proactively share information with customers.

Dell was off and running, to the amazement of many industry watchers. But to Menchaca and the rest of the team, it felt like they were coming home. It was natural for Dell to call on the core company value of being "direct" to drive the goal of being more open, and I believe this is one of the key reasons why Dell has been so successful at being open—it's in their DNA.

In January 2007, Michael Dell returned to the CEO position, and he quickly refocused the organization on engaging directly with customers. One example of the company redefining the relationships was Michael Dell's personal push for IdeaStorm, the site I discussed in Chapter Two, where people can submit, vote, and comment on ideas for Dell to adopt. Richard Binhammer, senior manager at Dell, recalled how IdeaStorm was started: "We were not sure what direction it was going to take, and I was worried. What if someone had a great idea—how were we going to be able to close the loop? How are we going to be able to manage all types of ideas that were going to come through? And Michael Dell just brushed aside those concerns and said, 'Don't worry. If it fails, we will learn and we will try again.' He's willing to support employees who are eager to test or experiment, to learn quickly and fail fast. It has been fantastic." I believe that kind of leadership support and commitment from the very top sets the stage for the company's initial foray into being open and also sustains it as the efforts mature.

By October 2007, the company had moved so far along that when Jeff Jarvis was invited to visit the Dell headquarters, he not only readily accepted the invitation, but also wrote in his blog post describing the visit, ". . . it's a big deal that a company that was vilified as the worst at blogs, social media, and customer relations in the broad sense is now, one could argue, the best at this. The company's executives wouldn't acknowledge this, but I wonder whether falling so far is just what set them up to be so bold in the blogosphere."[13] Although I wouldn't go so far as to say that you should set yourself up for a big fall in order to jump-start your social media efforts, I do believe that it helped focus Dell on the fundamental problem—that it hadn't grasped the fact that relationships had changed.

Although having a leader like Michael Dell is a huge advantage when undergoing a transformation, the team at Dell also made sure that systems and structures were in place to sustain and spread openness and engagement throughout the organization. Manish Mehta describes it as the inhalation and exhalation of the organization, saying, "In the beginning a lot of our efforts were run from the center—everything from governance and strategy to operations and resources. We then exhaled some of the knowledge out to the business units, where they started to experiment and test. We then inhaled it back in a bit as the experiments started to go awry."

One example is the social media and community governance council chaired by Mehta, which consists of representatives from each business unit and meets weekly. The council owns the social media strategy for the entire company, but each business unit in turn has its own council that implements the strategy throughout the division. Menchaca reflected on where the company is today in terms of its transformation: "We're taking what we have learned over the past few years in the central greenhouse, and we are now replanting all those pots all over the organization. We are scaling social media by making it part of everybody's job."

Transformation at Dell was a jarring process at the beginning, but made less so over time because of the leadership's ability to leverage deep-seated values of connecting directly with customers. But I also believe that the company's commitment to codifying and structuring being open—while at the same time remaining open to rapid changes and iterations—was a key to its moving forward so aggressively. Notably, although Dell has accomplished so much, there is also great humility in the organization—and recognition that they still have much to learn. Spend any time with Lionel Menchaca and his colleagues, or read their posts and tweets, and you realize that Dell has been successful in its transformation because these open leaders personally set the tone to be a learning organization, eager to continue the transformation process.

U.S. DEPARTMENT OF STATE: TRANSFORMING DIPLOMACY

Our last example is a study in progress, with the transformation more about changing the overall relationship between the organization and its constituents. The U.S. Department of State is using openness in pursuit of its Public Diplomacy mission—improving diplomatic relationships with the rest of the world. When Secretary Hillary Clinton came into office, she had the support of President Barack Obama to make government more transparent, collaborative, and participatory. Lovisa Williams, the deputy director of the Office of Innovative Engagement in the International Information Program Bureau at the Department, recalled, "When the secretary first came into the Department, on the very first day when she walked in the door, she said that social media is important and that it was something she was willing to advocate on our behalf."

Williams faced an uphill battle, though, as government bureaucracy rarely tackles reorganization or reengineering of its processes. Add to that the Department's security protocols, privacy concerns, and an international environment that isn't always receptive to American outreach, and you have a mentality that quashes experimentation and risk taking. Williams recalled the early days, trying to get a foothold in the Department: "I would run around saying, 'Please, try my social media Kool-Aid, you will like it!' And I would get fifty doors slammed in my face, pretty much every day. People all around me were saying, 'No, I'm not interested, this is crazy!'"

But she persisted and was able to find a few people in different areas willing to try something new.

In particular, she found a foothold in the diplomatic corps stationed overseas, Foreign Service Public Affairs Officers and Information Resource Officers. These diplomats were trying to reach out to ordinary people who have never been reached out to before, to extend the existing relationship beyond face-to-face engagement to one of building communities around common topics and interests. The challenge for them was how to reach more people with fewer resources. But also, how could they get feedback from people to not only demonstrate transparency but also influence real policy?

One thing that Williams' team did was to develop a Social Media Field Guide for Facebook pages, making it easy for embassies to create their own pages that comply with all policy and legal issues.[14] One of the most active is the U.S. Embassy Jakarta page, which is written in the local language and has almost twenty thousand fans.[15] Williams published a social media field guide that provides detailed do's and don'ts on how to engage with people, but for the most part the offices have the language expertise and cultural sensitivity to know what is appropriate for their situations and geographical location. Information security became a nonissue once it became clear that the staff was posting only information that was being developed for public consumption—there was little risk if it was compromised, and the cost of developing and maintaining this information was marginal.

The primary risk the organization faced was loss of reputation. Williams explained, "International relationships sometimes change very quickly, so we always have to be thinking about situations. The good thing is that everybody in the Department—from the secretary down through to the janitors—is trained to be a diplomat. You are expected to have a certain presence, to be very diplomatic about everything that you do. This is part of our 'corporate culture.' It's especially true for Public Affairs Officers who are very accustomed to working with the public and having little to no control over an event. An example would be a press conference in the local town square. We cannot control who attends, their reaction, or what they will say. The same is true for relationships online." Extending the diplomatic culture to the online space helped many staffers get over their fear of being open, as they were able to relate to something they were already familiar with.

But the biggest impact that I saw within the Department of State was how it started to use social technologies as a way to connect with people in new and innovative ways. When President Obama visited Ghana as the first black American President, the Department ran a program inviting Africans to use their mobile phones to text message questions to President Obama, to which he would respond in a radio program.[16] Those responses were recorded in both video and audio format and distributed to radio stations throughout Ghana and neighboring countries.[17] And as an experiment, a map mashing up the locations of the texted questions was also created to show the geographic diversity of the thousands of questions submitted.

Compared to some of the other examples in the book and in this chapter, the Department of State may look like it's just beginning on the journey to openness. But what I find most interesting is that it is actually far ahead of many organizations in terms of being open and using social technologies—even though, being part of a government agency, staff face many restrictions and have far more at risk in terms of international engagement. That's because individuals at the Department—especially those in foreign posts—already had tremendous freedom to act independently and in accordance with the circumstances they face on the ground. With guidelines and training in place, they are trusted to developed the relationships they think are best suited to achieve their diplomatic goals. But more important, they are—post by post, tweet by tweet—changing the relationships with local people, creating greater trust and transparency through the development of long-lasting communities.

The unifying theme across all of these transformations is that a fundamentally new relationship is being formed, often with the help and support of social technologies, but always with the intention of being more open. These types of trusting relationships form the foundation of culture and transformation—and without them, all of your efforts to achieve audacious goals will be for naught.

ACTION PLAN: STARTING THE TRANSFORMATION

There have been many books written about how to manage organizational and cultural change, and I'm joining that chorus in offering up advice on how to get started with a transformation.[18] From the case studies discussed here, I draw the following recommendations:

- *Create a sense of urgency with information sharing.* From SBI to the State Department, a common theme was communicating the *need* for change. The opportunity with today's open technologies is that you can share the data and information needed to make your case not only vivid but also personal. Rather than hearing the need for urgency from the top, you can also hear your colleagues and peers join in on the discussion. So when you start making your case for transformation, be sure to bolster the impact of your message with the voices of others in the organization.
- *Identify the values that will carry you through the transformation.* At its core, the most successful transformations were those that had visions and missions rooted in existing core values. Every organization has a set of core values, even if they are not expressly laid out, that you as a leader will be able to tap. Decide which ones will form the basis for the new culture and, using social technologies, demonstrate your commitment and connection to those core values in

(Continued)

(Continued)

authentic ways. And by all means, ask that people join you in spreading those core values to others.

- *Lead by example.* From Chambers to Lafley, from Best Buy to the State Department, the leaders themselves exemplify openness. To have credibility in the new culture, the leaders have to demonstrate the attitudes and behaviors that will be positively received and rewarded. If you find it personally hard to be open and share, it will be nearly impossible for the rest of your organization to take on the burden.
- *Encourage risk taking; reward risks taken.* Transformations require that things be done in new ways, ways that are uncomfortable and unfamiliar. It's important to encourage trials and, more important, reward risks that are taken but end in failure—otherwise no one will be willing to be the first to stick his or her neck out and make the transition.
- *Start small to win big.* Small steps are easier than big ones; little risks and failures are easier to swallow than big ones. Building up confidence in the transformation and the new culture with little steps will actually speed up the transition, not slow it down.
- *Institutionalize systems and structures.* Transformations take time and will be experienced differently as change management takes place. Processes, procedures, and guidelines all help institutionalize the change so that it becomes not only easier, but routine.
- *Be patient.* This is somewhat counter to the first action point of creating urgency. The reality is that although you need to create urgency to spur action, you need patience to guide the change through its sometimes achingly slow first steps.

As you set off on your transformation journey, I wish you all the best. You'll make a lot of mistakes; these are indications that you are working toward real change. And at times you will feel alone on this journey—when that happens, know that you are never really alone, because there are many others going through the same transitions. Seek out and consult with your peers who have already traveled this road. Talk with the customers and employees who want you to accomplish your goal. The advantage of pursuing an open strategy is that you will do it in the company of people who wish you the best, who will be there to support you and will count themselves among the many who will benefit from your success.

ENDNOTES

INTRODUCTION

1. In addition to its main Web site at redcross.org, the American Red Cross has the following online presences: blog.redcross.org, redcrossyouth.org, youtube.com/amredcross, twitter.com/redcross, flickr.com/groups/americanredcross, linkedin.com/static?key=groups_giving_arc, and socialvibe.com/#/causes/38.

2. The American Red Cross Social Media Strategy Handbook is available at http://sites.google.com/site/wharman/social-media-strategy-handbook.

3. A list of American Red Cross chapter blogs is at http://redcrosschat.org/chapter-blogs and a list of chapter Twitter accounts is at http://redcrosschat.org/twitter.

4. More information about how the Red Cross used mobile donations, as well as Facebook and Twitter, is available at http://mashable.com/2010/01/13/haiti-red-cross-donations and http://www.techcrunch.com/2010/01/15/haiti-text-donations.

CHAPTER ONE

1. "United Breaks Guitars, Dave Carroll Keeps Playing," http://www.petergreenberg.com/2009/08/11/united-breaks-guitars-dave-carroll-keeps-playing/, August 2009.

2. United explained that this policy was in place to accurately assign responsibility for the damage, and to address the many fraudulent claims it receives every year.

3. The first of what would be eventually a series of three videos, the "United Breaks Guitars" video is available at http://www.youtube.com/watch?v=5YGc4zOqozo.

4. More information about Dave Carroll is available at davecarrollmusic.com.

5. Dave Carroll's video comment is available at http://www.youtube.com/ watch?v=T_X-Qoh__mw/.

6. According to Internet World Stats, 1.7 billion people were online as of September 30, 2009, which represented 25.6 percent penetration. More information is available at http://www.internetworldstats.com/stats.htm.

7. Universal McCann Social Media Tracker, Wave 4, July 2009, available at http://universalmccann.bitecp.com/wave4/Wave4.pdf.

8. Verizon recently introduced the ability to access sites like Facebook and Twitter via their Verizon FIOS service. More information is available in this article at http://www.readwriteweb.com/archives/facebook_and_twitter_on_ tv_hands-on_with_verizon_fios_widgets.php.

9. Services like Gcast.com, Gabcast.com, and Hipcast.com allow podcasters to simply call a number and record the podcast; the file is then available for them to use.

10. James M. Kouzes and Barry Z. Posner, *The Leadership Challenge* (San Francisco: Jossey-Bass, 2007), p. 24.

11. The headline for a marketing conference email promotion read, "It's time to take back control!" More information is available in the blog post, "Can you control your customers?" at http://www.altimetergroup.com/2009/10/ can-you-control-your-customers.html.

12. Disclosure: I was active as a precinct manager and volunteer on the Obama campaign.

13. Obama campaign manager David Plouffe shares the campaign strategy on YouTube at http://www.youtube.com/watch?v=a6bp0B61rNk.

14. "Crush on Obama" by Obama Girl is available at http://www.youtube .com/watch?v=wKsoXHYICqU, "Wassup 2008" is available at http://www .youtube.com/watch?v=Qq8Uc5BFogE, and will.i.am's video "Yes We Can" is at http://www.youtube.com/watch?v=jjXyqcx-mYY.

15. Samuel P. Huntington, *Political Order in Changing Societies* (New Haven: Yale University Press, 1968).

16. Peter Drucker, *Concept of the Corporation* (New York: John Day, 1946).

17. Robert K. Greenleaf's essay *The Servant as Leader* first appeared in 1970; a copy of the essay is available at greenleaf.org. Greenleaf published *Servant Leadership: A Journey Into The Nature Of Legitimate Power And Greatness* (New York: Paulist Press) in 1977.

18. Thomas J. Peters, *In Search of Excellence: Lessons from America's Best-Run Companies* (New York: HarperCollins, 1982).

CHAPTER TWO

1. One blogger asked half-seriously if there were Cylons (alien species from the TV show *Battlestar Galactica*) on board, a question that stumped everyone from the captain to the public affairs officers. And they confirmed that there aren't any Cylons on the ship.

2. An excellent recap and photos of the USS *Nimitz* blogger embark is available at http://blog.guykawasaki.com/2009/06/24-hours-at-sea-on-the-uss-nimitz.html.

3. From an interview conducted by Jennifer Jones aboard the USS *Nimitz* on May 29, 2009. The interview is available at http://www.jenniferjones.com/MarketingVoices/5869/a-candid-perspective-from-fighter-pilot-lieutenant-luis-delgado.

4. John Case, *Open Book Management: The Coming Business Revolution* (New York: Harper Paperbacks, 1996). OBM involves four basic practices: (1) training employees so they become business literate and can understand financial statements, (2) empowering them to use that information in cost cutting and quality improvement, (3) trusting them as business partners on equal footing, and (4) rewarding them fairly for the firm's success. http://www.businessdictionary.com/definition/open-book-management-OBM.html.

5. See, for example, John Case, *Open-Book Management*; Thomas J. McCoy, *Creating an "Open Book" Organization: .Where Employees Think and Act Like Business Partners* (New York: AMACOM, 1996); and John P. Schuster, Jill Carpenter, and M. Patricia Kane, *The Open-Book Management Field Book* (Hoboken, NJ: Wiley, 1997).

6. Andrew Grove. *Only the Paranoid Survive* (New York: Doubleday Business, 1996).

7. Facebook's mission statement is available at http://www.facebook.com/facebook?ref=pf#/facebook?v=info&ref=pf. A look at the evolution of Facebook's mission statement is available at http://www.observer.com/2009/media/evolution-facebooks-mission-statement.

8. The Facebook Platform and Facebook Connect enable companies to take Facebook assets (like profiles and friend relationships) and use them on their own sites. Developers can also create applications that run on Facebook itself. Companies like game application developer Zynga are being valued well into the hundreds of millions because of the audience they have been able to amass on Facebook's platform.

9. Details of Facebook's short-term future plans are available at http://wiki
.developers.facebook.com/index.php/Developer_Roadmap.

10. Paul Levy's blog is at http://runningahospital.blogspot.com/. These specific
posts are at http://runningahospital.blogspot.com/2009/10/5s-projects-are-
spreading.html, http://runningahospital.blogspot.com/2009/10/icu-i-really-
care-for-you-and-your.html, and http://runningahospital.blogspot.com/2007/
01/do-i-get-paid-too-much.html.

11. From Paul Levy's first blog post, August 2, 2006, at http://runningahospital
.blogspot.com/2006/08/running-hospital.html.

12. Weber, Larry. *Sticks & Stones: How Digital Reputations Are Created Over Time
and Lost in a Click* (Hoboken, NJ: Wiley), 2009, 35.

13. Frank Eliason and the ComcastCares Twitter page are available at http://
twitter.com/comcastcares.

14. Micah Laaker contributed an essay "What It Means to Be Open" that appears
on pages 443–444 in Christian Crumlish and Erin Malone, *Designing Social
Interfaces* (O'Reilly/Yahoo! Press, 2009).

15. Randy Pausch's Last Lecture is at http://www.youtube.com/watch?v=ji5_
MqicxSo; "JK Wedding Entrance Dance" is at http://www.youtube.com/
watch?v=4-94JhLEiN0; inserting a central line how-to is at http://www
.youtube.com/watch?v=1xsgE7ueaek; Hamster On A Piano is at http://www
.youtube.com/watch?v=rfqNXADl3kU&feature=fvw.

16. Chris Morrow's reporting is available at http://www.ireport.com/people/
ChrisMorrow.

17. The *USA Today* Ad Meter results for the 2009 Super Bowl is available at
http://www.usatoday.com/money/advertising/admeter/2009admeter.htm.

18. Disclosure: The logo for Altimeter Group, which was founded by Charlene
Li, was designed and obtained on crowdspring.com.

19. The term *spec work* is applied to unscrupulous method of getting work
completed for free under the guise of a contest. Usually the designer signs
over all rights to the work. A group called "No! Spec" has advocated strongly
for an end to such practices. See http://www.no-spec.com/. The author
believes that sites like crowdspring.com and 99designs.com serve the interests
of designers by making clear the relationship and ownership of the designs at
the outset of the engagement.

20. An excellent overview of openness in technology appears in Chapter
Seventeen of Crumlish and Malone's *Designing Social Interfaces*.

21. For example, Facebook's platform has extended itself into thousands of other sites
via a program called "Facebook Connect" because it was able to quickly and

clearly lay out its own standards. In contrast, the rival OpenSocial API protocol has yet to reach a 1.0 release as of the writing of this book, primarily because it must reach agreement with partners like Google, Yahoo, Microsoft, and MySpace. More information about OpenSocial is available at opensocial.org.

22. The Do Us A Flavour Web site is at http://www.walkers.co.uk/flavours/#/howitworks/.

23. The *Financial Times* offers a quick overview of W. L. Gore's organizational structure and decision making at http://www.ft.com/cms/s/0/32fba7da-bfc9–11dd-9222–0000779fd18c.html.

24. Gary Hamel, *The Future of Management* (Cambridge, MA: Harvard Business School Press, 2007), p. 88.

25. Details on how Mozilla manages distributed decision making and module ownership is available at http://www.mozilla.org/hacking/module-ownership.html.

CHAPTER THREE

1. Google Blog Search is at blogsearch.google.com; Twitter search is at search.twitter.com. Both of these tools are free to use.

2. There are hundreds of social media and brand monitoring tools available. A report with a comprehensive list can be found at open-leadership.com.

3. Microsoft's Looking Glass and Salesforce's Chatter are just a few examples that were announced as this book was going to press.

4. Kohl's Facebook Wall is at http://www.facebook.com/kohls#/kohls?v=wall. These observations were made on November 14, 2009.

5. For more about the participation inequality theory, see http://www.useit.com/alertbox/participation_inequality.html. Jake McKee also captured this on his site at www.90-9-1.com.

6. The ShareThis report was a commissioned study by Forrester Research, "The Ins And Outs Of Online Sharing: How And When Consumers Share Content," July 7, 2008.

7. Based on activities in the preceding month, from Trendstream.net. Additional information about the survey data and for sixteen countries is available at open-leadership.com.

8. Southwest Airline employee Bill Owen's post is at http://www.blogsouthwest.com/blog/march-schedule-now-bookableso-go-somewhere.

9. SAP EcoHub is available at http://ecohub.sdn.sap.com.

10. crowdSPRING (crowdspring.com) provides design services, uTest (www.uTest.com) provides software and usability testing services, and InnoCentive (innocentive.com) crowdsources problem solving.

11. "P&G's New Innovation Model," HBS Working Knowledge, March 20, 2006. Available at http://hbswk.hbs.edu/archive/5258.html.

12. iTunes is at http://www.facebook.com/iTunes on Facebook. iTunes also has Twitter accounts at http://twitter.com/iTunesMusic, http://twitter.com/iTunesPodcasts, http://twitter.com/iTunesMovies, and http://twitter.com/iTunesTV. Apple Students also has a presence on Facebook at http://www.facebook.com/applestudents.

CHAPTER FOUR

1. American Express CMO John Hayes made this comment at the Brandworks University conference, June 2, 2009, in Madison, Wisconsin. More information is available at http://www.lsb.com/brandworks-brandworks-2009.

2. According to The American Customer Satisfaction Index, Comcast scored 54 out of 100 in 2008, tied with Charter for last in the cable and satellite TV industry. Note that Comcast did improve its score significantly in 2009. For more information, see http://www.theacsi.org/index.php?option=com_content&task=view&id=147&Itemid=155&i=Cable+%26+Satellite+TV.

3. The Grannie Annie blog post is available at http://grannieannies.blogspot.com/2008/03/i-dont-like-comcast.html.

4. Dell Outlet's Twitter page is at twitter.com/delloutlet.

5. Dell wrote a blog post about the linkage between its Dell Outlet Twitter account and sales, which can be found at http://en.community.dell.com/blogs/direct2dell/archive/2009/06/11/delloutlet-surpasses-2-million-on-twitter.aspx.

6. It's presumed that Dell's Twitter sales were incremental and didn't cannibalize sales that would have taken place anyway. Regardless, the minimal amount of resources taken up by Nelson is far outweighed by the benefit to Dell.

7. One site that aggregates Twitter deals is Cheaptweet.com.

8. The Ford Fiesta Movement campaign can be found online at www.fiestamovement.com.

9. The study is available at http://www.engagementdb.com.

10. Eighty-six of the 100 brands evaluated are publicly traded, so year-on-year financial data on revenue, gross margin, and gross profit were compared.

11. The most deeply and broadly engaged companies saw year-on-year increases in revenue, gross margin, and gross profit of +18 percent, +15 percent, and +4 percent, respectively. By comparison, the least deeply and broadly engaged companies saw year-on-year decreases of –6 percent, –9 percent, and –11 percent on the same respective metrics. More information is available online at www.engagementdb.com.

12. Jim Collins, *Good to Great: Why Some Companies Make the Leap . . . And Others Don't* (HarperBusiness, 2001).

13. The Ranger Station is available at http://www.therangerstation.com/. Thanks to Ron Ploof who captured the details of this case study in a document, "The Ranger Station Fire: How Ford Motor Company Used Social Media To Extinguish a PR Fire in less than 24 Hours," available at http://www.scribd .com/doc/9204719/The-Ranger-Station-Fire.

14. "Gold in Them Hills: Computing ROI for Support Communities," Lithium Technologies and FT Works, 2008. Available at http://pages.lithium.com/ gold-in-them-hills.html.

15. A PDF of Cisco's cost savings calculations is available at open-leadership .com.

16. More details are available in an interview with TransUnion CTO John Parkinson in Internet Evolution, http://www.internetevolution.com/document.asp?doc_ id=173854.

17. There are many ways to calculate lifetime value (LTV), and many use discount rates to calculate net present value (NPV). The model used here was based on information at http://www.dbmarketing.com/articles/Art129.htm and http:// hbswk.hbs.edu/archive/1436.html, but simplifies the calculation by not using NPV.

18. More information about the Net Promoter Score is available at http://www .netpromoter.com.

19. Satmetrix's 2009 Net Promoter Score Benchmark Rankings Report is available at http://www.satmetrix.com/satmetrix/news_events.php?page=1&pid=72.

CHAPTER FIVE

1. An October 6, 2009, press release from Robert Half Technology containing details about the survey is available at http://rht.mediaroom.com/index .php?s=131&item=790.

2. The Deloitte study, "Social Networking and Reputational Risk in the Work-place," can be found at http://www.complianceweek.com/s/documents/ DeloitteSocialNetworking.pdf.

3. HP's social media policy is an internal document; this excerpt was provided as a courtesy and appears with their permission.

4. The Razorfish Employee Social Influence Marketing Guidelines are available at http://www.razorfish.com/img/content/RazorfishSIMguideWebJuly2009 .pdf.

5. The Participation Guidelines for Mayo Employees is available at http:// sharing.mayoclinic.org/guidelines/for-mayo-clinic-employees/.

6. Details on the Accord Crosstour Facebook incident are available in an article at http://www.autoblog.com/2009/09/03/honda-purges-some-comments-from-crosstour-facebook-page/.

7. Honda's response on the Accord Crosstour Facebook page is available at http://www.facebook.com/accordcrosstour?v=wall&viewas=725095119#/accordcrosstour?v=app_6009294086.

8. Kodak's Social Media Tips are available at http://www.kodak.com/US/images/en/corp/aboutKodak/onlineToday/Kodak_SocialMediaTips_Aug14.pdf.

9. The Kaiser Permanente Social Media Policy is available at http://xnet.kp.org/newscenter/media/downloads/socialmediapolicy_091609.pdf.

10. Ibid.

11. A list of Kaiser Permanente doctors who have Twitter accounts can be found at http://twitter.com/htpotter/permanente-physicians. One of the most prolific blogging doctors is Dr. Ted Eytan, whose blog is available at http://www.tedeytan.com/.

12. Cisco's Internet Postings Policy is available at http://blogs.cisco.com/news/comments/ciscos_internet_postings_policy.

13. The U.S. Air Force includes guidelines in the document "New Media and the Air Force," available at http://www.af.mil/shared/media/document/AFD-090406–036.pdf.

14. Intel's Social Media Guidelines are available at http://www.intel.com/sites/sitewide/en_US/social-media.htm.

15. The IBM Social Computing Guidelines are available at http://www.ibm.com/blogs/zz/en/guidelines.html.

16. DePaul University's policy is available at http//brandresources.depaul.edu/vendor_guidelines/g_socialmedia.aspx.

17. Dell's Online Communications Policy is available at http://www.dell.com/content/topics/global.aspx/policy/en/policy.

18. IBM's Social Computing Guidelines are available at http://www.ibm.com/blogs/zz/en/guidelines.html. For comparison purposes, the 2005 version of the Guidelines is available as a PDF at http://www.wordbiz.com/x9ksp38/IBM_Blogging_Policy_and_Guidelines.pdf.

19. From an interview I conducted with Ed Terpening, available at http://vator.tv/news/show/2009-03-04-using-blogs-in-a-public-relations-crisis. In another interview, Terpening discusses how Wells Fargo successfully blogs; see http://vator.tv/news/show/2009-02-19-how-wells-fargo-successfully-blogs. Wells Fargo's Community Guidelines are available at http://blog.wellsfargo.com/community-guidelines.html.

20. Intel's Social Media Guidelines are available at http://www.intel.com/sites/ sitewide/en_US/social-media.htm.

21. GetSatisfaction's "The Company-Customer Pact" is available at http:// getsatisfaction.com/ccpact.

22. HP's Blogging Code of Conduct is available at http://www.hp.com/hpinfo/ blogs/codeofconduct.html.

23. Hill & Knowlton's Social Media Principles are available at http://www .hillandknowlton.com/principles.

24. The Social Media Business Council's Disclosure Best Practices Toolkit is available at http://www.socialmedia.org/disclosure/.

25. The Kilmer House blog is available at http://www.kilmerhouse.com.

26. The JNJ BTW blog is available at http://www.jnjbtw.com.

27. Netflix published a presentation that explains their company culture at http:// www.netflix.com/Jobs?lnkceData=22&lnkce=ftrlnk&trkid=912834. Slide 61 has more details on what Netflix considers "good" and "bad" processes.

CHAPTER SIX

1. The theory of "network neighbors" holds that people who are closely connected to each other have similar interests, tastes, and behaviors. So Toyota, knowing that I drive a Prius, could show people in my network an ad for a Prius and get much better results than a control group. Vendors like Media6Degrees provide such services.

2. More information about the U.S. Air Force Blog Assessment chart is available at http://www.globalnerdy.com/2008/12/30/the-air-forces-rules-of-engagement-for-blogging/.

3. More information about Cisco's "Connected Sports" offering is available at http://cisco.com/web/strategy/sports/index.html.

4. Humana's health question video is available at http://www.youtube.com/ user/staysmartstayhealthy.

5. Humana's Facebook page is at http://www.facebook.com/pages/Humana-Military/144152068725.

6. Starbucks' Facebook and Twitter pages are at http://www.facebook.com/ Starbucks and http://twitter.com/starbucks, respectively.

7. Links to all of Starbucks' international Facebook pages are available at http:// www.facebook.com/Starbucks?v=app_142063194423.

8. The Abrams Research Social Media Survey—February, 2009 results are available at http://www.abramsresearch.com/files/abrams_research_social_media_ survey_0209.pdf.

9. The American Red Cross Social Media Strategy Handbook is available at http://sites.google.com/site/wharman/social-media-strategy-handbook.

10. For a list of Red Cross chapter blogs, visit http://blog.redcross.org/chapter-blogs/.

11. The HP Blogging Code of Conduct is available at http://www.hp.com/hpinfo/blogs/codeofconduct.html.

12. A list of HP's blogs is available at http://www.communities.hp.com/online/blogs/Bloggers.aspx.

13. The Social Computer Lab research group at HP Labs provides one example: it led to the launch of Watercooler, an internal collaboration tool, and Friendlee, a mobile social application. More can be found at http://www.hpl.hp.com/research/scl/.

14. A list of Wells Fargo blogs can be found at http://blog.wellsfargo.com/. Other sites include http://www.youtube.com/user/wellsfargo, facebook.com/wellsfargo, http://www.myspace.com/stagecoachisland, and twitter.com/ask_wellsfargo. Stagecoach Island can be accessed at http://blog.wellsfargo.com/stagecoachisland.

CHAPTER SEVEN

1. Adam Bryant, "You Want Insights? Go to the Front Lines," *New York Times*, August 26, 2009, p. B2.

2. Jim Collins, *Good to Great: Why Some Companies Make the Leap . . . And Others Don't* (HarperBusiness, 2001).

3. Jeff Hayzlett's Twitter feed is available at http://twitter.com/JeffreyHayzlett; his blog is at http://jeffreyhayzlett.1000words.kodak.com/.

CHAPTER EIGHT

1. Warren Bennis, *On Becoming a Leader* (New York: Basic Books, 1994), page 39 and later passages.

2. Rob Goffee and Gareth Jones, "Managing Authenticity: The Paradox of Great Leadership." *Harvard Business Review* (December 2005), available at http://hbr.org/2005/12/managing-authenticity/ar/1.

3. The phrase "checking it at the door" is used to describe what a person does to assimilate into a specific world that may not be accepting of their differences. See the report, "Do We Check It at the Door?" by Keith Woods at http://www.namme.org/career/publications/report_checkit.pdf.

4. Barry Judge's first blog post is available at http://barryjudge.com/hello-world.

5. I wrote my first blog post in September 2004 and was indeed absolutely terrified to click "Publish." To this day, I have a small moment of panic before posting, but now I know from experience that everything will be fine.

6. The press release announcing Brian Moynihan's appointment as CEO of Bank of America is available at http://multivu.prnewswire.com/mnr/bankofamerica/41726.

7. Bill Marriott's blog is at http://www.blogs.marriott.com.

8. Bill Marriott, "Why Do I Blog?" http://www.blogs.marriott.com/marriott-on-the-move/2007/08/why-do-i-blog.html.

9. Chambers typically video blogs internally, but you can see his first external video blog at http://blogs.cisco.com/news/comments/john_chambers_video_blog_if_there_is_a_killer_application_its_video.

10. Ram Charan, Stephen Drotter, and James Noel, *The Leadership Pipeline: How to Build the Leadership-Powered Company* (San Francisco: Jossey-Bass, 2000) p. 35.

11. Ori Brafman and Rod A. Beckstrom, *The Starfish and the Spider* (Portfolio, 2006), 98.

12. To learn more about Best Buy's open strategy, see the video "Open for Business: Best Buy's Social Technology Strategy" at http://www.youtube.com/watch?v=whzN-7uCiZw.

13. A list of Sodexo's social media channels is available at http://www.sodexousa.com/usen/careers/network/network.asp.

14. Max Chafkin, "The Zappos Way of Managing," *Inc.* (May 2009), 66; available at http://www.inc.com/magazine/20090501/the-zappos-way-of-managing.html.

15. The Russell Herder study, "Social Media: Embracing the Opportunities, Averting the Risks," is available at http://www.russellherder.com/SocialMediaResearch/TCHRA_Resources/RHP_089_WhitePaper.pdf.

16. Hat tip to Erica Driver at ThinkBalm for the coining the phrase "Convincing the Curmudgeon," the topic of a discussion forum she hosted. For more details, see http://www.thinkbalm.com/2008/12/17/thinkbalm-storytelling-series-1-role-play-redux-convince-the-curmudgeon.

17. Adam Bryant, "In a Near-Death Event, a Corporate Rite of Passage," *New York Times*, August 2, 2009, B2.

CHAPTER NINE

1. Several books have been written about Google's reach and success. For example, check out *What Would Google Do?* by Jeff Jarvis (New York: Collins Business, 2009) and *Googled: The End of the World as We Know It* by Ken Auletta (New York: Penguin Press, 2009).

2. Adam Lashinsky, "Chaos by Design: The Inside Story of Disorder, Disarray, and Uncertainty at Google. And Why It's All Part of the Plan. (They Hope.),"

Fortune, October 2, 2006, http://money.cnn.com/magazines/fortune/fortune_archive/2006/10/02/8387489.

3. The *Consumerist* post is at http://consumerist.com/2009/02/facebooks-new-terms-of-service-we-can-do-anything-we-want-with-your-content-forever.html#comments-content.

4. Mark Zuckerberg's post, "On Facebook, People Own and Control Their Information" is at http://blog.facebook.com/blog.php?post=54434097130.

5. Zuckerberg's second post "Update on Terms" is available at http://blog.facebook.com/blog.php?post=54746167130. The group "Facebook Bill Of Rights And Responsibilities" is available at http://www.facebook.com/group.php?gid=69048030774.

6. You can read more about Walmart's "The Hub" in this story, "Walmart's MySpace Clone Dead On Arrival" at http://mashable.com/2006/10/03/walmarts-myspace-clone-dead-on-arrival.

7. See the *BusinessWeek* article, "Wal-Mart's Jim and Laura: The Real Story," October 9, 2006 at http://www.businessweek.com/bwdaily/dnflash/content/oct2006/db20061009_579137.htm.

8. Details on Walmart's "Roommate Style Match" is at http://mashable.com/2007/08/08/wal-marts-facebook-group-for-back-to-school-shopping. And more information on what went wrong with Walmart's initial Facebook foray is at http://social-media-optimization.com/2007/10/a-failed-facebook-marketing-campaign.

9. Walmart's Facebook page can be found at www.facebook.com/walmart and a list of Walmart Twitter accounts is available at http://walmartstores.com/twitter.

10. You can see the Motrin commercial at http://www.youtube.com/watch?v=XO6SlTUBA38.

11. Details on how the Motrin Mom incident began are available at http://www.scientificamerican.com/blog/60-second-science/post.cfm?id=motrin-moms-a-twitter-over-ad-take-2008-11-17.

12. The YouTube video of Motrin Mom tweets is available at http://www.youtube.com/watch?v=LhR-y1N6R8Q.

13. McNeil's response to the Motrin Moms controversy can be found at http://jnjbtw.com/2008/11/mcneil-meets-twitter-we-hear-you.

14. The Spy application was created by Best Buy employee Ben Hedrington and is available at http://spy.appspot.com.

15. You can see a copy of the email with the erroneous offer at http://www.crunchgear.com/2008/09/03/best-buy-intros-premier-black-reward-zone-program.

16. Barry Judge's blog post "Trust and the Reward Zone Black Card Test" is available at http://barryjudge.com/trust-and-the-reward-zone-black-card-test.

17. You can read Jeremiah Owyang's post "Expect Changes at Mzinga" at http://www.web-strategist.com/blog/2009/03/16/expect-changes-at-mzinga.

18. Owyang's post "A Public Apology to Mzinga" is available at http://www.web-strategist.com/blog/2009/03/17/a-public-apology-to-mzinga.

19. Ralph Heath, *Celebrating Failure: The Power of Taking Risks, Making Mistakes, and Thinking Big* (The Career Press, 2009).

CHAPTER TEN

1. T. E. Deal and A. A. Kennedy, *Corporate Cultures: The Rites and Rituals of Corporate Life* (Harmondsworth, UK: Penguin Books, 1982).

2. The State Bank of India's situation is detailed in a *McKinsey Quarterly* interview with Om Bhatt, available at http://www.mckinseyquarterly.com/Remaking_a_government-owned_giant_An_interview_with_the_chairman_of_the_State_Bank_of_India_2249.

3. A summary of *The Bhagavad Gita* is available at http://www.hinduwebsite.com/summary.asp. The book *Gita on the Green: The Mystical Tradition Behind Bagger Vance* by Stephen J. Rosen (Continuum, 2008) explores the connection between *The Legend of Bagger Vance* and *The Bhagavad Gita.*

4. The State Bank of India case is based on Tamal Bandyopadhyay, "Om Prakash Bhatt: The Chairman in a Hurry," http://www.livemint.com/2008/05/03000522/Om-Prakash-Bhatt--The-chairma.html; Vivek Kaul, "The elephant can dance: O P Bhatt," http://www.dnaindia.com/money/report_the-elephant-can-dance-o-p-bhatt_1201401; "It is Parivartan time at SBI," http://www.financialexpress.com/news/it-is-parivartan-time-at-sbi/208256/#; Ryan Rodrigues, "Change Manager," *Business India*, August 23, 2009, 58–76.

5. The presentation "An Open, Social Approach" is available at http://www.slideshare.net/garykoelling/thebigslideshow1-presentation.

6. Best Buy Remix is available at http://remix.bestbuy.com/.

7. From Barry Judge's blog post, "Twelpforce—Blurring the Lines Between Customer Service and Marketing," available at http://barryjudge.com/twelpforce---blurring-the-lines-between-customer-service-and-marketing.

8. A. G. Lafley and Ram Charan, *The Game-Changer: How You Can Drive Revenue and Profit Growth with Innovation* (Crown Business, 2008).

9. From a presentation by Jeff Weedman, April 3, 2009, available at http://cusli.org/conferences/annual/annual_2009/presentations/Weedman%20Canada.pdf.

10. Jarvis's first post, "Dell Lies. Dell Sucks," is available at http://www.buzzmachine.com/archives/2005_06_21.html#009911.

11. Engadget has a post titled "Dude, Your Dell Is on Fire" that describes the incident; it's available at http://www.engadget.com/2006/06/22/dude-your-dell-is-on-fire.

12. Menchaca's "Flaming Notebook" post is available at http://en.community.dell.com/blogs/direct2dell/archive/2006/07/13/431.aspx.

13. Jeff Jarvis's visit to Dell, entitled "Dell Hell: The End?" is available at http://www.buzzmachine.com/2007/10/18/dell-hell-the-end.

14. The main State Department Facebook page is at facebook.com/usdos with links to over forty embassies and topics.

15. The US Jakarta embassy Facebook page can be found at http://www.facebook.com/jakarta.usembassy.

16. Details on the "Global Conversations" conducted by Obama are available at http://www.america.gov/st/africa-english/2009/July/20090708145523SztiwomoD0.258053.html.

17. A transcript of Obama's responses is available at http://www.america.gov/st/texttrans-english/2009/July/20090713000019ptellivremos0.3191645.html.

18. One of my favorites in the genre of change management is *Leading Change* by John P. Kotter (Harvard Business Press, 1996).

ACKNOWLEDGMENTS

Every book is a collaborative effort, and none more so than a book about being open. So although my name is the only one that appears on the book, there are many others to whom credit should go. First and foremost, I am grateful to my husband, Côme Laguë, who provided the encouragement to write the book and took care of me and our family during countless evenings, weekends, and family vacations spent researching and writing. To our kids, thank you for your patience and encouraging hugs—they were much appreciated!

Wally Wood, my writer and researcher, served as the sounding board for my wacky ideas and provided calm wisdom in the face of daunting deadlines. Our regular meetings were a welcome relief from the isolation of writing! Larry Weber introduced me to Wally and has always been a wonderful friend and advisor. Mary Maki transcribed every interview we did for the book, capturing the ideas and voices of the open leaders for these pages.

My partners at Altimeter Group—Deb Schultz, Jeremiah Owyang, and Ray Wang—provided ideas, contacts, edits, and most important, their friendship and support. Each day, they help me learn how to be a better open leader. And the seemingly endless supply of dates, nuts, and other "brain food" also helped considerably! Denise Aday, my virtual assistant, not only kept me on track and organized throughout the entire process, but also provided peace of mind that everything would be done just right.

Special thanks go to Susan Williams for believing in the book, and to Mark Karmendy, Kristi Hein, and the rest of the amazing team at Jossey-Bass, who not only accommodated an impossible publishing schedule but did so with amazing grace. And warm thanks go to Byron Schneider for editing the manuscript and holding my hand (and ego) throughout the process—your suggestions were spot on, and your attention to detail made the book far better.

Kevin Small, my agent, provided the guidance that gave birth to *Open Leadership.* From our initial brainstorms to working with publishers, you have been at my side providing wise counsel. Together with Carolyn Monaco and the rest of the ResultSource team, Kevin also managed the publicity and marketing of the book in coordination with Jossey-Bass.

The many people who were interviewed and mentioned in this book gave generously not only of their time but also their keen advice and wisdom. Thank you for being open about your experiences, especially about your failures.

There were countless other people who have helped me along the way, from casual comments to pointed conversations. Thanks to Steve Farber and Stephen Caldwell for brainstorming the original concepts for the book and to Mel Blake and Chris Meyer (Monitor), Allen Morgan (Mayfield Fund), Giovanni Rodriguez (The Conversation Group), and Larry Weber (Racepoint Group) for reading the proposal. Susan Etlinger (Horn Group) and many others provided feedback on the book outline that I published early in the process on my blog. And Caroline Ogawa did much of the original research on social media policies.

My fellow book author friends—Guy Kawasaki, Chris Anderson, Adam Metz, Tara Hunt, Shel Israel, Beth Kanter, Brian Solis, Peter Simms, and especially my *Groundswell* coauthor, Josh Bernoff—all provided encouraging pats on the back and advice along the way. Having gone through the joys and trials of writing a book, they knew just what to say at the appropriate moments to keep me going.

Ben Elowitz and Kevin Flaherty at Wetpaint were my research partners on the Engagementdb report. Without their initiative and insight, that groundbreaking report would never have seen the light of day. Rick Murray (Edelman), Jack Holt (Department of Defense), Ravishankar Gundlapalli (Turningpoint), Tracy Sjogreen (Jive Software), Diane Hessan (Communispace), and Sanjay Dohlakia's team at Lithium Technologies all made invaluable introductions to people and companies interviewed for the book. And I'm grateful to Scott Cook (Intuit), Soumitra Dutta (INSEAD), Jeff Gaus (Prolifiq) and Sangeeth Varghese (Leadcap) for providing early fodder for my thinking on open organizations.

Last, but far from least, I am grateful to the many people who reached out to me on my blog or Twitter account, as well as in person at events and conferences. Your questions and concerns resonated in my mind and were the constant standard against which I measured the quality of the work.

Charlene Li, San Mateo, California

THE AUTHOR

CHARLENE LI is one of the leading independent voices in business today, with a special focus on the strategic use of emerging technologies.

Her expertise spans the most critical areas that drive sustainable success—leadership, strategy, innovation, interactive media, and marketing. An established thought leader, Charlene is frequently quoted on these specialties by leading media channels such as the *Wall Street Journal,* the *New York Times, USA Today,* Reuters, and the Associated Press. She has appeared on 60 Minutes, PBS NewsHour, ABC News, CNN, and CNBC. And as a noted social technologist, Charlene has earned a vast following through her blogs, Twitter, Web site, articles, and keynotes.

Charlene has been widely recognized as a driving force of innovation by the business community: as one of the "Most Influential Women in Technology in 2009" and "12 Most Creative Minds in 2008" by *Fast Company* magazine; as one of the "Top 40 Women to Watch in 2008" by Ad Age; and as one of the "50 Most Influential People in Silicon Valley in 2008" by NowPublic. That same year, she was named "Visionary of the Year" (alongside Josh Bernoff) by Society for New Communications.

Charlene is coauthor of *Groundswell: Winning in a World Transformed by Social Technologies,* named by both Amazon and *strategy+business* magazine as one of the best business books of 2008.

A seminal book filled with case studies, *Groundswell* was named one of the "Best Innovation and Design Books of 2008" by *Business Week,* who also deemed it a bestseller. In 2009, the book was also awarded the prestigious Berry-AMA Prize for the best book in marketing.

Charlene is founder of Altimeter Group, a strategy consulting firm with a pragmatic approach to using emerging technologies for competitive advantage (altimetergroup.com). Clients include Fortune 1000 companies across a range of industries including retail, financial services, travel, technology, and consumer package goods.

Previously, she was a vice president and principal analyst at Forrester Research. She joined Forrester in 1999, after spending five years in online and newspaper publishing with *San Jose Mercury News* and *Community Newspaper Company.* She was also a consultant with Monitor Group in Boston and Amsterdam. Charlene is a graduate of Harvard Business School, as well as Harvard College.

To follow Charlene and to get a number of free resources to help you start transforming the way you lead, visit open-leadership.com.

AUTHOR'S WORK WITH CLIENTS

Open Leadership author Charlene Li is founder of Altimeter Group, a strategy consulting firm with a pragmatic approach to using emerging technologies for competitive advantage. The firm focuses on four areas:

- Leadership and Management
- Customer Strategy
- Enterprise Strategy
- Innovation and Practices

Clients include Fortune 1000 companies worldwide—across a range of industries including retail, financial services, travel, technology, and consumer package goods.

Engagements range from short-term projects to long-term retainer relationships. Some clients work with Altimeter Group to revamp their social media policies. Others need to formulate a coherent social strategy that aligns with their strategic objectives. And others seek advice on how best to organize for openness. Altimeter Group is also known for running workshops with executive teams to introduce open leadership and social technologies as a way to kick off a new strategy process.

In every engagement, Altimeter Group believes that community is a strength in our fast-changing world. That speed is a competitive advantage. And that excellence is paramount.

Learn how Altimeter Group can help your organization move forward, faster, by contacting Charlene Li directly:

charlene@altimetergroup.com

OPEN LEADERSHIP RESOURCES...FREE

Author Charlene Li created eight critical resources
you need to start your transformation to open leadership.

→ **Visit open-leadership.com**

THE CHALLENGES
Answer eight questions about the challenges of social technologies –
and define your starting point. Then compare your answers to other
readers in this dynamic survey.

OPENNESS AUDIT
Find out *why* you are more or less open in one area or another. And
are you as open as you need to be to achieve your goals? Assess the
openness of your organization – and your competitors, or the
companies you admire.

ENGAGEMENT PYRAMID DATA
Get data on each of the five levels of engagement for sixteen different
countries.

BENEFITS AND LIFETIME VALUE CALCULATOR
Download spreadsheets for four different benefit calculators, as well as
Charlene Li's new lifetime value (LTV) tool, and measure the real value
of social technologies.

SOCIAL MEDIA POLICY DIRECTORY
See the guidelines used by companies, ranging from industries such as health care and finance to retail and manufacturing. Also submit your policy for inclusion in this directory.

READINESS CHECKLIST
Move your open strategy to operations using this detailed plan covering seven major areas. The downloadable checklist includes descriptions and details on how to get started with your open strategy.

OPEN LEADERSHIP SELF-ASSESSMENT
Take this assessment test to reveal your true leadership archetype, and understand how to best pair with other leadership types to become more open.

OPEN LEADERSHIP SKILLS ASSESSMENT
Score yourself – and measure your results against others – on the key skills and behaviors required for open leadership.

Get all eight resources FREE at **open-leadership.com**

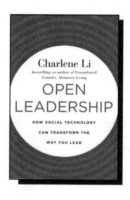

CHARLENE LI is frequently quoted in the national media including the *Wall Street Journal*, the *New York Times*, *USA Today*, 60 Minutes, PBS NewsHour, ABC News, and CNN.

Charlene Li is founder of Altimeter Group, a strategy consulting firm with a pragmatic approach to using emerging technologies for competitive advantage.

Her honors are many:

{
One of the 12 Most
Creative Minds
—Fast Company, 2008
}

{
One of the Most Influential
Women in Technology
—Fast Company, 2009
}

{
Groundswell,
BusinessWeek Bestseller
—BusinessWeek
}

{
Groundswell,
Top Business Book
—Amazon, 2009
}

Bring Charlene and her powerful message to your organization or next event.

Contact her directly at charlene@altimetergroup.com

SUBJECT INDEX

A

Abrams Research, 148

Accountability: about, 15; covenants and, 109–110; failure and, 227–228, 237–238

Altimeter Group, 86, 143

American Express, 76

American Idol, 38, 39

American Red Cross, 149, 175–176, 184

Apple: NPS scores for, 100; open architecture used by, 34–35; openness and control at, 70–71

Assessments: mind-sets, 180–181; open leader skills, 212, 214–215; open leadership archetypes, 179–183

Association of American Advertising Agencies, 23

Audit: compiling failure, 239; conducting social, 134–135; customer and employee engagement, 135; influence, 135; openness, 44–48

Authenticity: gauging personal, 196–197; open leadership and, 190–193

B

Bank of America, 193

Bazaarvoice, 122–123

Benefits of openness: adopting NPS metric, 98, 100; calculating, 89, 90–91, 100–103; collaborative technology's savings, 93; difficulties measuring, 75–77; engagement and, 85–87; finding customer lifetime value, 96, 98, 99; innovation benefits, 94, 95–96, 97; measuring for learning, 78–82, 83; support, 89, 91–94, 95

Best Buy: apologizing for mistakes, 235–237; encouraging employee passion, 253–256; executive blogging at, 192–193; finding open leaders at, 171–172, 201–202; hiring Realist Optimists, 184; open data access on, 35–36

Beth Israel Deaconess Medical Center, 26

Bhagavad Gita, 247

Blogging Code of Conduct (HP), 126

Blogs: Best Buy's executive, 192–193; Cisco's, 199; developing trust with, 126; employee guidelines for, 108, 113, 115; garnering insights from, 55–56; IBM's guidelines for, 121–122; Johnson & Johnson, 128–129; producing, 60; responding to crises via, 261; Southwest Airline's, 63–64;

NAME INDEX

ADDITIONAL READING RECOMMENDATIONS

I read a huge pile of business, strategy, and leadership books while writing *Open Leadership*. Here are some of my favorites:

- *Switch*, by Chip and Dan Heath [Culture]. This book went to press just as I was finishing up the book. It's essential reading if you trying to get real change done within your organization.
- *Mindset*, by Carol Dweck [Psychology]. If you want more on how mind-sets are developed and how they can change, then this book is for you. Focus on Chapter 5, as it's oriented to how mind-sets impact business.
- *Transparency*, by Warren Bennis, Daniel Goleman, and James O'Toole [Culture]. This slim volume packs a punch and it's excellent reading for executives who want to understand how to build a "culture of candor."
- *Good for Business*, by Andrew Benett, Cavas Gobhai, Ann O'Reilly, and Greg Welch [Branding]. The authors provide a compelling, absorbing read on what it means to develop an authentic corporate brand.
- *Enterprise 2.0*, by Andrew McAfee [Collaboration]. This book provides a deep dive into the use of social and collaboration technologies inside organizations, and is filled with case studies and implementation details.
- *The Facebook Era*, by Clara Shih [Social networking]. If you're looking over your teenager's shoulder to understand Facebook, you need to read this book. Get smart and up to speed on the business of social networks.
- *Twitterville*, by Shel Israel [Twitter, of course]. This book stands out because it explains why Twitter matters to business and communications. (Disclosure: I wrote the Introduction).